From The Library of
Joe C Miller
From The Library of

The
PROPHET'S
MANUAL

JOHN ECKHARDT

CHAR
HOI

D0905755

Most CHARISMA HOUSE BOOK GROUP products are available at special quantity discounts for bulk purchase for sales promotions, premiums, fund-raising, and educational needs. For details, write Charisma House Book Group, 600 Rinehart Road, Lake Mary, Florida 32746, or telephone (407) 333-0600.

THE PROPHET'S MANUAL by John Eckhardt
Published by Charisma House
Charisma Media/Charisma House Book Group
600 Rinehart Road
Lake Mary, Florida 32746
www.charismahouse.com

This book or parts thereof may not be reproduced in any form, stored in a retrieval system, or transmitted in any form by any means—electronic, mechanical, photocopy, recording, or otherwise—without prior written permission of the publisher, except as provided by United States of America copyright law.

Unless otherwise noted, all Scripture quotations are taken from the Holy Bible, Modern English Version. Copyright © 2014 by Military Bible Association. Used by permission. All rights reserved.

Scripture quotations marked AMPC are from the Amplified Bible, Classic Edition. Copyright © 1954, 1958, 1962, 1964, 1965, 1987 by The Lockman Foundation. Used by permission.

Scripture quotations marked CEB are from the Common English Bible. Copyright © 2011 Common English Bible. Used by permission.

Scripture quotations marked CEV are from the Contemporary English Version, copyright © 1995 by the American Bible Society. Used by permission.

Scripture quotations marked CJB are from the Complete Jewish Bible. Copyright © 1998 by David H. Stern. All rights reserved.

Scripture quotations marked ERV are from the Easy-to-Read Version. Copyright © 2006 by Bible League International. Used by permission.

Scripture quotations marked EXB are from The Expanded Bible. Copyright ©2011 by Thomas Nelson. Used by permission. All rights reserved.

Scripture quotations marked GNT are from the Good News Translation, copyright © 1992 American Bible Society. Used by permission.

Scripture quotations marked GW are taken from GOD'S WORD, © 1995 God's Word to the Nations. Used by permission of Baker Publishing Group.

Scripture quotations marked HCSB are taken from the Holman Christian Standard Bible®, Copyright © 1999, 2000, 2002, 2003, 2009 by Holman Bible Publishers. Used by permission. Holman Christian Standard Bible®, Holman CSB®, and HCSB® are federally registered trademarks of Holman Bible Publishers.

Scripture quotations marked ISV are from the International Standard Version. Copyright © 1995–2014 by ISV Foundation. All rights reserved internationally. Used by permission of Davidson Press, LLC.

Scripture quotations marked JUB are from the Jubilee Bible (from the Scriptures of the Reformation), edited by Russell M. Stendal. Copyright © 2000, 2001, 2010 by LIFE SENTENCE Publishing, LLC. Used by permission.

Scripture quotations marked KJV are from the King James Version of the Bible.

Scripture quotations marked NIV are taken from the Holy Bible, New International Version®, NIV®. Copyright © 1973, 1978, 1984, 2011 by Biblica, Inc.™ Used by permission of Zondervan. All rights reserved worldwide. www.zondervan.com. The "NIV" and "New

Scripture quotations marked NIV are taken from the Holy Bible, New International Version®, NIV®. Copyright © 1973, 1978, 1984, 2011 by Biblica, Inc.™ Used by permission of Zondervan. All rights reserved worldwide. www.zondervan.com. The "NIV" and "New International Version" are trademarks registered in the United States Patent and Trademark Office by Biblica, Inc.™

Scripture quotations marked NKJV are from the New King James Version of the Bible. Copyright © 1979, 1980, 1982 by Thomas Nelson, Inc., publishers. Used by permission.

Scripture quotations marked PHILLIPS are from *The New Testament in Modern English*, Revised Edition. Copyright © 1958, 1960, 1972 by J.B. Phillips. Macmillan Publishing Co. Used by permission.

Scripture quotations marked THE MESSAGE are from *The Message: The Bible in Contemporary English*, copyright © 1993, 1994, 1995, 1996, 2000, 2001, 2002. Used by permission of NavPress Publishing Group.

Scripture quotations marked WEB are taken from the World English Bible. Public domain.

Scripture quotations marked WYC are taken from the Wycliffe's Old Testament. Copyright © 2010 by Terence P. Noble. All rights reserved.

Cover design by Justin Evans

Copyright © 2017 by John Eckhardt
All rights reserved

Visit the author's websites at www.johneckhardt.global and www.prophetsmanual.com.

Library of Congress Cataloging-in-Publication Data:
Names: Eckhardt, John, 1957- author.
Title: The prophet's manual / John Eckhardt.
Description: Lake Mary, Florida : Charisma House, 2017. | Includes
   bibliographical references and index.
Identifiers: LCCN 2017017638| ISBN 9781629990934 (trade paper : alk. paper) |
   ISBN 9781629990941 (ebook : alk. paper)
Subjects: LCSH: Prophecy--Christianity.
Classification: LCC BR115.P8 E365 2017 | DDC 234/.13--dc23
LC record available at https://lccn.loc.gov/2017017638

This publication is translated in Spanish under the title *El manual del profeta*, copyright © 2017 by John Eckhardt, published by Casa Creación, a Charisma Media company. All rights reserved.

Portions of this book were previously published by Charisma House as *God Still Speaks*, ISBN 978-1-59979-475-4, copyright © 2009, *Prophet Arise*, ISBN 978-1-62998-638-8, copyright © 2015, *Prophetic Activation*, ISBN 978-1-62998-709-5, copyright © 2016, and *Deliverance and Spiritual Warfare Manual*, ISBN 978-1-62136-625-6, copyright © 2014.

While the author has made every effort to provide accurate Internet addresses at the time of publication, neither the publisher nor the author assumes any responsibility for errors or for changes that occur after publication.

19 20 21 22 23 — 10 9 8 7 6
Printed in the United States of America

CONTENTS

Part IV: Stay in the Flow

INTRODUCTION

PROPHETS, IT IS TIME TO ARISE!

Arise, shine, for your light has come, and the glory of the
LORD has risen upon you. For the darkness shall cover the earth
and deep darkness the peoples; but the LORD shall rise upon
you, and His glory shall be seen upon you. The nations shall
come to your light and kings to the brightness of your rising.

—ISAIAH 60:1–3

G OD STIRS His prophets whenever there is darkness. When you look
around at all that is stirring in the earth, your spirit will begin to
testify that the light of God is needed now more than ever. God uses
His prophets to shine His light in places of darkness, dispelling wickedness
and oppression of all kinds. From nations to communities to individual lives,
those who are in darkness need light. Those in darkness need to hear the voice
of the Lord.

There is a new glory coming upon prophets. There is a new honor and
favor coming upon them. Those who have been ignored and oppressed are
now coming forth. Those who have been in despair are now being encouraged.
There is a global community of prophets that is being challenged and called.
They are in every nation and city. They will not be hidden anymore. The
nations will see you. Your cities will hear you. The churches will acknowledge
you. Prophet, your light has come.

I have prepared *The Prophet's Manual* as a resource to help equip and
encourage you in your prophetic call. In this book you will learn the true
nature of a prophet's call, the prophet's role in the body of Christ and the world,
how a prophet can be activated in specific areas of prophetic ministry, and how
a prophet can stay in the flow of accurate and edifying prophetic utterance.

As you may have felt and experienced yourself, many prophets have been in
the dark and have not known their true calling. Religion and tradition have
hindered them. But no more. It is time for prophets to see and to come out of
the dark and out of the caves.

As the Lord moved upon Obadiah to hide and feed one hundred prophets
escaping Jezebel (1 Kings 18:4), God has also sustained you in the cave. He has
fed you bread and water. He would not let you die. But it is time to come out

of your cave. It is time to come out of the shadows. It is time to prophesy. It is time to fulfill your call.

This book is also about a prophet's need to be restored, reset, relaunched, and reequipped for the changing seasons ahead. Prophets who have been hurt, discouraged, frustrated, cast out, mistreated, and persecuted are being touched by heaven. Though persecution and tribulation are part of the call, there are much-needed times when the prophet must seek healing and deliverance. In this book we will look at ways for prophets to be healed and made whole.

> For I will restore health to you, and I will heal you of your wounds, says the LORD, because they called you an outcast, saying, "This is Zion whom no man cares for."
>
> —JEREMIAH 30:17

GET READY FOR FRESH OIL

If you've been wondering where your fire has gone, know that by your stirring up your gift all over again, people will once again seek after you. They will say, "What is the word of the Lord?" You will no longer be an outcast.

Let any harvest the enemy has stolen be restored.

> And I will compensate you for the years the locusts have eaten—the larval locust, the hopper locust, and the fledging locust—My great army which I sent against you.
>
> —JOEL 2:25

Fresh oil is coming to the prophets from heaven. God is pouring it out upon His prophets. God has seen you, and your cup will overflow. God is the God of the overflow.

> But my horn You have exalted like the horn of the wild ox; You have anointed me with fresh oil.
>
> —PSALM 92:10

There is a fresh anointing coming upon you, prophet. You may have been anointed once before, but get ready for something new. David was anointed three times. Each anointing took him to another level of power and authority.

Get ready for new levels of power and authority. Get ready for a new flow of prophecy. Your utterances will get stronger and deeper. Your ear will become more sensitive to the voice of God.

> You shall arise, and have mercy upon Zion, for the time to favor her, indeed, the appointed time has come.
>
> —PSALM 102:13

This is the set time of favor. This is the set time to arise and shine. This is a new season for the prophets. The winter is over, and spring has arrived.

> The flowers appear on the earth; the time of the singing has come, and the voice of the turtledove is heard in our land.
> —SONG OF SONGS 2:12

God loves His prophets. He has seen your condition. He speaks now to arise and shine. Your light has come, and the glory of the Lord has risen upon you.

PART I

The Prophet's Call to Ministry

CHAPTER 1

ARE YOU A PROPHET?

The spirits of the prophets are subject to the prophets.
—1 CORINTHIANS 14:32

A s you've begun to read this book, you may be wondering about the nature of your call as a prophet. You may be wondering if you are called to the office of a prophet or to be a believer who speaks as God moves upon them. These are indeed very different prophetic functions, but what I have come to realize throughout my years as a prophetic minister is that whether you are a prophetic believer or functioning in the role of a prophet, there are characteristics that we all share.

Prophetic people are the same all over the world. Every nation has them. Every city has them. Every region has them. They exist in every generation. You are not alone. You are a part of a global company of prophets. The same things grieve them, stir them, give them joy, and cause them to weep. The following pages of this chapter list, identify, and describe common characteristics prophets and prophetic people share. This knowledge will give you strength and confidence to be the prophet God has called you to be and to recognize and validate the other prophets in your life.

Are you ready to find out if you are a prophet? Well, you may be a prophet if...

You will take a stand.

Prophets will stand up against the workers of iniquity when no one else will. Prophets will answer the call and rise against evildoers.

> Who will rise up for me against the wicked? Who will stand up for me against those who do iniquity?
>
> —PSALM 94:16

You are different.

Prophets are not normal. Prophets are different. They are configured differently. They don't think like everyone else. They see things differently. They do not like people saying, "This is just the way it is," or "We have always done it this way."

They see what others do not see. They are not satisfied with the status quo.

They see God's agenda of advancement and change. They desire new moves and new things. They often have a holy discontent. Prophets are change agents.

If this is you, then know that there are many just like you. You are not crazy, and you are not alone.

> Still, I have preserved seven thousand men in Israel for Myself, all of whose knees have not bowed to Baal and whose mouths have not kissed him.
>
> —1 Kings 19:18

You march to the beat of a different drummer.

Prophets are motivated by a different set of values than the average person.

You are motivated by love.

Prophets have a love for God, His people (the church), and the world. They will stand against anything that comes to kill, steal, and destroy.

This love makes them protectors, defenders, deliverers, and intercessors.

A prophet's core message is love God and love one another. Prophets will deal with anything that keeps us from loving God and from loving one another.

> Jesus said to him, "'You shall love the Lord your God with all your heart, and with all your soul, and with all your mind.' This is the first and great commandment. And the second is like it: 'You shall love your neighbor as yourself.'"
>
> —Matthew 22:37–39

You extend mercy.

Sometimes prophets are portrayed as only being harsh and mean, but prophets are merciful. Prophets are uncompromising, but there is room for mercy and redemption in their messages. Prophets represent the heart of God, and God is merciful.

> It is of the Lord's mercies that we are not consumed; His compassions do not fail.
>
> —Lamentations 3:22

> Go and proclaim these words toward the north, and say: Return, backsliding Israel, says the Lord, and I will not cause My anger to fall on you. For I am merciful, says the Lord, and I will not keep anger forever.
>
> —Jeremiah 3:12

> In a little wrath I hid My face from you for a moment; but with everlasting kindness I will have mercy on you, says the Lord your Redeemer.
>
> —Isaiah 54:8

You see the potential in small things.

Prophets can see the beginning and where a thing is going. They can see potential when others see smallness.

> For who has despised the day of small things? These seven will rejoice and see the plumb line in the hand of Zerubbabel. These are the eyes of the LORD, which survey to and fro throughout the earth.
> —ZECHARIAH 4:10

You see hidden things.

Prophets see what is hidden from most. They discern when things are not right and are out of order. They often wonder why everyone does not see it. They often think, "Am I crazy? Am I really seeing this?" Prophets hate spiritual blindness. They are grieved when leaders and believers cannot see what is so obvious to them. Some people see what they want to see, and some don't see what they don't want to see, but the prophet can't help but to see.

Be encouraged, prophets. There are many seeing the same things you are seeing. There are many praying about the same things. You are not crazy, and you are not alone.

You see things from heaven's perspective.

Prophets say to us, "Come up higher."

> After this I looked. And there was an open door in heaven. The first voice I heard was like a trumpet speaking with me, saying, "Come up here, and I will show you things which must take place after this."
> —REVELATION 4:1

You can access God's thoughts.

Prophets know what God is thinking, and they speak what God is thinking. God's thoughts are not man's thoughts. Prophets think differently. Prophets are not limited to the way man thinks.

> For My thoughts are not your thoughts, nor are your ways My ways, says the LORD. For as the heavens are higher than the earth, so are My ways higher than your ways, and My thoughts than your thoughts.
> —ISAIAH 55:8–9

You know God's ways.

Israel knew the acts of God, but Moses knew His ways. Scripture says, "He made known His ways [of righteousness and justice] to Moses, His acts to the children of Israel" (Ps. 103:7, AMPC). It is not enough to know the acts of God; we must also know His ways.

You wait on God.

You have an expectation of what the Lord will do. You wait for Him to act. You wait for Him to judge. You wait for Him to reveal Himself. You wait for Him to fulfill His word.

> My soul waits for the Lord, more than watchmen for the morning, more than watchmen for the morning.
>
> —Psalm 130:6

> I will wait on the Lord, who hides His face from the house of Jacob, and I will eagerly look for Him.
>
> —Isaiah 8:17

You ask the hard questions.

Prophets want to know why. They desire insight and understanding when life seems confusing. They don't settle for the religious saying, "You never can really know the mind of God." Prophets are friends of God. They want insight into perplexing questions and challenges in their generation and society.

> I will stand at my watch and station myself on the watchtower; and I will keep watch to see what He will say to me, and what I will answer when I am reproved. And the Lord answered me: Write the vision, and make it plain on tablets, that he who reads it may run. For the vision is yet for an appointed time; but it speaks of the end, and does not lie.
>
> —Habakkuk 2:1–3

You ask, "Who has bewitched you?"

> Who has bewitched you that you should not obey the truth? Before your eyes Jesus Christ was clearly portrayed among you as crucified.
>
> —Galatians 3:1

The Galatians had been bewitched by legalistic teachers. The Amplified Version, Classic Edition says, "Who has fascinated or bewitched or cast a spell over you…?" Another translation says, "Who has hypnotized you…?" (HCSB).

You oppose the wisdom of the world.

The church cannot operate in worldly wisdom but in godly wisdom. God's wisdom is higher than man's, whose wisdom is earthly, sensual, and devilish.

> Therefore I will once again do a marvelous work among this people, even a marvelous work and a wonder; for the wisdom of their wise men shall perish, and the understanding of their prudent men shall be hidden.
>
> —Isaiah 29:14

> Where is the wise? Where is the scribe? Where is the debater of this age? Has God not made the wisdom of this world foolish?
>
> —1 Corinthians 1:20

You uproot what God has not planted.

> But He answered, "Every plant which My heavenly Father has not planted will be uprooted."
>
> —Matthew 15:13

You are used by God to release other people into their assignments and destinies.

Prophets know the people whom God has called and appointed. They know the ones who are called and the ones who are not called. They love to see people released into their purpose. Prophets are not selfish. They want to see others fulfill their purpose.

> The LORD said to him, "Go, return on the road through the Wilderness of Damascus, and when you arrive, anoint Hazael to be king over Aram."
>
> —1 Kings 19:15

You are a spiritual midwife.

Midwives assist in delivery. Prophets assist us in bringing forth the plans of God for our lives through prayer, preaching, teaching, and prophesying—birthing.

> So it happened that because the midwives feared God, He gave them families.
>
> —Exodus 1:21

You are inspired.

Prophets are moved by inspiration. Once they get inspired to do something, they are hard to stop. Once they get stirred up, watch out. They will fight through every obstacle once they know something is of God. Don't underestimate the power of inspiration.

You know the power of inspiration.

Inspiration is the process of being stimulated to do or feel something, especially to do something creative. Prophets are inspired to speak, pray, sing, and worship.

You are feared.

Herod was afraid of John. God uses prophets to release a holy fear, which is needed today. Let the prophets arise and bring a holy fear to this generation.

> For Herod feared John, knowing that he was a righteous and holy man, and protected him. When he heard him, he was greatly perplexed, but heard him gladly.
>
> —Mark 6:20

You call out sin.

God has always used prophets to call out sin.

> Cry aloud, do not hold back; lift up your voice like a trumpet, and show My people their transgression and the house of Jacob their sins.
>
> —ISAIAH 58:1

> If I had not come and spoken to them, they would not have had sin. But now they have no excuse for their sin.
>
> —JOHN 15:22

You fight carnality.

Carnality has always been a problem with churches. *Carnal* means "fleshly or worldly." Prophets will oppose carnality. It causes people to become sectarian and to exalt men. Carnality includes envy, strife, and division.

> Brothers, I could not speak to you as to spiritual men, but as to worldly, even as to babes in Christ. I have fed you with milk and not with solid food. For to this day you were not able to endure it. Nor are you able now, for you are still worldly. Since there is envy, strife, and divisions among you, are you not worldly and behaving as mere men?
>
> —1 CORINTHIANS 3:1–3

You call for fasting, prayer, and humility.

Prophets often call the church to humility. Repentance from pride, disobedience, and rebellion is needed. Fasting is one of the biblical ways to humble the soul. Humility, repentance, and fasting are keys to breakthrough.

> Consecrate a fast, call a sacred assembly, assemble the elders and all the inhabitants of the land to the house of the LORD your God, and cry out to the LORD.
>
> —JOEL 1:14

> Yet even now, declares the LORD, return to Me with all your heart, and with fasting and with weeping and with mourning....Blow the ram's horn in Zion, consecrate a fast, call a sacred assembly.
>
> —JOEL 2:12, 15

You offend people.

People can be offended by prophets. Prophets can rub people the wrong way. Some people hate truth. They don't like what prophets say. Remember, Jesus offended the people in His hometown. He offended the Pharisees and the religious leaders of His day. He did not "butter them up," but He spoke the truth. If you don't want to offend anyone, you cannot be a prophet.

And they took offense at Him. But Jesus said to them, "A prophet is not without honor except in his own country and in his own house."

—MATTHEW 13:57

Then His disciples came and said to Him, "Do You know that the Pharisees were offended after they heard this saying?"

—MATTHEW 15:12

You speak what some people do not want to hear.

And the king of Israel said to Jehoshaphat, "There is still one man, Micaiah the son of Imlah, by whom we can inquire of the LORD. But I hate him because he never prophesies good for me, but always evil." And Jehoshaphat said, "Let not the king say so."

—1 KINGS 22:8

You tell the truth.

Israel went into captivity because of bad prophetics (false and vain prophets). These so-called prophets did not tell Israel the truth. Jeremiah stood against them and told Israel the truth. Tell the truth, prophets.

Your prophets have seen for you false and deceptive visions; they have not revealed your iniquity, to bring back your captives, but have seen for you oracles that are false and misleading.

—LAMENTATIONS 2:14

You are fervent.

Fervent means "having or showing great emotion or zeal; ardent…extremely hot, glowing."[1] Prophets are sometimes called "too emotional" or "too zealous," but it is the nature of prophets to be fervent.

Fervent in prayer, love, preaching, teaching, and worship, they often wonder why everyone is not fervent.

Confess your faults to one another and pray for one another, that you may be healed. The effective, fervent prayer of a righteous man accomplishes much.

—JAMES 5:16

Epaphras greets you. He is one of you, a servant of Christ, always laboring fervently for you in prayers, that you may stand mature and complete in the entire will of God.

—COLOSSIANS 4:12

Above all things, have unfailing love for one another, because love covers a multitude of sins.

—1 PETER 4:8

You have zeal.

Zeal is passion and jealousy. Jesus had zeal for the house of God. This zeal caused Him to drive the moneychangers from the temple.

The house of God is the church. Prophets have a zeal (passion, jealousy) for the church. Zeal will consume prophets. They cannot sit by and watch the house of God be destroyed. They must act.

> My strong love [jealousy; passion; zeal] for your Temple [house] completely controls [consumes] me [John 2:17]. When people insult you, it hurts me [The reproaches/scorn of those who reproach/scorn you fall on me; Rom. 15:3].
>
> —Psalm 69:9, exb

You are radical.

The word *radical* means "departing markedly from the usual or customary; extreme or drastic." [2]

You can be set like flint.

Flint is a very hard stone that symbolizes being set and unchangeable. Prophets will set their faces like flint when they know something is of God. They will stand against the world if they have to. Prophets take a stand with the help of God.

> For the Lord God will help me; therefore, I shall not be disgraced; therefore, I have set my face like a flint, and I know that I shall not be ashamed.
>
> —Isaiah 50:7

You need to understand when things don't make sense.

This can be very frustrating to a prophet. A prophet likes to make sense of things. He or she wants to know why.

You are sometimes too hard on yourself.

Prophets can be hard on themselves because of the nature of their gift. For this reason, it is sometimes difficult to restore prophets when they fail. Sometimes prophets can be too hard on themselves because of the way they view things. Don't come down too hard on yourself, prophet, if you make a mistake. There is room for mercy on others as well as yourself.

You tend to be intense.

Intense means "having or showing strong feelings or opinions; extremely earnest or serious." [3] Prophets are not laid back. They have a difficult time understanding believers who have no intensity.

You are human.

Prophets are subject to similar passions as others, yet they walk in power and authority by God's grace and calling. They don't allow their passions to stop them from doing what needs to be done. They've learned how to bring their passions under the rule of God and submit to His will. They pray harder.

> Elijah was a man subject to natural passions as we are, and he prayed earnestly that it might not rain, and it did not rain on the earth for three years and six months.
>
> —JAMES 5:17

You are tenacious in prayer.

Once prophets get a burden, they will pray it through, no matter how long it takes. They will hold on to a prayer assignment for years if they have to. If you want a strong prayer ministry in your church, get some prophets together.

When prophets get a burden, they cannot shake it. They carry that burden. That burden is their assignment from the Lord. They try sometimes to shake it, but it will not leave them. You might as well deal with the burden because it is not going anywhere. A burden is a weight, something the prophet carries. It can be a message, a ministry, or an assignment.

> The burden which Habakkuk the prophet did see.
>
> —HABAKKUK 1:1, KJV

You like holy interruptions.

Prophets love it when God interrupts a service and does something new. Prophets get bored with routine and tradition. They don't like being stuck to an "order of service." They love the "suddenlies" of God.

> Suddenly a sound like a mighty rushing wind came from heaven, and it filled the whole house where they were sitting.
>
> —ACTS 2:2

God does some things suddenly. Sometimes what prophets speak "tarries," but other times it comes "suddenly."

You are sensitive to the spirit realm.

Prophets are the most sensitive of the fivefold ministry. God has configured prophets to have spiritual sensitivity. Prophets have to learn how to handle this increased sensitivity. They tend to "pick up things" without trying to. Their sensitivity is related to being extremely intuitive, highly aware, and keenly observant.

Prophets move in the Spirit…

Move immediately in the Spirit…

Are carried away in the Spirit…

Pray in the Spirit…

Sing in the Spirit…
Walk in the Spirit…
Dance in the Spirit…

> The hand of the LORD was upon me, and He carried me out in the Spirit of the LORD and set me down in the midst of the valley which was full of bones.
>
> —EZEKIEL 37:1

> I was in the Spirit on the Lord's Day, and I heard behind me a great voice like a trumpet.
>
> —REVELATION 1:10

> Immediately I was in the Spirit. And there was a throne set in heaven with One sitting on the throne!
>
> —REVELATION 4:2

> And he carried me away in the Spirit to a great and high mountain, and showed me the Holy City, Jerusalem, descending out of heaven from God.
>
> —REVELATION 21:10

You are spontaneous.

Spontaneity is the result of inspiration. *Spontaneous* means "performed or occurring as a result of a sudden impulse or inclination and without premeditation or external stimulus."[4] Sometimes churches don't care much for spontaneity. Some want everything preplanned.

You expect new bottles and new wine.

> And it will be that in that day the mountains will drip sweet wine, and the hills will flow with milk, and all the streambeds of Judah will flow with water; a spring will proceed from the house of the LORD and will water the Valley of Shittim.
>
> —JOEL 3:18

> But new wine must be put into new wineskins, and both are preserved.
>
> —LUKE 5:38

You smell uncleanness.

Did you know that prophets can smell? They can smell uncleanness. They can smell sin. They can also smell the sweet aroma of prayer and worship. They can smell bread where the Word is preached. They can smell the fragrance of the Lord when He is present in a church.

Prophet, don't be afraid to smell; you are not crazy.

If the whole body were an eye, where would the hearing be? If the whole body were hearing, where would the sense of smell be?

—1 Corinthians 12:17

I rose up to open to my beloved, and my hands dripped with myrrh, my fingers with liquid myrrh on the handles of the bolt.

—Song of Songs 5:5

You know Jezebel.

Jezebel is a false prophetess. Elijah knew Jezebel, and Jezebel knew Elijah. Prophets hate when Jezebel is allowed to run rampant in the church. Jezebel represents a spirit of control, manipulation, seduction, intimidation, and whoredom.

But I have a few things against you: You permit that woman Jezebel, who calls herself a prophetess, to teach and seduce My servants to commit sexual immorality and eat food sacrificed to idols.

—Revelation 2:20

When Joram saw Jehu he said, "Is it peace, Jehu?" And he said, "What peace, so long as the harlotries of your mother Jezebel and her sorceries are so many?"

—2 Kings 9:22

You cry out against abominations.

An abomination is that which is disgusting and detestable. Here is what is abominable to God: pride, lying, murder, evil imaginations, mischief, false witness, and discord.

These six things the Lord hates, yes, seven are an abomination to him: a proud look, a lying tongue, and hands that shed innocent blood, a heart that devises wicked imaginations, feet that are swift in running to mischief, a false witness who speaks lies, and he who sows discord among brethren.

—Proverbs 6:16–19

For the sons of Judah have done evil in My sight, says the Lord. They have set their abominations in the house which is called by My name, to pollute it.

—Jeremiah 7:30

You detect when thing are out of order.

Prophets discern when situations are encased in disorder and confusion or when there is misalignment.

For this reason I left you in Crete, that you should set in order the things that are lacking, and appoint elders in every city, as I commanded you.

—Titus 1:5

For though I am absent in the flesh, yet I am with you in spirit, rejoicing and seeing your orderliness and the steadfastness of your faith in Christ.

—COLOSSIANS 2:5

We have diverse gifts according to the grace that is given to us: if prophecy, according to the proportion of faith.

—ROMANS 12:6

You are not impressed with buildings.

Prophets are not impressed with religious adornment. They understand that God does not dwell in temples made with hands. They look for the true temple, which is the people of God filled with the Holy Spirit.

However, the Most High does not dwell in houses made with hands. As the prophet says...

—ACTS 7:48

As some spoke of how the temple was adorned with beautiful stones and gifts, He said, "As for these things which you see, the days will come when not one stone shall be left on another that will not be thrown down."

—LUKE 21:5–6

You are contagious.

The prophet's spirit is strong and influences others. God has called prophets to be contagious. You cannot keep this to yourself. You are an influencer. You can impart.

After that you will come to the hill of God, where the garrison of the Philistines is. And when you come there to the city, you will meet a group of prophets coming down from the high place with a harp, a tambourine, a flute, and a lyre before them. And they will prophesy. And the Spirit of the LORD will come upon you, and you will prophesy with them. And you will be turned into another man.

—1 SAMUEL 10:5–6

Prophets should want everyone to hear from and speak for God. Prophets should not want the prophetic to be a club for a few "anointed" people. Prophets want the leaders to be prophetic and the people to be prophetic. Prophets love it when people hear, speak, and obey the word of the Lord. Prophets are not jealous when God uses other people.

Sometimes when you ask a prophet, "What is God saying?" they will answer, "What is God saying to you?"

> Moses said to him, "Are you jealous for my sake? Oh, that all the people of the LORD were prophets, and that the LORD would put His Spirit upon them!"
>
> —NUMBERS 11:29

You are concerned about God's agenda, purposes, and plans.

God's agenda is the priority of the prophet, not the agenda of man. The prophet knows that only the plans and purposes of the Lord will stand, and anything else is a waste of time. Prophets don't like to waste time on things that are not ordained by God.

> Many plans are in a man's mind, but it is the LORD's purpose for him that will stand.
>
> —PROVERBS 19:21, AMPC

> Jesus said to them, "My food is to do the will of Him who sent Me, and to finish His work."
>
> —JOHN 4:34

> The LORD of Hosts has sworn, saying: Surely as I have thought, so shall it come to pass, and as I have purposed, so shall it stand.
>
> —ISAIAH 14:24

You listen for a sound.

Sounds are important to prophets. The prophet's ears are opened to the sounds of heaven. Certain sounds stir prophets. Anointed music stirs prophets. The wrong sound is a sign that something is wrong. Some churches and ministries have an old sound.

> Elijah said to Ahab, "Get up, eat and drink, for there is a sound of a heavy rainfall."
>
> —1 KINGS 18:41

> Hear attentively the thunder of His voice, and the sound that goes out of His mouth.
>
> —JOB 37:2

> The clouds poured out water; the skies thundered. Your arrows flashed about.
>
> —PSALM 77:17

Here are examples of sounds that stir prophets:

- Sound of the trumpet
- Sound of many waters
- Sound of rain
- Sound of the alarm

- Sound of wind
- Sound of battle
- Sound of shouting
- Sound of praise
- Sound of music
- Sound of preaching
- Sound of singing

You are a great helper.

Prophets help build. They help leaders. They help churches. They help in prayer. They help in worship. They help us transition. They help us move into the new. It is the nature of a prophet to be a helper and to have a desire to help. Prophets provide supernatural assistance. If you need help, get a prophet.

> Then Zerubbabel the son of Shealtiel and Joshua the son of Jozadak rose up and began to build the house of God which is at Jerusalem, and the prophets of God were with them, helping them.
>
> —Ezra 5:2

You step up in crisis.

When others run from crisis, prophets step up. They are built and designed to bring solutions and order when there is crisis and chaos.

You release courage.

Courage is important, especially for leaders. Asa took courage after he heard the word of Oded the prophet. He then pressed forward in removing the idols from the land. Prophets will encourage leaders to do what God desires.

> And when Asa heard these words of the prophecy of Azariah son of Oded the prophet, he was encouraged and removed the detestable idols from the entire land of Judah and Benjamin and from the cities that he captured in the hills of Ephraim. And he repaired the altar of the LORD that was before the vestibule of the LORD.
>
> —2 CHRONICLES 15:8

You speak peace.

Shalom is the Hebrew word for peace, healing, wholeness, and prosperity.

> I will hear what God the LORD will speak, for He will speak peace to His people and to His saints, but let them not turn again to folly.
>
> —PSALM 85:8

You speak to the gods.

The gods are the judges, the mighty, and the rulers. God stands in the congregation of the gods. We are the assembly of the gods (the rulers, the mighty, the sons and daughters of God). We are the judges, and God is in our midst. We issue verdicts and pass sentences. Rise up, saints; you are the gods.

> God stands among the divine council; He renders judgment among the gods.
>
> —PSALM 82:1

> Elohim [God] stands in the divine assembly; there with the elohim [judges], he judges.
>
> —PSALM 82:1, CJB

> I have said, "You are gods, sons of the Most High, all of you."
>
> —PSALM 82:6

> Jesus answered them, "Is it not written in your law, 'I said, "You are gods"'? If He called them 'gods,' to whom the word of God came, and the Scripture cannot be broken..."
>
> —JOHN 10:34–35

You are focused on the heart.

Prophets are concerned about the heart (motives). Outward shows don't impress them. They hate it when people honor God with their lips but their hearts are far from Him. Prophets look for purity of heart. Prophets discern the heart. God looks at the heart.

> Therefore, the Lord said: Because this people draw near with their mouths and honor Me with their lips, but have removed their hearts far from Me, and their fear toward Me is tradition by the precept of men...
>
> —ISAIAH 29:13

> But the LORD said to Samuel, "Do not look on his appearance or on the height of his stature, because I have rejected him. For the LORD sees not as man sees. For man looks on the outward appearance, but the LORD looks on the heart."
>
> —1 SAMUEL 16:7

You are tenderhearted.

Although prophets can be tough and strong, they are also tenderhearted. David was tenderhearted when he was challenged by Nathan.

Tender means "showing gentleness and concern or sympathy." Synonyms include caring, kind, kindly, kindhearted, softhearted, tenderhearted, compassionate, sympathetic, warm, warmhearted, solicitous, fatherly, motherly, maternal, gentle, mild, benevolent, generous, giving, and humane.

> Because your heart was tender and you humbled yourself before God when you heard His words against this place and those who dwell here, and you have brought yourself low before Me and torn your clothes and wept before Me, I have heard you, declares the LORD.
>
> —2 CHRONICLES 34:27

You are God's representative.

Prophets have a passion to see God represented correctly. They don't like it when God is misrepresented. They are fierce defenders of the truth and the truth of God. Don't misrepresent the Lord!

You have godly jealousy.

Jealousy, in this case, really just shows you care about something passionately and don't want to see it destroyed. Prophets are protective. They are protective of God's people and God's truth. They are protective of God's honor. Prophets will fight against anything that comes to kill, steal, and destroy. They will not just stand by and watch the enemy come in. They will raise their voices and do what is necessary.

> And he said, "I have been very zealous for the LORD, Lord of Hosts, for the children of Israel have forsaken Your covenant, thrown down Your altars, and killed Your prophets with the sword, and I alone am left, and they seek to take my life."
>
> —1 KINGS 19:10

You are faithful (loyal).

Faithfulness and loyalty to God are important to prophets. They call back the backsliders. They challenge the church when there is unfaithfulness and disloyalty to God and His truth. Prophets preach commitment. They challenge anyone and anything that would draw the church away from God. They emphasize wholehearted loyalty and devotion to God despite changing times and what the world teaches.

You are often considered too strict.

Prophets often ask themselves, "Am I being too strict? Am I being too dogmatic?" With prophets, it is either obedience or disobedience. They have a standard, and that standard is obedience.

Prophets know the blessings of obedience and the trouble with disobedience. Rebellious and disobedient people have a hard time with prophets.

Although prophets can sometimes seem strict, prophets are also merciful. They have the heart of God, which is both holiness and mercy.

> If you are willing and obedient, you shall eat the good of the land; but if you refuse and rebel, you shall be devoured with the sword; for the mouth of the LORD has spoken it.
>
> —ISAIAH 1:19–20

You want people to experience the blessing of obedience.

Prophets are not mean or mean-spirited. What prophets really desire is for us to be blessed and to prosper through obedience. Prophets know that if we are willing and obedient, we will eat the good of the land (Isa. 1:19). Prophets want the best for the church and God's people. Prophets desire us to be above and not beneath, the head and not the tail, blessed coming in and blessed going out, lending and not borrowing, healthy, whole, peaceful, joyful, and wealthy.

You have a high standard of holiness.

This can cause relationship issues with people who do not have high standards. Some people will consider prophets to have standards that are too high. Some will consider prophets too strict and too judgmental.

> Pursue peace with all men, and the holiness without which no one will see the Lord.
>
> —Hebrews 12:14

You raise and carry the standard.

A standard is a flag, a banner, a signal, an ensign. Standards draw, gather, and rally people to a cause. Banners can be seen from a distance. We need standard bearers. Standard bearers are those who gather and rally people for a godly cause. Prophets are standard bearers.

> We no longer see our own banners; there is no longer any prophet: neither is there among us any that knows. How long shall this be?
>
> —Psalm 74:9, jub

> We will rejoice in your salvation, and in the name of our God we will set up our banners
>
> —Psalm 20:5

> You have given a banner to those who fear You, that they may flee to it from the bow.
>
> —Psalm 60:4

> Go through, go through the gates. Prepare the way of the people; build up, build up the highway. Remove the stones; lift up a standard over the peoples.
>
> —Isaiah 62:10

You want things done God's way.

God gives patterns and blueprints to prophets.

> See that you make them according to their pattern which was shown to you on the mountain.
>
> —Exodus 25:40

You are an example.

Prophets are to be examples to others: "My brothers, take the prophets, who spoke in the name of the Lord, as an example of suffering and patience" (James 5:10).

Prophets are examples of how to endure suffering and how to exercise patience, perseverance, and steadfastness.

You are an equalizer.

John the Baptist came to fill the valleys and bring down the mountains. Prophets help bring down the proud and lift up the humble. This is leveling—equalization, demolishing, razing, grading, leveling, tearing down.

> Every valley shall be filled and every mountain and hill shall be brought low; and the crooked shall be made straight and the rough ways shall be made smooth.
>
> —Luke 3:5

You understand the severity of God.

> Therefore consider the goodness and severity of God—severity toward those who fell, but goodness toward you, if you continue in His goodness. Otherwise, you also will be cut off.
>
> —Romans 11:22

Severity is God's strict justice. Prophets understand the severity of God toward those with hard and impenitent hearts. We don't hear much about severity today. *Severe* means "strict in judgment or discipline."[5] God is merciful, but He is also at times severe.

Prophets must walk in balance between God's mercy and His severity.

You are awake.

Prophets are awake to the things of the Spirit, and they cannot stand it when churches are asleep. They are awake to what God is doing. When others are sleeping, the prophet is awake. Prophets wonder why others are sleeping. Prophets can't sleep like everyone else. God does not let them sleep. They can't slumber. Prophets cry, "Wake up!"

> Therefore He says: "Awake, you who sleep, arise from the dead, and Christ will give you light."
>
> —Ephesians 5:14

> Awake, awake! Put on your strength, O Zion; put on your beautiful garments, O Jerusalem, the holy city. For the uncircumcised and the unclean will no longer enter you.
>
> —Isaiah 52:1

You are concerned about the glory of God.

God's glory is important to prophets. They want God to be glorified in all things, and they will oppose anything or anyone who tries to take away from His glory. God's glory is His honor, power, fame, holiness, majesty, and authority. Prophets are promoters and defenders of the glory of God. They will pull down anything that exalts itself and tries to take the glory of God.

> If anyone speaks, let him speak as the oracles of God. If anyone serves, let him serve with the strength that God supplies, so that God in all things may be glorified through Jesus Christ, to whom be praise and dominion forever and ever. Amen.
>
> —1 Peter 4:11

You have sharp discernment (or radar).

This is a strong point in prophets. They discern. This is sometimes hard to handle because they are sensitive to the spirit realm.

Discernment in the Greek language means "judicial estimation, discern, disputation." It comes from a word meaning "to separate thoroughly, withdraw, oppose, discriminate, decide, hesitate, contend, make to differ, doubt, judge, be partial, stagger, and waver."

When the discerner is confronted with something that appears good on the outside, but isn't, it becomes a stumbling block to his spirit. His flesh sees good signs, but his spirit is disputing, opposing, hesitating, contending, differing, doubting, staggering, and wavering against the outward appearance. Discernment is an internal war as one grapples to line up what they perceive with who God is and what is being offered.[6]

> But solid food belongs to those who are mature, for those who through practice have powers of discernment that are trained to distinguish good from evil.
>
> —Hebrews 5:14

You know when it's time to move in a new direction.

Prophets hate going around in circles. They know when it's time to stop circling the mountain.

> You have circled this mountain long enough. Now turn north.
>
> —Deuteronomy 2:3

You see the measure.

Ezekiel saw the measuring rod of the house of the Lord. He also saw the measure of the river (depth of the waters—ankle high, knee high, shoulder high). *Measure* means "to ascertain the dimensions, quantity, or capacity of."[7] Prophets can see the depth of holiness, prayer, worship, revelation, love, outreach, and the like. Measuring helps us know where we are and in what areas we need to increase.

> The man said to me, "Son of man, look with your eyes, and hear with your ears, and set your heart on all that I shall show you. For you have been brought here to show it to you. Declare all that you see to the house of Israel."
> There was a wall all around the outside of the temple. In the man's hand was a measuring reed of six cubits long, each being a cubit and a handbreadth. So he measured the width of the building, one reed. And the height, one reed.
>
> —EZEKIEL 40:4–5

> Again he measured a thousand and brought me through the water. The water reached the knees. Again he measured a thousand and brought me through the water. The water reached the loins. Afterward he measured a thousand. And it was a river that I could not pass over, for the water had risen, enough water to swim in, a river that could not be passed over.
>
> —EZEKIEL 47:4–5

You are a good evangelist.

Everyone should evangelize, including prophets. Prophets are good at evangelizing because they have discernment and sensitivity to the conditions of people, including the lost. Prophets bring conviction when they minister, and conviction is a part of successful evangelism.

Prophetic churches will also have many salvations because of a strong presence of God and the convicting power of the Holy Spirit.

Prophets will also carry the burden of the Lord for the lost.

> But if all prophesy [giving inspired testimony and interpreting the divine will and purpose] and an unbeliever or untaught outsider comes in, he is told of his sin and reproved and convicted and convinced by all, and his defects and needs are examined (estimated, determined) and he is called to account by all.
>
> —1 CORINTHIANS 14:24, AMPC

Sometimes nonbelievers respond to prophets better than believers. Someone pointed this out to me. The city of Nineveh repented at the preaching of Jonah. Jesus said that Sodom would have repented at His works. Elijah was sent to a Gentile widow. Elisha healed a Gentile leper.

> He also said, "Truly, I say to you, no prophet is accepted in his own country. But I tell you truthfully, many widows were in Israel in the days of Elijah, when the heavens were closed for three years and six

months, when great famine was throughout all the land. Yet to none of them was Elijah sent except to Zarephath, a city of Sidon, to a woman who was a widow.

—Luke 4:24–26

And you, Capernaum, who is exalted toward heaven, will be brought down to Hades. For if the mighty works which have been done in you had been done in Sodom, it would have remained until this day.

—Matthew 11:23

You are a good deliverance minister.

Prophets generally operate with the gifts of discerning of spirits and the word of knowledge, which are invaluable when ministering deliverance. Prophets can "hit the nail on the head" when it comes to demons and casting them out. Their spiritual insight and sensitivity help greatly when ministering deliverance. I have also seen many people delivered through the prophetic word.

He sent His word and healed them and delivered them from their destruction.

—Psalm 107:20

You are cutting edge.

Prophets are usually the first ones to embrace change and the new thing that God is doing. They understand and embrace new moves of God. If you want to be a part of cutting-edge people of the Spirit, then get around prophets. Prophets hate stagnation and old wine. Prophets love new wine and new wineskins.

Prophets release freshness.

You fear the Lord.

Prophets understand and promote the fear of the Lord. They stand up when people lose the fear of the Lord. Prophets promote reverence for God and the things of the Spirit. To a prophet there cannot be true success and blessing without the fear of the Lord.

Sanctify the Lord of Hosts Himself, and let Him be your fear, and let Him be your dread.

—Isaiah 8:13

You bring reverence (trembling) for God.

Many have lost reverence for God. What has happened to trembling? Prophets stand up when reverence is lost.

Serve the Lord with fear; tremble with trepidation!

—Psalm 2:11

Do you not fear and reverence Me? says the Lord. Do you not tremble before Me? I placed the sand for the boundary of the sea, a perpetual barrier beyond which it cannot pass and by an everlasting ordinance beyond which it cannot go? And though the waves of the sea toss and shake themselves, yet they cannot prevail [against the feeble grains of sand which God has ordained by nature to be sufficient for His purpose]; though [the billows] roar, yet they cannot pass over that [barrier]. [Is not such a God to be reverently feared and worshiped?]

—JEREMIAH 5:22, AMPC

Therefore, my beloved, as you have always obeyed, not only in my presence, but so much more in my absence, work out your own salvation with fear and trembling.

—PHILIPPIANS 2:12

You expose idolatry.

Idolatry is more than worshipping images. Idolatry is anything that replaces God. Worship and exaltation of men, ministry, power, possessions, groups, and fame is nothing but idolatry. Covetousness is called idolatry. Prophets are fierce opponents of idols. Prophets stand against idolatry creeping into the church.

You shall have no other gods before Me.

—EXODUS 20:3

Little children, keep yourselves from idols. Amen.

—1 JOHN 5:21

Therefore put to death the parts of your earthly nature: sexual immorality, uncleanness, inordinate affection, evil desire, and covetousness, which is idolatry.

—COLOSSIANS 3:5

You expose reprobates (continual rejection of God).

A reprobate is a morally unprincipled person; one who is shameless; a depraved, unprincipled, or wicked person; someone rejected by God and without hope of salvation. Continual rejection of God and His Spirit is dangerous and wicked. (See Acts 7:51.)

And since they did not see fit to acknowledge God, God gave them over to a debased mind, to do those things which are not proper.

—ROMANS 1:28

Now as Jannes and Jambres resisted Moses, so these also resist the truth, men of corrupt minds and worthless concerning the faith.

—2 TIMOTHY 3:8

Examine yourselves, seeing whether you are in the faith; test yourselves. Do you not know that Jesus Christ is in you?—unless indeed you are disqualified.

—2 CORINTHIANS 13:5

They profess that they know God, but in their deeds they deny Him, being abominable, disobedient, and worthless for every good work.

—TITUS 1:16

You expose foxes (craftiness).

A fox is a crafty, sly, or clever person. This craftiness can also be personified by a weasel, which is a person regarded as sneaky or treacherous.

He perceived their craftiness and said to them, "Why do you test Me?"

—LUKE 20:23

He said to them, "Go and tell that fox, 'Look, I cast out demons. And I perform healings today and tomorrow, and on the third day I shall be perfected.'"

—LUKE 13:32

O Israel, your prophets are like the foxes in the ruins.

—EZEKIEL 13:4

Catch the foxes for us, the little foxes that spoil the vineyards, for our vineyards are in blossom.

—SONG OF SONGS 2:15

You expose seducers and seducing spirits.

Seduce means "to attract or lead (someone) away from proper behavior or thinking; to induce (someone) to engage in sexual activity, as by flirting or persuasion; to entice into a different state or position." [8]

But evil men and seducers will grow worse and worse, deceiving and being deceived.

—2 TIMOTHY 3:13

I have written these things to you concerning those who deceive you.

—1 JOHN 2:26

But I have a few things against you: You permit that woman Jezebel, who calls herself a prophetess, to teach and seduce My servants to commit sexual immorality and eat food sacrificed to idols.

—REVELATION 2:20

> Now the Spirit clearly says that in the last times some will depart from the faith and pay attention to seducing spirits and doctrines of devils.
>
> —1 TIMOTHY 4:1

You expose the spirit of mammon.

Mammon is greed, covetousness, and the love of money. Jesus exposed it among the leaders in Israel. You cannot serve God and mammon. False prophets are controlled by mammon. True prophets expose mammon.

> No man can serve two masters: for either he will hate the one, and love the other; or else he will hold to the one, and despise the other. Ye cannot serve God and mammon.
>
> —MATTHEW 6:24, KJV

> For the love of money is the root of all evil. While coveting after money, some have strayed from the faith and pierced themselves through with many sorrows.
>
> —1 TIMOTHY 6:10

You expose hidden things.

Prophets will see hidden pride, hidden ambition, hidden lust, hidden witchcraft, hidden wickedness, hidden agendas, and hidden lies.

> Woe to those who deeply hide their counsel from the LORD and whose works are done in the dark, and they say, "Who sees us?" and "Who knows us?"
>
> —ISAIAH 29:15

> How the things of Esau have been ransacked! How his hidden treasures hunted out!
>
> —OBADIAH 6

You expose hypocrisy.

Notice in Matthew 6:2–16, Matthew 23:3–29, and other places throughout Matthew how much Jesus (the Prophet like unto Moses) spoke about hypocrisy. Hypocrisy is the "practice of claiming to have moral standards or beliefs to which one's own behavior does not conform; pretense."[9]

> You hypocrites, Isaiah well prophesied of you.
>
> —MATTHEW 15:7

> And in the morning, "It will be foul weather today, for the sky is red and overcast." O you hypocrites, you can discern the face of the sky, but you cannot discern the signs of the times.
>
> —MATTHEW 16:3

But Jesus perceived their wickedness and said, "Why test Me, you hypocrites?"

—Matthew 22:18

Therefore, whatever they tell you to observe, that observe and do, but do not do their works. For they speak, but do nothing.

—Matthew 23:3

Woe to you, scribes and Pharisees, hypocrites! You shut the kingdom of heaven against men. For you neither enter yourselves, nor allow those who are entering to go in.

—Matthew 23:13

And will cut him in pieces and appoint him his portion with the hypocrites, where there shall be weeping and gnashing of teeth.

—Matthew 24:51

You want people to experience God.

Jacob called the name of the place Peniel, saying, "I have seen God face to face, and my life has been preserved."

—Genesis 32:30

Dreams, visions, glory, weeping, visitations at night, under the power for long periods of time, angels—these are what prophets want others to experience in the presence of God.

You want to see something done.

When there is a need, a problem, a situation, or an error, prophets don't just want to talk about it. They want action! They sometimes get into trouble because they press for action and change. They hate when nothing is done and people just cover up and delay.

You are focused and like praying the plans and purposes of God.

Prophets don't want to just pray about anything and everything. Prophets want to "zero in" on what God wants to do. They want to hit the "bull's-eye." Prophets are focused on the will of God in a situation. If you want to hit the target, ask a prophet to pray.

You look for spiritual rivers.

Prophets like the flow of the Spirit. The flow of the Spirit is likened unto a river. The river of God is important to prophets. They like river churches and river believers. They want to know where God's power is flowing.

Prophets don't like when the flow of the Spirit is blocked. Prophets work to remove the obstacles that block the river. They like to be in services where there is a strong flow of the Spirit. Prophets want to see the river of God flow in their regions and territories.

There is a river whose streams make glad the city of God, the holy dwelling place of the Most High.

—Psalm 46:4

He who believes in Me, as the Scripture has said, out of his heart shall flow rivers of living water.

—John 7:38

Prophets look for rivers, currents, flow, living water, river churches, and spiritual dams.

You dig wells.

Prophets will dig wells where there is no water. They don't like when the things of the Spirit are plugged and stopped up. They are like Isaac, who redug the wells the Philistines had stopped up. Prophets will redig the wells that have been stopped up in a region by sin, apathy, and compromise. They dig new wells and open old wells. Prophets will get the water flowing.

If you want the wells unstopped and the water released, get a prophet.

Isaac dug again the wells of water, which they had dug in the days of Abraham his father, for the Philistines had stopped them up after the death of Abraham. He called their names after the names his father had called them.

—Genesis 26:18

You build the waste places.

Like Nehemiah, prophets rebuild. They build the old waste places. They raise up the former desolations. They repair the waste cities. Prophets repair, rebuild, and restore.

They shall build the old ruins; they shall raise up the former desolations, and they shall repair the waste cities, the desolations of many generations.

—Isaiah 61:4

You are a repairer of the breach and a restorer of paths to dwell in.

Prophets deal with ruins, broken walls, lost paths, and fallen foundations in the lives of people. Prophets are all about rebuilding, repairing, and restoring the lives of the broken.

Those from among you shall rebuild the old waste places; you shall raise up the foundations of many generations; and you shall be called, the Repairer of the Breach, the Restorer of Paths in which to Dwell.

—Isaiah 58:12

You stand in the breach.

This is intercession. This is pleading on the behalf of people. This is standing in the gap. This is asking for mercy.

> Blessed are those who keep justice and who do righteousness at all times.
>
> —Psalm 106:3

> Therefore He said that He would destroy them, had not Moses, His chosen one, stood before Him to intercede, to turn away His wrath from destroying them.
>
> —Psalm 106:23

> I sought for a man among them who would build up the hedge and stand in the gap before Me for the land so that I would not destroy it, but I found no one.
>
> —Ezekiel 22:30

You repair altars.

An altar is a place of sacrifice, consecration, worship, prayer, glory, and manifestation.

> Elijah said to all the people, "Come near to me." And all the people came near to him. And he repaired the altar of the Lord that was broken down.
>
> —1 Kings 18:30

> Then I will go to the altar of God, to the God of my joyful gladness; with the harp I will give thanks to You, O God, my God.
>
> —Psalm 43:4

You want to see deliverance and restoration.

> But this is a people robbed and despoiled; they are all snared in holes, and they are hidden in prison houses; they are for a prey, and no one delivers, for a spoil, and no one says, "Restore them."
>
> —Isaiah 42:22

You turn hearts (reconciliation).

Prophets deal with heart issues. The prophet's ministry turns the heart and brings reconciliation between those who have been separated.

> And he shall turn and reconcile the hearts of the [estranged] fathers to the [ungodly] children, and the hearts of the [rebellious] children to [the piety of] their fathers [a reconciliation produced by repentance of the ungodly], lest I come and smite the land with a curse and a ban of utter destruction.
>
> —Malachi 4:6, ampc

You have intimacy with God.

Intimacy is a strength of a prophet. The prophet knows how to withdraw and get with God. Intimacy is about a close, familiar, and usually affectionate or loving personal relationship with another person or group. Prophets love being alone with God. Prophets love ministering to the Lord (worshipping).

Prophets cultivate intimacy with the Father and the ability to hear His voice. Fasting, prayer, and ministering to the Lord are all part of how prophets draw near to God.

> As they worshipped the Lord and fasted, the Holy Spirit said, "Set apart for Me Barnabas and Saul for the work to which I have called them."
>
> —Acts 13:2

> My beloved speaks and says to me: "Rise up, my love, my fair one, and come away."
>
> —Song of Songs 2:10

You are covenant messengers.

The prophets were sent by the king to call Israel back to covenant. Prophets are concerned about covenant. The church is the New Testament covenant community. Broken covenant (fellowship) will grieve prophets. Prophets demand that we live up to our covenant obligations.

> The earth also is defiled by its inhabitants because they have transgressed the laws, violated the ordinances, broken the everlasting covenant.
>
> —Isaiah 24:5

> Now may the God of peace, who through the blood of the eternal covenant brought again from the dead our Lord Jesus, the Great Shepherd of the sheep...
>
> —Hebrews 13:20

You look for fruit.

Jesus came to Israel looking for fruit. Jesus cursed the fig tree because it had no fruit. Israel was religious but fruitless. Fruit is important to God and to the prophet. Prophets hate barrenness. Prophets need more than talk, sermons, prayers, and religious activity. Prophets look for fruit. Prophets are grieved at fruitlessness.

> Therefore, bear fruit worthy of repentance.
>
> —Matthew 3:8

> So he said to the vinedresser of his vineyard, "Now these three years I have come looking for fruit on this fig tree, and I find none. Cut it down. Why should it deplete the soil?"
>
> —LUKE 13:7

> When He saw a fig tree by the road, He went to it but found nothing on it except leaves. He said to it, "Let no fruit ever grow on you again." Immediately the fig tree withered away.
>
> —MATTHEW 21:19

You look for works.

The prophet says, "Faith without works is dead." Prophets hate the claim to faith without corresponding actions. I like the Amplified Version, Classic Edition of James 2:17, "So also faith, if it does not have works (deeds and actions of obedience to back it up), by itself is destitute of power (inoperative, dead)."

> So faith by itself, if it has no works, is dead.
>
> —JAMES 2:17

You look at deeds.

Prophets don't go by what people say but what they do (their deeds). A deed is something that is carried out; an act or action.[10] They either produce evil deeds or righteous deeds.

> Not everyone who says to Me, "Lord, Lord," shall enter the kingdom of heaven, but he who does the will of My Father who is in heaven.
>
> —MATTHEW 7:21

> For everyone who does evil hates the light and does not come to the light, lest his deeds should be exposed. But he who does the truth comes to the light, that it may be revealed that his deeds have been done in God.
>
> —JOHN 3:20–21

> "You are doing the works of your father." Then they said to Him, "We were not born of sexual immorality. We have one Father: God."
>
> —JOHN 8:41

> My little children, let us love not in word and speech, but in action and truth.
>
> —1 JOHN 3:18

> …and blasphemed the God of heaven because of their pains and their sores, and did not repent of their deeds.
>
> —REVELATION 16:11

You look for sincerity.

Sincere means "not feigned or affected; genuine; being without hypocrisy or pretense; true; pure; unadulterated." [11]

> Therefore let us keep the feast, not with old yeast, nor with the yeast of malice and wickedness, but with the unleavened bread of sincerity and truth.
>
> —1 Corinthians 5:8

> For we are not as many are who peddle the word of God. Instead, being sent by God, we sincerely speak in Christ in the sight of God.
>
> —2 Corinthians 2:17

> In all things presenting yourself as an example of good works: in doctrine showing integrity, gravity, incorruptibility.
>
> —Titus 2:7

You look for tears (weeping).

Tears (weeping) are a sign of a contrite spirit. Prophets look for real repentance and tears when there is a need to return to the Lord.

> The sacrifices of God are a broken spirit; a broken and a contrite heart, O God, You will not despise.
>
> —Psalm 51:17

> Those who sow in tears shall reap in joy.
>
> —Psalm 126:5

> Yet even now, declares the Lord, return to Me with all your heart, and with fasting and with weeping and with mourning.
>
> —Joel 2:12

You don't judge by outward appearance.

Prophets look at what is inside. They are not fooled by the outward appearance.

> Woe to you, scribes and Pharisees, hypocrites! You are like whitewashed tombs, which indeed appear beautiful outwardly, but inside are full of dead men's bones and of all uncleanness.
>
> —Matthew 23:27

You hunger and thirst for righteousness.

One of the prime motivations of prophets is a desire to do and see what is right. Prophets hate unrighteousness. Prophets have a strong desire to see things done and set right. This is what satisfies the prophet.

> Blessed are those who hunger and thirst for righteousness, for they shall be filled.
>
> —Matthew 5:6

> Great blessings belong to those who want to do right more than anything else. God will fully satisfy them.
>
> —Matthew 5:6, erv

You can identify children of the devil.

In other words, prophets can identify people who are being used and controlled by the devil to bring harm and destruction. Jesus identified people this way. Paul identified Elymas the sorcerer this way. Prophets can identify the enemies of God and His kingdom.

> You are of your father the devil, and you want to do the desires of your father. He was a murderer from the beginning, and does not stand in the truth, because there is no truth in him. When he lies, he speaks from his own nature, for he is a liar and the father of lies.
>
> —John 8:44

> You son of the devil, enemy of all righteousness, full of deceit and of all fraud, will you not cease perverting the right ways of the Lord?
>
> —Acts 13:10

You cannot tolerate evil.

Tolerate means "to allow the existence, presence, practice, or act of without prohibition or hindrance; permit."[12] Prophets will speak up against evil.

> Whoever privately slanders his neighbor, him I will destroy; whoever has a haughty look and a proud heart I will not endure.
>
> —Psalm 101:5

> For [you seem readily to endure it] if a man comes and preaches another Jesus than the One we preached, or if you receive a different spirit from the [Spirit] you [once] received or a different gospel from the one you [then] received and welcomed; you tolerate [all that] well enough!
>
> —2 Corinthians 11:4, ampc

> But I have a few things against you: You permit that woman Jezebel, who calls herself a prophetess, to teach and seduce My servants to commit sexual immorality and eat food sacrificed to idols.
>
> —Revelation 2:20

You battle (contend) against the wicked.

> Those who abandon Instruction praise the wicked, but those who follow Instruction battle them.
>
> —PROVERBS 28:4, CEB

> Those who abandon God's teachings praise wicked people, but those who follow God's teachings oppose wicked people.
>
> —PROVERBS 28:4, GW

> I confronted the officials and asked, "Why is the house of God forsaken?" So I gathered them and stationed them at their posts.
>
> —NEHEMIAH 13:11

> You shall seek them and shall not find them, even those who contended with you. Those who war against you shall be as nothing, as a thing of nonexistence.
>
> —ISAIAH 41:12

You don't whitewash evil.

Whitewash is a mixture of lime and water, often with whiting, size, or glue added, that is used to whiten walls, fences, or other structures. It means to conceal or gloss over (wrongdoing, for example).

> When the wall has fallen, will you not be asked, "Where is the whitewash with which you daubed it?"
>
> —EZEKIEL 13:12

You speak when the wicked prosper.

Prophets speak and pray when the wicked prosper. They stand up when it seems as if the wicked are prospering and the righteous are struggling. Prophets remind us that it will not go well with the wicked and the righteous should not fret.

> Rest in the LORD, and wait patiently for Him; do not fret because of those who prosper in their way, because of those who make wicked schemes.
>
> —PSALM 37:7

> Hope in the LORD, and keep His way, and He will exalt you to inherit the land; when the wicked are cut off, you will see it. I have seen the wicked in great power, and spreading himself like a luxuriant tree. Yet he passed away, and he was not; I sought him, but he could not be found.
>
> —PSALM 37:34–36

> For I was envious at the boastful; I saw the prosperity of the wicked.
>
> —PSALM 73:3

> Observe, these are the wicked, always at ease; they increase in riches.
>
> —Psalm 73:12

You take a stand against immorality.

Prophets will not stand for sexual sin, greed, wasteful living, impurity, and other immoralities.

> Shun immorality and all sexual looseness [flee from impurity in thought, word, or deed]. Any other sin which a man commits is one outside the body, but he who commits sexual immorality sins against his own body.
>
> —1 Corinthians 6:18, ampc

> But immorality (sexual vice) and all impurity [of lustful, rich, wasteful living] or greediness must not even be named among you, as is fitting and proper among saints (God's consecrated people).
>
> —Ephesians 5:3, ampc

> Let us live and conduct ourselves honorably and becomingly as in the [open light of] day, not in reveling (carousing) and drunkenness, not in immorality and debauchery (sensuality and licentiousness), not in quarreling and jealousy.
>
> —Romans 13:13, ampc

You don't walk and agree with just anyone.

Prophets don't agree with everything. *Agree* means "to accept or support a policy or program."[13]

> Do two people walk together, if they have not agreed?
>
> —Amos 3:3

> What agreement has the temple of God with idols? For you are the temple of the living God. As God has said: "I will live in them and walk in them. I will be their God, and they shall be My people."
>
> —2 Corinthians 6:16

You understand God-ordained relationships.

Relationships are very important to prophets. Relationships are important to destiny. God-ordained relationships are a part of fulfilling your destiny and purpose. These relationships include:

- Husband-wife relationships
- Ministry relationships
- Father-son relationships
- Covenant relationships

The prophet asks, "Are you connected to the right people?"

> As they worshipped the Lord and fasted, the Holy Spirit said, "Set apart for Me Barnabas and Saul for the work to which I have called them."
>
> —ACTS 13:2

You let people know when they are connected to the wrong people.

Eliezer prophesied to Jehoshaphat concerning his connection with the wicked king Amaziah. This connection caused his works to fail. People who want to be in relationships that are not ordained of God may resent this. Prophets will let you know when you are bound by bad soul ties or ungodly connections.

> And Eliezer son of Dodavahu from Mareshah prophesied against Jehoshaphat saying, "Because you have joined with Ahaziah, the LORD will tear down your works." So the ships were wrecked, so that they were not able to journey to Tarshish.
>
> —2 CHRONICLES 20:37

> Do not be so deceived and misled! Evil companionships (communion, associations) corrupt and deprave good manners and morals and character.
>
> —1 CORINTHIANS 15:33, AMPC

You are an iconoclast (Nehushtan).

An iconoclast is a breaker of idols. The children of Israel began to worship the brazen serpent that God instructed Moses to raise in the wilderness. The brazen serpent became an idol. It was later smashed. Sometimes old moves of God have become idols. The prophet will smash these idols.

An iconoclast is a person who attacks cherished beliefs, traditional institutions, and the like as being based on error or superstition. These iconoclast characteristics apply to apostles as well.

> He removed the high places, broke down the sacred pillars, cut down the Asherah poles, and crushed the bronze serpent that Moses had made, for until those days the children of Israel had made offerings to it. *They called it Nehushtan.*
>
> —2 KINGS 18:4, EMPHASIS ADDED

You are an insider who thinks like outsider.

God uses prophets to keep the church on course. Sometimes it takes a person on the outside to see clearly and press for change. I call the prophet an insider who sees like an outsider. The prophet sometimes feels like an outsider, although the prophet is a member of the faith community. Insiders tend to be nearsighted and sometimes cannot see the forest for the trees. I want to emphasize that the prophet is a member of the church. I call them the insider who sometimes feels like an outsider.

Outsiders can be critical of what is happening because they see things differently. Outsiders can be more objective. Sometimes insiders reject all critique from outsiders, but often the outsider is right. The outsider has nothing to lose. The outsider is not invested like the insider.

You think outside the box.

This is a metaphor that means to think differently, unconventionally, or from a new perspective. Prophets cannot fit in the box. Prophets stretch us. Prophets help us break limitations. They are visionaries. They help us move out of ruts and routine. They not only think outside the box, but they also help us break out of the box.

Religion and tradition can become a box. Limitations, thinking, mind-sets, barriers, and so on are other boxes.

You are a problem solver.

When Pharaoh had a problem (a dream), he called Joseph. When King Nebuchadnezzar had a problem (a dream), he called Daniel. Daniel was described as a man that solved "knotty problems."

If you have a problem, get with a prophet. Prophets have solutions.

> Because an excellent spirit, knowledge, and understanding to interpret dreams, clarify riddles, and solve knotty problems were found in this same Daniel, whom the king named Belteshazzar. Now let Daniel be called, and he will show the interpretation.
> —Daniel 5:12, ampc

You are a person of vision.

Prophets have to have vision. They cannot live aimless lives. They want to know what the vision is. They want to know where we are going. They want to know where the church is going. They ask, "What does the future hold?"

> Where there is no vision, the people perish; but happy is he who keeps the teaching.
> —Proverbs 29:18

> And the Lord answered me: Write the vision, and make it plain on tablets, that he who reads it may run.
> —Habakkuk 2:2

You are a spark plug.

A spark plug is one who gives life or energy to an endeavor. Prophets are catalysts. Synonyms for *catalyst* include stimulus, stimulation, spark, spark plug, spur, incitement, and impetus.

Prophets help get things moving. Prophets like to get things moving. They hate when things are stagnant and not moving. They are like a spark that ignites. Their words ignite. Their prayers ignite. Their songs ignite.

You don't settle for less.

Prophets know there is more to come.
Prophets know there is more to do.
Prophets know there is more to experience.
Prophets know there is more to know.
Prophets know there is more to believe.
Prophets know there is more to happen.
Prophets know there is more to see.
Prophets know there is more to hear.

> Now to Him who is able to do exceedingly abundantly beyond all that we ask or imagine, according to the power that works in us.
>
> —EPHESIANS 3:20

You are a contender (fighters).

Contend means "struggle to surmount (a difficulty or danger)."[14] To contend is to fight or battle. Contenders are overcomers. Contenders fight for truth. Contenders fight for justice. Prophets always seem to be fighting something. Prophets can sometimes think, "Am I the only one fighting this?" That is the nature of a prophet: they are fighters.

> Beloved, while I diligently tried to write to you of the salvation we have in common, I found it necessary to write and appeal to you to contend for the faith which was once delivered to the saints.
>
> —JUDE 3

> Those who forsake instruction praise the wicked, but such as keep instruction contend with them.
>
> —PROVERBS 28:4

You are a Zadok.

Zadoks were the faithful priests who did not go astray like other Levites. God commended them for their faithfulness and obedience. Faithfulness to God is a priority with prophets. Zadok was also a seer.

> The king also said to Zadok the priest, "Are you not a seer? Return to the city in peace with your two sons, your son Ahimaaz and Jonathan the son of Abiathar."
>
> —2 SAMUEL 15:27

> But the Levitical priests, the sons of Zadok, who kept the charge of My sanctuary when the sons of Israel went astray from Me, they shall

come near to Me to minister to Me, and they shall stand before Me to
offer to Me the fat and the blood, says the Lord GOD.

—EZEKIEL 44:15

It shall be for the priests who are sanctified of the sons of Zadok, who
have kept My charge, who did not go astray when the sons of Israel
went astray as the Levites went astray.

—EZEKIEL 48:11

You know your people.

Prophets know the people they are assigned to. They know their good
points, and they know their bad points. Jesus knew the Jews and dealt with
them strongly. Prophets are honest. Prophets tell their people the truth.

One of them, a prophet of their own, said, "The Cretans are always
liars, evil beasts, and idle gluttons!" This witness is true. So rebuke
them sharply that they may be sound in the faith.

—TITUS 1:12–13

You speak to the remnant.

Prophets spoke to the remnant in Israel. There was always a true Israel
within Israel. They were promised salvation, deliverance, and restoration. The
remnant are the faithful. Prophets bless and encourage the remnant.

Still, I have preserved seven thousand men in Israel for Myself, all
of whose knees have not bowed to Baal and whose mouths have not
kissed him.

—1 KINGS 19:18

For from Jerusalem shall go out a remnant, and those who escape out
of Mount Zion. The zeal of the LORD of Hosts shall do this.

—ISAIAH 37:32

Then the dragon was angry with the woman, and he went to wage war
with the remnant of her offspring, who keep the commandments of
God and have the testimony of Jesus Christ.

—REVELATION 12:17

You challenge those who claim to be God's people.

Prophets were sent to challenge those who claimed to be God's people. Israel
claimed it in name but denied it in action. Hosea named one of his children
Lo-Ammi, which meant "not My people." Prophets are concerned about those
who are supposed to be God's people. A common phrase throughout Scripture
is "you shall be My people, and I will be your God."

Prophets want your action to line up with your claim.

Then the LORD said: "Call his name Lo-Ammi, for you are not My people, and I am not your God."

—HOSEA 1:9

You plead.

Plead means "to present and argue for (a position), especially in court or in another public context." Prophets plead for those that have no advocate. They plead for those who have no voice. They plead in prayer. They plead with their voice. Prophets also plead for the righteous.

No one calls for justice, nor does anyone plead for truth. They trust in vanity and speak lies; they conceive mischief and bring forth iniquity.

—ISAIAH 59:4

Open your mouth, judge righteously, and plead the cause of the poor and needy.

—PROVERBS 31:9

Learn to do good; seek justice, relieve the oppressed; judge the fatherless, plead for the widow.

—ISAIAH 1:17

You are a servant.

Prophets are God's servants, and they also serve man. The term *servant* implies subservience and humility. The Hebrew term is *ebed*, which also has the connotation of an official or an officer, especially an officer of a royal court. The greatest in the kingdom is the servant. Prophets serve in an official capacity.

Surely the Lord GOD does nothing without revealing His purpose to His servants the prophets.

—AMOS 3:7

We have not listened to Your servants the prophets, who spoke in Your name.

—DANIEL 9:6

You are a burning one.

In Isaiah 6:1–8 *seraphim* is the word Isaiah used to describe fiery beings that fly around God's throne singing, "Holy, holy, holy." It translates in Hebrew to literally "burning ones." There is a new breed of prophets arising in this season who are sent out by the throne of heaven to deliver the word of the Lord. These prophets are the burning ones for this age. They will speak as the prophets of old, burning with a fire that will not be contained. The word of the Lord in their hearts is like a burning fire. They will ignite the world with this word.

> But if I say, "I will not make mention of Him nor speak any more in His name," then His word was in my heart as a burning fire shut up in my bones; and I was weary of forbearing it, and I could not endure it.
>
> —JEREMIAH 20:9

You preach the reality not the shadow.

The Law was a shadow, but Christ is the reality. The shadows (types and symbols) are fulfilled in Christ. Prophets help us get away from the shadows so we can experience the fulfillment in Christ. Prophets deal with spiritual realities, not shadows and types such as Passover, Pentecost, Day of Atonement, dietary laws, circumcision, sabbaths, and the like.

You have ears to hear.

If anyone has ears to hear what the Lord is saying to the church, it should be the prophets. Where were the prophets in the seven churches of Asia (Rev. 1–3)? The Lord sent a word to the seven churches and was speaking to those who had ears to hear. The Lord sends His word to churches and looks for those who have ears to hear.

> He who has an ear, let him hear what the Spirit says to the churches. To him who overcomes I will give permission to eat of the tree of life, which is in the midst of the Paradise of God.
>
> —REVELATION 2:7

You hear the still, small voice.

Sometimes the Lord is not in the wind, the earthquake, or the fire, but in the still small voice. The prophet can hear the still, small voice in the midst of the wind, the earthquake, and the fire. The prophet does not get caught up in the dramatic, but he can hear the still, small voice. The prophet sometimes has to get quiet to hear this voice, "What is God saying that I can hear only when I quiet down and listen to what He is saying deep within?"

Get quiet, prophets, and let God speak to you in the still, small voice.

> He said, "Go and stand on the mountain before the LORD." And, behold, the LORD passed by, and a great and strong wind split the mountains and broke in pieces the rocks before the LORD, but the LORD was not in the wind. And after the wind, an earthquake came, but the LORD was not in the earthquake. And after the earthquake, a fire came, but the LORD was not in the fire, and after the fire, a still, small voice. When Elijah heard it, he wrapped his face in his cloak and went out and stood in the entrance to the cave. And a voice came to him and said, "Why are you here, Elijah?"
>
> —1 KINGS 19:11–13

You remind people that power (strength) belongs to God.

Strength comes from God. God is the source of power and strength. Prophets encourage us to draw from God's strength.

> God says there is one thing you can really depend on, and I believe it: "Strength comes from God!"
>
> —Psalm 62:11, erv

> God has spoken once, twice have I heard this: that power belongs to God.
>
> —Psalm 62:11

> O God, You are awesome from Your sanctuaries; the God of Israel is He who gives strength and power to people. Blessed be God!
>
> —Psalm 68:35

> Do not fear, for I am with you; do not be dismayed, for I am your God. I will strengthen you, I will help you, yes, I will uphold you with My righteous right hand.
>
> —Isaiah 41:10

You remind people that it's by the Spirit.

No program can replace the power of the Spirit. Entertainment does not replace the power of the Spirit. Prophets will cry out whenever churches move away from the power of the Spirit.

> And he said to me: "This is the word of the Lord to Zerubbabbel, saying: Not by might nor by power, but by My Spirit, says the Lord of Hosts."
>
> —Zechariah 4:6

CHAPTER 2

WHAT MOVES YOUR HEART?

*God gave Solomon wisdom and great depth of understanding
as well as compassion, as vast as the sand on the seashore.*
—1 KINGS 4:29

ONTINUING OUR LOOK into what characteristics are common among prophets, we go deeper into the prophet's heart. In prophets we see many sides to God's heart—compassion, hatred of sin and unrighteousness, holiness, grief, encouragement, power, joy, zeal, and so on. Prophets carry within them the heart of the Father. They feel what the Father feels at different times.

This can be a difficult thing for prophets to learn to handle. They can feel as if they are on an emotional roller coaster.

Don't fret, prophet, and don't be confused. You are special. You carry within you the heartbeat of God.

David was a man after God's own heart.

The LORD has sought for Himself a man after His own heart and the LORD has commanded him to be prince over His people.
—1 SAMUEL 13:14

Prophets have big hearts. This chapter reveals how deep and wide the prophet's heart is. God gives prophets His heart. Prophets are in tune with the heartbeat of God. Their hearts beat in rhythm with the heart of God. They love what God loves and hate what He hates. This is what makes prophets unique: their heart. Read on to see if you find yourself on these pages.

THE HEART OF THE PROPHET

Jesus wept over the city of Jerusalem because they missed their time of visitation. This is the heart of the prophet. The prophet grieves and weeps when people miss what God has for them. This is what breaks the prophet's heart.

And when he was come near, he beheld the city, and wept over it,
Saying, If thou hadst known, even thou, at least in this thy day, the

things which belong unto thy peace! but now they are hid from thine eyes.

—LUKE 19:41–42, KJV

WHAT STIRS PROPHETS

Prophets are stirred by other prophets. Prophets benefit from being in a prophetic community. Hearing another prophet's revelation stirs the prophet.

Let two or three prophets speak, and let the others judge. If anything is revealed to another that sits by, let the first keep silent. For you may all prophesy one by one, that all may learn and all may be encouraged.

—1 CORINTHIANS 14:29–31

WHAT MATTERS TO PROPHETS

The things that matter to other people do not matter to prophets. Prophets are concerned about things that others overlook. They are not concerned about carnal things. They are concerned about the things of the Spirit. They are often considered "too deep" by carnal people. They are often considered "troublemakers." Prophets are often considered "crazy" by the disobedient and rebellious.

When Ahab saw Elijah, Ahab said to him, "Are you he that troubles Israel?"

—1 KINGS 18:17

The days of punishment have come; the days of recompense have come. Israel knows! The prophet is a fool; the man of the spirit is insane, because of your great iniquity and great hatred.

—HOSEA 9:7

Judgment (justice), mercy, faith, humility, compassion, love, and truth matter greatly to prophets.

Woe to you, scribes and Pharisees, hypocrites! You tithe mint and dill and cumin, but have neglected the weightier matters of the law: justice and mercy and faith. These you ought to have done without leaving the others undone.

—MATTHEW 23:23

He has told you, O man, what is good—and what does the Lord require of you, but to do justice and to love kindness, and to walk humbly with your God?

—MICAH 6:8

Thus says the LORD of Hosts: Execute true justice, show mercy and compassion, every man to his brother.

—ZECHARIAH 7:9

No one calls for justice, nor does anyone plead for truth. They trust in vanity and speak lies; they conceive mischief and bring forth iniquity.

—ISAIAH 59:4, KJV

Character is also important to prophets, not just charisma.

WHAT GIVES PROPHETS JOY

- Prophets are stirred and joyful when they see revival and glory.
- They are stirred and joyful when they see God's people moving and advancing.
- They get excited and joyful when they see the people of God and the church breaking through barriers and obstacles.
- They are stirred and joyful when they see the release of power and miracles.
- They love to see people saved, delivered, and healed.
- They love it when backsliders return.
- They are joyful when they see the things for which they have been praying for years manifest.
- They are joyful when they see the poor and neglected lifted.
- They are joyful when they see wickedness defeated and righteousness prevailing.

WHAT CAUSES PROPHETS TO GRIEVE

Prophets are grieved and bothered by what others overlook. Prophets have a sensitivity to the things that grieve God:

- Injustice
- When things are out of order
- When the wicked prosper and the righteous suffer
- When the poor and helpless are taken advantage of and mistreated
- When the church is not fulfilling its call and purpose
- When the wrong people are in authority
- Hypocrisy
- False teaching

- Carnality and apostasy (departure from God and the truth)
- Unfairness and abuse
- Religious tradition and religious control
- Pride, vanity, and arrogance
- False worship and wolves (false ministries)
- Greed, covetousness, corruption, crookedness, and theft
- Lukewarmness
- Lying and deception
- Rebellion, witchcraft, and divination

These are the things that drive the prophet to prayer. These are the things that drive them to their prayer closet. They pray for change. They cannot stand the way things are. They cry out to God. They weep in their prayer closet. Praying prophets bring change.

> I behold the transgressors with disgust, because they have not kept Your word.
>
> —Psalm 119:158

Be encouraged, prophets. Your prayers make a difference. Joy will come when they are answered.

> But if you will not listen to it, my soul will weep in secret places for your pride; and my eyes will weep sorely and run down with tears, because the flock of the LORD is carried away captive.
>
> —Jeremiah 13:17

When there is no love

Love is important to prophets. You can have activity, but if there is no love, the prophet is grieved. Strife, division, rudeness, and hatred are grievous sins to a prophet. Prophets know that if you don't have love, you don't know God.

> Beloved, let us love one another, for love is of God, and everyone who loves is born of God and knows God. Anyone who does not love does not know God, for God is love.
>
> —1 John 4:7–8

Hardness of heart

A hard heart is a stony heart. It is a stubborn and unbelieving heart. It is an unyielding heart. Prophets look for soft and tender hearts. Prophets look for broken and contrite hearts.

Jesus became angry at the hardened hearts of the Pharisees.

> When He had looked around at them with anger, being grieved for the hardness of their hearts, He said to the man, "Stretch your hand forward." He stretched it out, and his hand was restored as whole as the other.
>
> —MARK 3:5

> Being aware of it, Jesus said to them, "Why do you reason that you have no bread? Do you still not perceive or understand? Are your hearts still hardened?"
>
> —MARK 8:17

When there is no prayer

Prophets know the house of God is a house of prayer. Prophets call for prayer. Prophets call the church back to prayer.

> Even them I will bring to My holy mountain and make them joyful in My house of prayer. Their burnt offerings and their sacrifices shall be accepted on My altar; for My house shall be called a house of prayer for all people.
>
> —ISAIAH 56:7

When people miss God

Jesus wept over Jerusalem because they had missed the time of their visitation. Divine opportunities can be missed.

> They will dash you, and your children within you, to the ground. They will not leave one stone upon another within you, because you did not know the time of your visitation.
>
> —LUKE 19:44

WHAT PROPHETS LOVE

Symbols and symbolic acts

Symbolism is important to prophets. Sometimes the things of the Spirit are difficult to articulate with your known language and must be acted out or relayed through symbols. Symbols can become the language of the Spirit. The spirit realm is different from the natural realm, and God gives the prophet other ways of relaying a message than the limitations of human language.

> Then he said, "Open the east window." So he opened it. Then Elisha said, "Shoot." So he shot. Then he said, "The arrow of the deliverance of the LORD, and the arrow of deliverance from Aram; for you must strike Aram in Aphek until you have destroyed them."
>
> —2 KINGS 13:17

Prophets love symbols such as banners, flags, oil, swords, crowns, and so on.

The presence of God

God's presence is the oxygen prophets breathe. They hate it when the presence of God is not in the church. They can't abide programs without presence. They can't stay in places that have become an Ichabod. They don't have a problem being in long services when the presence of God is there.

David, a prophet, loved God's presence. His prophecies came out of being in God's presence.

> I have seen You in the sanctuary, to see Your power and Your glory.
> —Psalm 63:2

The bruised and hurting

Prophets won't disregard and overlook those who are broken, bruised, and hurting. They have an eye to see them. They can pick them out of a crowd. They can see those in need of healing and restoration when others overlook them and pass them by.

> He won't brush aside the bruised and the hurt and he won't disregard the small and insignificant, but he'll steadily and firmly set things right. He won't tire out and quit. He won't be stopped until he's finished his work—to set things right on earth.
> —Isaiah 42:3–4, The Message

Worship

Prophets love the glory and presence of God. Prophets are inspirational by nature, and prophets love inspired worship. Prophets love new songs and new sounds. The song of the Lord stirs prophets. Prophets make great worship leaders.

Some of the greatest worshippers in the Bible were prophets. David, Asaph, Heman, and Jeduthun were worshippers who were prophets (1 Chron. 25:1–6). Worship is connected to the spirit of prophecy.

Israel's worship was established by prophets.

> And he set the Levites at the house of the Lord with cymbals, harps, and lyres according to the commandment of David, and Gad the seer of the king, and Nathan the prophet. For the commandment came from the Lord through His prophets.
> —2 Chronicles 29:25

> I fell at his feet to worship him. But he said to me, "See that you not do that. I am your fellow servant, and of your brothers who hold the testimony of Jesus. Worship God! For the testimony of Jesus is the spirit of prophecy."
> —Revelation 19:10

Worship creates an atmosphere for the spirit of prophecy. Prophets and prophetic people thrive in the atmosphere of worship. Prophets can function as worship leaders, psalmists, and minstrels. They release prophetic sounds and prophetic songs that bring deliverance, healing, restoration, and refreshing.

There are also prophets who operate as seers. Seers have the ability to see into the spirit realm and then declare what they see. When seers are involved in our worship, they see what is taking place in the spirit realm while we worship and as a result of our worship. Seers have seen angels, smoke, fire, rain, demons, horses, armies, thrones, jewels, judgments, colors, and so on. They can declare what they see to the congregation and encourage the saints to act on what they see. This results in great freedom and breakthroughs.

We need to make room for seers in our worship services. Any believer can see if God permits, but seers are proven prophetic ministers who are recognized by the leadership of the church.

Anointed music and musicians quicken the prophetic word.

> 2 Kings 3:11–16. King Jehoshaphat desired a prophetic word to give him direction. He inquired for a prophet (vs. 11), and Elisha was brought forward. Elisha sought for a minstrel...[and] the hand of the Lord came upon him (vs. 15). The anointed music quickened the prophetic word to Elisha, and then he prophesied the Word of the Lord. Even a prophet such as Elisha had to have music to quicken the prophetic word.
>
> 1 Samuel 10:5–6, 10. A company of prophets are seen as coming down a road, preceded by those who played psalterys, tabrets, pipes, and harps. The result was that by the preceding of anointed music, not only did the prophets prophesy, but the spirit of prophecy came upon Saul, and he also prophesied. It was the presence of music that quickened the prophetic word to Saul and the prophets.[1]

Prophets, you are not crazy. You are just crazy about praise and worship.

> Praise the LORD! Praise God in His sanctuary; praise Him in the firmament of His power! Praise Him for His mighty acts; praise Him according to His excellent greatness! Praise Him with the sound of the trumpet; praise Him with the lyre and harp! Praise Him with the tambourine and dancing; praise Him with stringed instruments and flute! Praise Him with loud cymbals; praise Him with the clanging cymbals! Let everything that has breath praise the LORD. Praise the LORD!
>
> —PSALM 150:1–6

The dance

Prophets love the dance because they are people of movement. God is a God of movement, and anointed movement can release the blessing of God.

> Miriam the prophetess, the sister of Aaron, took a timbrel in her hand, and all the women went out after her with timbrels and with dancing.
>
> —Exodus 15:20

> Then you will go to the Hill of God in Gibeah, where there is a Philistine camp. At the entrance to the town you will meet a group of prophets coming down from the altar on the hill, playing harps, drums, flutes, and lyres. They will be dancing and shouting.
>
> —1 Samuel 10:5, gnt

> David danced before the Lord with all of his might, and he wore a linen ephod.
>
> —2 Samuel 6:14

Dancing is a symbol of victory, joy, and celebration. No dancing is a sign of defeat and mourning.

> Then the virgin shall rejoice in the dance, both young men and old together; for I will turn their mourning into joy, and will comfort them, and make them rejoice from their sorrow.
>
> —Jeremiah 31:13

> The joy of our hearts has ceased; our dancing has turned into mourning.
>
> —Lamentations 5:15

Musical instruments in the praise of God

Did you know that David made instruments for praise?

> Heman and Jeduthun had with them trumpets and cymbals to sound aloud and instruments for sacred song. The sons of Jeduthun were appointed to the gate.
>
> —1 Chronicles 16:42

> Four thousand shall be gatekeepers, and four thousand shall offer praises to the Lord with the instruments that I have made for praise.
>
> —1 Chronicles 23:5

Liberty

Freedom is the desire of prophets. Prophets hate bondage and control. Prophets hate when the Holy Spirit is quenched. Prophets want God's people to be free and enjoy liberty.

> Now the Lord is the Spirit, and where the Spirit of the Lord is, there is liberty (emancipation from bondage, freedom).
>
> —2 Corinthians 3:17, ampc

> For freedom Christ freed us. Stand fast therefore and do not be
> entangled again with the yoke of bondage.
>
> —GALATIANS 5:1

Rhema

The Bible is the logos. When God quickens a word from the logos, it becomes rhema. There are scriptures that are applicable at certain times in your life. Prophets release the rhema. What God is speaking from His Word (logos) today is rhema.

In Greek the word *rhema* means "an utterance." Therefore the rhema word in biblical terms refers to a portion of Scripture that "speaks" to a believer. Matthew 4:4 is an excellent example of its importance: "Man shall not live by bread alone, but by every word [rhema] that proceeds out of the mouth of God."

To a prophet there is nothing worse than stale preaching and teaching—yesterday's word, yesterday's anointing. Rhema is fresh and applicable in the now season.

We should all love and study the Word (logos). Prophets should study and know the Word (logos), but prophets should release rhema.

Deeper things of the Spirit

Prophets are not shallow. They like depth. They like to understand the deeper things of God. They understand the mysteries of God. They hate shallowness. They are the first to embrace deeper truths. They are called "too deep" by shallow people. Prophets understand that God is greater and deeper than most people understand. Prophets press the church to go deeper, higher, and wider in their understanding of the mysteries of God.

> But God has revealed them to us by His Spirit. For the Spirit searches
> all things, yes, the deep things of God.
>
> —1 CORINTHIANS 2:10

> O LORD, how great are Your works! Your thoughts are very deep!
>
> —PSALM 92:5

The babes

Although prophets love when the saints mature, they also love the babes. Prophets have a heart for the babes (the childish, unskilled, and untaught). The babes are those with childlike faith. The babes are the humble.

It is much easier to deal with babes than with some people who have been in the church for years. Babes are excited about the new things of the Spirit. Prophets love innocence, purity, and childlike faith.

> At that time Jesus rejoiced in the Holy Spirit and said, "I thank You,
> O Father, Lord of heaven and earth, because You have hidden these

things from the wise and intelligent and revealed them to infants. Yes, Father, for it was Your good pleasure."

—Luke 10:21

The faithful

Prophets look for the faithful. Prophets love faithfulness. Prophets love the faithful. The faithful are those who are steadfast with God. The faithful are the ones who serve God without compromise. Prophets grieve when there is no faithfulness.

Prophets encourage the faithful. They remind the faithful of God's blessings and faithfulness to them. They encourage the faithful to keep moving ahead in spite of any obstacles and persecutions. Prophets will preach faithfulness.

> Do not fear any of those things which you are about to suffer. Look, the devil is about to throw some of you into prison, that you may be tried, and you will have tribulation for ten days. Be faithful unto death, and I will give you the crown of life.
>
> —Revelation 2:10

> Help, Lord, for the godly man comes to an end, for the faithful disappear from sons of men.
>
> —Psalm 12:1

> A faithful man will abound with blessings, but he who makes haste to be rich will not be innocent.
>
> —Proverbs 28:20

WHAT PROPHETS HATE

Injustice and hypocrisy

> What do you mean that you beat My people to pieces and grind the faces of the poor? says the Lord God of Hosts.
>
> —Isaiah 3:15

> Woe to you, scribes and Pharisees, hypocrites! You devour widows' houses and for pretense make long prayers. Therefore you will receive the greater condemnation.
>
> —Matthew 23:14

Crookedness

> What is bent cannot be straightened, and what is missing cannot be counted.
>
> —Ecclesiastes 1:15

They have acted corruptly to Him; they are not His children, but blemished; they are a perverse and crooked generation.

—DEUTERONOMY 32:5

The way of peace they do not know, and there is no justice in their ways; they have made their paths crooked; whoever walks in them does not know peace.

—ISAIAH 59:8

Compromise

Prophets see things in black and white. There are no gray areas for prophets. They hate mixture. They often get in trouble for their stand.

Ephraim mixes himself with the people. Ephraim is a cake not turned.

—HOSEA 7:8

Prophets would rather walk alone than compromise. But they are never really alone, because they are the friends of God.

Look to Abraham your father and to Sarah who bore you; for I called him alone, and blessed him, and multiplied him.

—ISAIAH 51:2

Mixture

Mixtures such as...

- Law and grace
- Righteousness and unrighteousness
- Flesh and the Spirit
- Truth and tradition
- Church and the world
- Light and darkness
- Clean and unclean

...are revolting to prophets.

Your silver has become dross, your wine mixed with water.

—ISAIAH 1:22

They serve in a sanctuary that is an example and shadow of the heavenly one, as Moses was instructed by God when he was about to make the tabernacle, "See that you make all things according to the pattern shown you on the mountain."

—HEBREWS 8:5

For the law is a shadow of the good things to come, and not the very image of those things. It could never by the same sacrifices, which they offer continually year after year, perfect those who draw near.

—HEBREWS 10:1

Does a spring yield at the same opening sweet and bitter water?

—JAMES 3:11

A form of godliness with no power

…having a form of godliness, but denying its power. Turn away from such people.

—2 TIMOTHY 3:5

For [although] they hold a form of piety (true religion), they deny and reject and are strangers to the power of it [their conduct belies the genuineness of their profession]. Avoid [all] such people [turn away from them].

—2 TIMOTHY 3:5, AMPC

They will go on pretending to be devoted to God, but they will refuse to let that "devotion" change the way they live. Stay away from these people!

—2 TIMOTHY 3:5, ERV

The traditions of men

Prophets hate the traditions of men that make void the Word of God. Prophets will oppose anything that prevents God's people from obeying Him, including tradition. Prophets will oppose these traditions and warn people of the dangers of religious tradition.

But He answered them, "Why do you also violate the commandment of God by your tradition?"

—MATTHEW 15:3

…making the word of God of no effect through your tradition, which you have delivered. And you do many similar things.

—MARK 7:13

Beware lest anyone captivate you through philosophy and vain deceit, in the tradition of men and the elementary principles of the world, and not after Christ.

—COLOSSIANS 2:8

Religious control

It is wrong for leaders to use prophecy to pronounce judgments (doom and gloom) on people because they do not agree with them. This is a manifestation of control, and true prophets will cry against it. Prophets do not manipulate and control people through a word. This is unjust and will grieve and anger a true prophet.

There is no place for rudeness and arrogance in the prophetic ministry. Prophets can be firm, but all things must be done in love. There is no place for control, manipulation, and domination in the prophetic ministry.

> If I speak with the tongues of men and of angels, and have not love, I have become as sounding brass or a clanging cymbal. If I have the gift of prophecy, and understand all mysteries and all knowledge, and if I have all faith, so that I could move mountains, but have not love, I am nothing.
>
> —1 Corinthians 13:1–2

> It is not conceited (arrogant and inflated with pride); it is not rude (unmannerly) and does not act unbecomingly. Love (God's love in us) does not insist on its own rights or its own way, for it is not self-seeking; it is not touchy or fretful or resentful; it takes no account of the evil done to it [it pays no attention to a suffered wrong].
>
> —1 Corinthians 13:5, ampc

Witchcraft

Witchcraft is a work of the flesh, and it is also a demon. Witchcraft is domination, intimidation, manipulation, sorcery, divination, enchantment, spells, hexes, vexes, and legalism. Prophets will discern it and challenge it.

> And I will cut off witchcrafts out of thine hand; and thou shalt have no more soothsayers.
>
> —Micah 5:12, kjv

Evil and wickedness

> Do not I hate those, O Lord, who hate You? And do I not abhor those who rise up against You? I hate them with perfect hatred; I count them my enemies. Search me, O God, and know my heart; try me, and know my concerns.
>
> —Psalm 139:21–23

> You have loved righteousness and hated wickedness; therefore God, Your God, has anointed You with the oil of gladness more than your companions.
>
> —Hebrews 1:9

Maintaining things

If you give them something to maintain, prophets will want to improve it, change it, renew it, enlarge it, or simply quit. They don't do well in churches that are only maintaining and not changing, improving, and growing.

"Slight healing"

Prophets don't believe in putting a Band-Aid on a deep wound. Don't say, "All is well," when all is not well.

> They have healed also the brokenness of the daughter of my people superficially, saying, "Peace, peace," when there is no peace.
> —JEREMIAH 6:14

> They treat the wound of my people as if it were nothing: "All is well, all is well," they insist, when in fact nothing is well.
> —JEREMIAH 6:14, CEB

Ignorance

What really bugs a prophet is when people reject knowledge. This includes leadership, churches, and ministries that refuse truth and refuse to grow in knowledge. The knowledge of God is important to prophets.

> My people are destroyed for lack of knowledge. Because you have rejected knowledge, I will reject you from being My priest. And because you have forgotten the law of your God, I will also forget your children.
> —HOSEA 4:6

> Therefore My people go into captivity because they have no knowledge; and their honorable men are famished, and their multitude dried up with thirst.
> —ISAIAH 5:13

Lip service

Lip service means "verbal expression of agreement or allegiance, unsupported by real conviction or action; hypocritical respect."[2] Prophets hate when people say but do not do.

> Why do you call Me, "Lord, Lord," and not do what I say?
> —LUKE 6:46

> Therefore, whatever they tell you to observe, that observe and do, but do not do their works. For they speak, but do nothing.
> —MATTHEW 23:3

> This people draw near to Me with their mouth, and honor Me with their lips, but their heart is far from me.
> —MATTHEW 15:8

Flattery

Flattery is excessive and insincere praise, especially that given to further one's own interests. Prophets don't flatter. Prophets speak truth. Prophets don't come to "butter you up."

> For there shall be no more any vain vision nor flattering divination within the house of Israel.
>
> —Ezekiel 12:24

> They speak empty words, each with his own neighbor; they speak with flattering lips and a double heart.
>
> —Psalm 12:2

Playing favorites

This one really bugs prophets.

> You shall not show partiality in judgment, but you shall hear the small as well as the great. You shall not be afraid in any man's presence, for the judgment is God's. The case that is too hard for you, you shall bring it to me, and I will hear it.
>
> —Deuteronomy 1:17

> My brothers, have faith in our Lord Jesus Christ, the Lord of glory, without partiality.
>
> —James 2:1

> But if you show partiality, you are committing sin and are convicted by the law as sinners.
>
> —James 2:9

Thievery

Jesus drove the thieves out of the temple. This is the anger of the prophet. Prophets hate when the temple becomes a house of merchandise. This really bugs prophets. Prophets want the thieves out of the temple. They hate thievery and robbery.

> He said to them, "It is written, 'My house shall be called a house of prayer,' but you have made it 'a den of thieves.'"
>
> —Matthew 21:13

> Woe to the bloody city! It is all full of lies and plunder. The prey never departs.
>
> —Nahum 3:1

Slander

Slander is another thing that bugs prophets. Gossip, backbiting, rumors, and talebearing are sins that need to be exposed and stopped. Prophets can hear slander. They can hear the secret counsel of the wicked. They hate slander against God's leaders, His appointed. Prophets will expose slander. Slander has destroyed ministries, churches, leaders, and so many more.

> For I have heard the slander of many; fear was on every side; while they took counsel together against me, they planned to take away my life.
> —PSALM 31:13

> They are all stubborn rebels walking about practicing slander. They are bronze and iron; they are all corrupters.
> —JEREMIAH 6:28

> Let everyone be on guard against his neighbor, and do not trust in any brother; for every brother supplants, and every neighbor walks about with slanders.
> —JEREMIAH 9:4

Slander and evil speaking have brought much damage to leaders, churches, people, and relationships. It is an evil that must be rooted out. Prophets can detect slander, will pray against it, and help root it out. Slander and evil speaking reflect the condition of the heart. From the abundance of the heart the mouth speaks. Evil people cannot speak good things. Prophets wonder why this bothers them so much. The answer is "Because it is evil."

> You let loose your mouth to evil, and your tongue is bound to deceit. You sit and speak against your brother; you accuse your own mother's son.
> —PSALM 50:19–20

> The tongue is a fire, a world of evil. The tongue is among the parts of the body, defiling the whole body, and setting the course of nature on fire, and it is set on fire by hell.
> —JAMES 3:6

> A perverse man sows strife, and a whisperer separates the best of friends.
> —PROVERBS 16:28

Empty religion

Prophets challenge the church when it moves away from God's power and replaces it with man's agenda, human strength, and earthly wisdom.

Blasphemy

Blaspheme means "to dishonor and insult." Prophets have a passion for the name of the Lord to be honored and exalted.

> O God, how long will the adversary scorn? Will the enemy blaspheme Your name forever?
> —PSALM 74:10

Remember this, that the enemy has scorned, O Lord, and that the foolish people have blasphemed Your name.

—Psalm 74:18

Now therefore, what do have I here, says the Lord, seeing that My people have been taken away for nothing? Those who rule over them make them wail, says the Lord; and My name is continually blasphemed all day long.

—Isaiah 52:5

As it is written, "The name of God is blasphemed among the Gentiles because of you."

—Romans 2:24

Do not they blaspheme that worthy name by the which you are called?

—James 2:7

False discipleship

In other words, prophets hate when leaders make people their disciples instead of making them disciples of Christ.

Woe to you, scribes and Pharisees, hypocrites! You travel sea and land to make one proselyte, and when he becomes one, you make him twice as much a son of hell as yourselves.

—Matthew 23:15

False prophets

- A part of the prophet's ministry is to discern the true from the false. Prophets hate lies and deception.
- False prophets are greedy. True prophets hate greed.
- False prophets are covetous. True prophets hate covetousness.
- False prophets are abusive. True prophets hate abuse.
- False prophets are controlling. True prophets hate control.
- False prophets are arrogant. True prophets are humble.
- False prophets cannot produce good fruit. True prophets look for fruit.
- False prophets are deceptive. True prophets discern deception.

Beware of false prophets who come to you in sheep's clothing, but inwardly they are ravenous wolves. You will know them by their fruit. Do men gather grapes from thorns, or figs from thistles?

—Matthew 7:15–16

> For you permit it if a man brings you into bondage, if a man devours you, if a man takes from you, if a man exalts himself, or if a man strikes you on the face.
>
> —2 Corinthians 11:20

Prophets cannot abide false shepherds, false apostles, false prophets, false teachers, false bishops, false brethren, false accusers, and false witnesses. False doctrine will really bug prophets.

Prophets cannot abide false ministries. They will vex and upset prophets. Prophets want to rescue people from false ministries. A prophet will tell you to "leave." A prophet will help you get out.

> Transgressing and lying against the Lord, and departing away from our God, speaking oppression and revolt, conceiving and uttering from the heart words of falsehood.
>
> —Isaiah 59:13

> My people have been lost sheep. Their shepherds have caused them to go astray; they have turned them away on the mountains. They have gone from mountain to hill and have forgotten their resting place.
>
> —Jeremiah 50:6

> Son of man, prophesy against the shepherds of Israel. Prophesy and say to those shepherds, Thus says the Lord God: Woe to the shepherds of Israel who feed themselves! Should not the shepherds feed the flock?
>
> —Ezekiel 34:2

What Prophets Desire

Demonstration of the Spirit and power

Prophets are not impressed with enticing words of man's wisdom. Prophets want a move of the Spirit in demonstration and power. Man's doctrines and philosophies don't impress prophets. Prophets desire words that release power, healing, deliverance, and miracles.

> My speech and my preaching was not with enticing words of man's wisdom, but in demonstration of the Spirit and of power.
>
> —1 Corinthians 2:4

> I didn't speak my message with persuasive intellectual arguments. I spoke my message with a show of spiritual power.
>
> —1 Corinthians 2:4, gw

To see God's power and glory

> I have seen You in the sanctuary, to see Your power and Your glory.
>
> —Psalm 63:2

David was a prophet. You can learn a lot about the heart of a prophet by studying David. David's desire was to see God's power and glory. David yearned for the presence of God.

Prophets enjoy a lifestyle of power and glory. Prophets want everyone to experience God's power and glory. They cry out, "Lord, show me Your glory!"

> Then Moses said, "I pray, show me Your glory."
>
> —Exodus 33:18

> In the year that King Uzziah died I saw also the Lord sitting upon a throne, high and lifted up, and His train filled the temple.
>
> —Isaiah 6:1

To behold the beauty of the Lord

> One thing I have asked from the Lord, that will I seek after—for me to dwell in the house of the Lord all the days of my life, to see the beauty of the Lord, and to inquire in His temple.
>
> —Psalm 27:4

Prophets love the beauty of God. They want everyone to experience His beauty. God's beauty is His perfection and glory. This was the desire of David, who was a prophet.

The judgments of the Lord

> The fear of the Lord is clean, enduring forever; the judgments of the Lord are true and righteous altogether. More to be desired are they than gold, yes, than much fine gold; sweeter also than honey and the honeycomb.
>
> —Psalm 19:9–10

Prophets love the fear of the Lord and the judgments (ordinances) of the Lord. They desire them more than gold. They are sweeter than honey. Prophets seek and dig into the judgments (ordinances) of God. God's judgments are "a great deep."

> Your righteousness is like the great mountains, Your judgments like the great deep.
>
> —Psalm 36:6

Truth in the inward parts

> You desire truth in the inward parts, and in the hidden part You make
> me to know wisdom.
>
> —Psalm 51:6

Prophets want truth in the inward parts. The hidden part of man is the
prophet's focus. Prophets desire what God desires.

To know the will of God

> For this reason we also, since the day we heard it, do not cease to pray
> for you and to ask that you may be filled with the knowledge of His
> will in all wisdom and spiritual understanding.
>
> —Colossians 1:9

Prophets want to know God's will. They want to be filled with wisdom and
understanding of His will. They desire for God's people to know His will and
be filled with wisdom and spiritual understanding.

Sincere and pure devotion to Christ

Prophets desire a sincere and pure devotion to Christ. They do not want to
see the people of God corrupted from the simplicity of Christ. Simplicity is
sincerity. Prophets want to see an uncorrupted devotion to Christ...

> But [now] I am fearful, lest that even as the serpent beguiled Eve
> by his cunning, so your minds may be corrupted and seduced from
> wholehearted and sincere and pure devotion to Christ.
>
> —2 Corinthians 11:3, ampc

To see God pleased

Prophets are grieved when God is not pleased. Prophets rejoice when God is
pleased. Prophets will reveal what pleases God and what displeases Him.

> But with many of them God was not well pleased, and they were
> overthrown in the wilderness.
>
> —1 Corinthians 10:5

> Finally, brothers, we urge and exhort you by the Lord Jesus, that as
> you have learned from us how you ought to walk and to please God,
> you should excel more and more.
>
> —1 Thessalonians 4:1

CHAPTER 3

WE NEED YOU

See, I have this day set you over the nations and over the kingdoms, to root out and to pull down, to destroy and to throw down, to build and to plant.
—JEREMIAH 1:10

FOR MANY YEARS I have taught our congregation on the subject of prophecy, and I have seen the result of this teaching as thousands of people have been blessed and have learned to hear and move in prophecy. This is not theory to me, but rather it is a lifestyle. I cannot imagine my life without prophecy. This is why this book is in your hands. I want to encourage you to become a part of a worldwide movement that is blessing countless lives.

It is important that we remain scriptural in everything we do. The Word of God provides safety and protection from misuse and abuse of prophecy. This book is filled with scriptural references on the prophetic life, and I encourage you to meditate on these verses. God wants to use His Word of truth to make your way prosperous and to cause good success. In each generation God wants to develop a prophetic culture:

> Surely, the days are coming, says the LORD, when I will make a new covenant with the house of Israel and with the house of Judah. It will not be according to the covenant that I made with their fathers in the day that I took them by the hand to bring them out of the land of Egypt, because they broke My covenant, although I was a husband to them, says the LORD. But this shall be the covenant that I will make with the house of Israel after those days, says the LORD: I will put My law within them and write it in their hearts; and I will be their God, and they shall be My people. They shall teach no more every man his neighbor and every man his brother, saying, "Know the LORD," for they shall know Me from the least of them to the greatest of them, says the LORD, for I will forgive their iniquity, and I will remember their sin no more.
> —JEREMIAH 31:31–34

It is clear that the new covenant God established with Israel and Judah includes knowing the Lord. All believers, from the least of us to the greatest, can have the blessing of knowing God through the Holy Spirit. This includes knowing and recognizing the voice of the Lord. When we use the term *prophecy*, we are simply referring to hearing the voice of the Lord and speaking His word to others.

In other words, every believer has the opportunity to operate in the prophetic realm. Every believer should expect to hear the voice of God. This is because each of us is a new covenant believer. The foundation of the new covenant is the basis for developing your prophetic life.

Every believer should expect to speak as the oracle of God. The key is to develop this ability intentionally. It will not happen automatically. Some believers have doubts about whether God will speak to them. Others can hear His word, but they struggle with speaking out on the behalf of God. All of us need more faith in order to flow in prophecy. Each of us must believe what the Word of God says and then act on it.

It is true: God wants every single person to be a prophet. Remember what Moses said:

> Moses said to him, "Are you jealous for my sake? Oh, that all the people of the LORD were prophets, and that the LORD would put His Spirit upon them!"
>
> —NUMBERS 11:29

This should be the heart of every leader. Moses desired that all of God's people would share in the prophetic anointing through the Holy Spirit being upon them. This is now a reality under the new covenant. We can all have the Holy Spirit upon us, and we can all share in the prophetic anointing.

But the prophetic ministry is more than giving people "the word of the Lord" once in a while. In the context of a prophetic culture, the prophetic ministry will affect every area of the life of the local church. The prophetic ministry will affect the way people in a church live and operate.

Develop means "to build up or expand, to make stronger or more effective, to bring something that is latent into activity." The prophetic ministry is latent or dormant in the lives of many individuals and many churches, and as a result there is a great need for activation. I want to help you develop in the area of prophecy. I want to stir your faith, and I want to impart the necessary knowledge you need to develop prophetically.

PROPHETS ARE ESSENTIAL

In an article titled "Five-Fold Partnership: What Prophets Need," Eric Rafferty tells why prophets are essential to the body of Christ. He says that without the ministry of prophets, apostles, evangelists, shepherds, and teachers get caught up in their own agendas and can stray from the heart of God. "We should all welcome prophets to help our teams, our ministries, and our churches stay close to the heart of God in all that we do," he says. "Prophets create moments where people have an encounter with the living God."[1]

As I mentioned above, prophetic ministry is more than giving a word. Prophets help the body of Christ stay in tune with what the Spirit of God is doing. The tendency of men and movements to get off track in a short period of time is confirmed in the Bible and in the history of the church. The prophet is the one who warns and calls men and movements to get back on track.

During times of intercession and corporate prayer we like to pray for revival. We like for God to move. We pray for a new season, a fresh anointing, or confirmation of a new direction for our ministries. Prophets help to ensure that we stay on track with the specific movement God has ordained for the body of which we are members. Here are some things between men and movements that prophets help us guard against:

1. Men and movements can begin in the Spirit and quickly end up in the flesh.

2. Men and movements can get away from the mandate to advance the kingdom and instead begin to build empires.

3. Men and movements can become controlling and exclusive.

4. Greed and mammon can begin to manifest in men and movements.

5. The standards of righteousness and holiness can begin to fall in a short period of time.

6. Pride and vanity can begin to replace humility and meekness.

7. Error and false teaching can creep into men and movements quickly.

8. The traditions of men can be elevated to the position of Scripture.

9. Ungodly people can rise to leadership positions through manipulation and seduction.

10. Men and movements can stagnate and cease to progress.

11. Men and movements can become obsolete and irrelevant to the present generation in a short period of time.

12. Men and movements can cease to be the salt of the earth.

13. Men and movements can become carnal and worldly and begin to compromise.

14. Men and movements can lose their fire and zeal, and rest on past accomplishments.

WHEN THERE ARE NO PROPHETS

Prophets, along with other ministry gifts, are a sign of God's presence in the church (Ps. 68:18). Whenever the presence of God departed from Israel in Old

Testament times, one indication of His forsaking them was that "there was no longer any prophet" among them (Ps. 74:1, 9).

> You have ascended on high, You have led captivity captive; You have received gifts from people, yes, even from the rebellious, that the LORD God might dwell among them.
>
> —PSALM 68:18

> We do not see our signs; there is no longer any prophet, nor is there among us any who knows how long.
>
> —PSALM 74:9

There were no prophets in Israel when Samuel was born. The priesthood was corrupt, and the nation was in apostasy. Samuel brought a new level of blessing to Israel and transitioned Israel to one of its greatest periods of power and glory.

> Now the boy Samuel was ministering to the LORD before Eli. And the word of the LORD was rare in those days. There was no vision coming forth.
>
> —1 SAMUEL 3:1

When there are no prophets, then there is a famine.

> The time is coming, says the Lord GOD, when I will send a famine on the land, not a famine of bread, nor a thirst for water, but of hearing the words of the LORD. They will wander from sea to sea, and from north to east; they will run back and forth to seek the word of the LORD, but they will not find it.
>
> —AMOS 8:11–12

I believe that God is breaking the famine off of your life and the lives of those to whom you minister. Through His servants the prophets, famine is being broken over cities and regions where there is no prophetic release.

For these reasons we must always be praying for the Holy Spirit to release power through His prophets that they may protect, build, bless, and encourage God's people through His supernatural wisdom and revealed Word.

PROPHETS HELP US DISCERN OUR PART IN GOD'S PLAN

With revelation, apostles and prophets minister the purposes of the Lord for the church. The anointing gives them special insight into divine purposes. They have the ability to make the saints see their part and place in the purposes of God.

...which in other generations was not made known to the sons of men, as it is now revealed to His holy apostles and prophets by the Spirit....And to reveal for all people what is the fellowship of the mystery.

—EPHESIANS 3:5, 9

We all need to know our fellowship (part) in the plan of God. As individuals, churches, and families we need to know what our role is in the plan of God. Prophets deal with eternal purposes. (See Ephesians 3:11.) The eternal plans and purposes ordained by the Lord from before the foundation of the world apply to every person. Each one of us has been born with a part in the eternal purposes of God. We can choose to walk in that purpose or reject it through disobedience and rebellion—or through ignorance.

Prophets minister revelation concerning our fellowship (part) of the mystery (purpose) of the Lord, and those who have a desire to know and fulfill the will of the Lord need to avail themselves of true prophetic ministry. The enemy attempts to keep us ignorant of our part in the purposes of God. He tries to divert us from the will of God. He wants to destroy us and interfere with the establishment of the kingdom of God in the earth.

Therefore to reject the ministry of prophets is to reject the revelation the Lord desires to give us regarding our eternal purpose. As we honor and draw from the anointing of the prophet, we will walk in greater revelation of the purposes of the Lord. In other words, the prophet has been given as a gift to the body of Christ to bless us and perfect us. We can never be perfected without a revelation of the purposes of God.

PROPHETS HELP US TO FULFILL OUR MINISTRIES

Another way of saying that each of us was born with a part to play in God's eternal purpose is to say that we each have a destiny or a ministry to fulfill. Paul was referring to this when he wrote to a member of the Colossian church:

Tell Archippus, "Make sure that you fulfill the ministry which you have received in the Lord."

—COLOSSIANS 4:17

Prophets help us fulfill our ministries by imparting the revelation we need to know concerning the will of the Lord. Ignorance of the will of the Lord will hinder people from fulfilling their ministries. Many people spend too much of their time operating in the wrong places and doing the wrong things simply because they do not know the will of the Lord.

We are not called to do anything and everything, but rather we are called to fulfill a specific function within the body of Christ. The saints need to be fitly joined together and every part functioning properly (Eph. 4:16). I believe that prophets are the primary ones who can help us find our places in the body and learn to function properly, thus fulfilling the will of the Lord for the church.

Prophets in the local church

The saints learn from prophetic revelation, and they are "comforted":

> Let prophets speak two or three, and let the other judge. If any thing be revealed to another that sitteth by, let the first hold his peace. For ye may all prophesy one by one, that all may learn, and all may be comforted.
>
> —1 Corinthians 14:29–31, kjv

These verses are in reference to prophets ministering by revelation in the local church. Notice that prophets receive revelation, and they can all prophesy (speak forth the revelation) "that all may learn, and all may be comforted." Thus, prophetic revelation does not bring fear but comfort. The Phillips translation says that "everyone will have his faith stimulated" (v. 31). Another word for *comfort* is *encouragement*.

Often when one prophet is ministering, another prophet will begin to receive revelation as well. As the anointing flows, it will stir up others in their prophetic gift. If you are a prophet, you know what I mean. Prophets will find their gift stirred as they associate with other prophets. It should not be unusual for two or three prophets to speak out in sequence in a meeting of a local fellowship. And as one of them ministers, the others are to judge what is being said. Therefore prophetic revelation is subject to being weighed by others.

Local assemblies that allow prophets to minister freely will achieve a greater degree of revelation, spiritual knowledge, comfort, and encouragement as they move toward fulfilling God's purposes.

Prophets Bring Us Revelation From God

Before God does anything, He first reveals it to His servants the prophets. You have heard this line quoted often:

> Surely the Lord God does nothing without revealing His purpose to His servants the prophets.
>
> —Amos 3:7

Prophetic revelation can come in the form of dreams, visions, or the direct words of the Lord. Prophets are also known as "seers" because they see beforehand what the Lord will do, and they then speak forth what they have seen in dreams or visions or have heard in the spirit.

When a prophet speaks out what he or she has seen in the spirit, the Lord hastens to perform the words of the prophet because it is really His word and His will expressed through one of His servants. Because prophetic revelation gives us insight into the plans and purposes of God, it makes us able to bring our lives into agreement with what the Lord is doing.

> See then that you walk carefully, not as fools, but as wise men, making the most of the time because the days are evil. Therefore do not be unwise, but understand what the will of the Lord is.
> —EPHESIANS 5:15–17

It is not the will of the Lord for us to be ignorant of His plans and purposes. When we know the will of the Lord, we are then able to redeem the time and accomplish His intended will. Time will not be wasted on things the Lord has not called us to do.

Prophetic ministry is the means by which God will bring us the revelation of the will of the Lord for our lives and churches. When prophetic ministry is lacking, darkness and confusion concerning the will of the Lord will result. In other words, the will of the Lord is not only seen and heard in the spirit by prophets, but it is also spoken and activated by prophets.

When the Spirit of God moves and the prophets prophesy, light comes. The illumination power of revelation penetrates the darkness of confusion. The church begins to discern the will of the Lord. As soon as the word of the Lord is spoken, confusion and ignorance depart. How exciting it is to see saints receive prophetic ministry and their lives and ministries come into form. Without prophetic ministry, darkness and confusion are often present. With prophetic ministry, believers receive clarity of vision and energy of purpose.

We can know the general will of God through reading the Word of God. We need to study the Bible for this reason. However, the specific will of the Lord for individuals, families, churches, and nations can only be received through revelation, and this entails prophetic ministry.

I have received personal prophecy over a consistent period of time that has helped me to know the will of God for my life and ministry. This has enabled me to channel my time and energy into the perfect will of God for my life. It has eliminated double-mindedness and instability and has given me the faith and assurance I need to fulfill the purposes of God for my life.

I am not recommending that we replace an individual's personal responsibility to pray and seek the will of the Lord with the words of prophets. Each one of us is still responsible to pray and hear from the Lord concerning His will for our lives. But the prophets can minister revelation to us, giving us a clearer picture and understanding of what the Lord is leading us to do.

PROPHETS IMPART SPIRITUAL GIFTS AND ANOINTING

One of the abilities of prophets is to impart blessings to other people. We see this in Romans 1:11, where the apostle Paul said, "For I long to see you, that I may impart to you some spiritual gift, so that you may be strengthened." Paul had a desire to come to the church at Rome so that he could impart spiritual gifts to the church members and help them be established in mature strength. It was the anointing of the prophet that gave him the ability to impart spiritual gifts and anointings to people through prophetic utterances and through the laying on of hands.

Timothy received an impartation of a gift and the anointing of God through prophecy and the laying on of hands:

> Do not neglect the gift that is in you, which was given to you by prophecy, with the laying on of hands by the elders.
>
> —1 TIMOTHY 4:14

There was a transference of spiritual power, authority, ability, and grace. Paul then told Timothy not to neglect what he had received through impartation.

All of us need impartations of the anointing. You can receive some things directly from God; other things will come through the channel of another individual. Although most people received gifts and callings when they were born again and baptized in the Holy Spirit, additional anointings can come through the avenue of laying on of hands and prophecy.

When this avenue is lacking, the result will be a lack of strong ministries and anointings in the local assembly. We need this blessing of impartation given to us by the Lord Jesus Christ. It is important that the body of Christ discern and embrace this function of prophets. Otherwise we will miss the deposit of anointings and gifts that could have come through prophetic impartation. All of the ministry gifts, especially those who are young, can benefit from receiving additional supernatural gifts and anointings through prophesying and praying with the laying on of hands.

I personally feel that every ministry gift needs the ministry of the prophet. As we allow prophets to minister unto us by the Spirit of God, the Lord can impart or deposit things into our lives. We need these impartations to make our ministries effective. Some ministry gifts lack because they have not come into contact with or allowed prophets to prophesy into their lives. In other words, what may be lacking in the operation of a ministry gift in the local assembly may be a lack of prophetic ministry. Without prophetic impartation, individuals will not have the necessary equipping they need for fruitful and powerful ministries.

This ability to impart is different from the simple gift of prophecy, which is meant for edification, exhortation, and comfort. Those who have the simple gift of prophecy may not have the ability to impart the way the prophet does. A person with the office of prophet does more than prophesy; he or she also imparts. You can see the difference when a prophet prophesies. The words will do more than edify, exhort, and comfort. They will also impart spiritual grace into individuals and assemblies.

Equipping the saints for ministry is more than just teaching them how to do it; it also involves impartation. The Word of God is effective, but it is not enough by itself. In fact, it says so through all the examples of prophetic activity that it includes for our instruction. In other words, when you equip someone, you not only give them the Word of God, but you also impart to them the necessary gifts they need to do the work of the ministry, and the prophet has a vital part in equipping the saints for the work of the ministry.

A good example of impartation is when Elijah was taken up into heaven and his mantle fell so that Elisha could retrieve it (2 Kings 2). As a direct result, Elisha received a double portion of Elijah's spirit. Another example of an impartation was when Moses, through the laying on of hands, imparted wisdom into Joshua (Deut. 34:9).

You can see that prophets do more than just prophesy. They also impart, transfer, and transmit anointings and gifts as the Spirit of God leads.

Establishment

According to Romans 1:11, the result of this impartation is establishment. You can be established, firm and strong, in your ministry as the prophets impart unto you through prophecy and the laying on of hands.

It is quite likely that the reason many gifts are not established in local churches is because of the lack of the prophetic anointing, which releases impartation, which in turn causes God's provision to be established in local assemblies.

I believe that every local assembly needs the prophet's ministry of impartation. Without the anointing of the prophet, certain things will not be established, be strong, or be made firm in the local church.

Power

Another direct result of prophetic impartation is spiritual power. The Lord Jesus gave His disciples power over unclean spirits and sickness (Matt. 10:1). He imparted this power to them.

In 1 Samuel 10, we find impartation coming to Saul as he met the company of prophets prophesying. The Spirit of the Lord came into him, and this resulted in his being "turned into another man" (v. 6). When individuals come into contact with those who have a prophetic anointing, there will be a powerful impartation.

Character

A word needs to be added about the importance of good, upstanding, personal character. The Word of God tells us to lay hands suddenly upon no man (1 Tim. 5:22). Prophets should lay hands on and prophesy impartation to people who have been faithful and have developed good character. Individuals who have not developed Christlike character should not receive impartation of this kind because they will end up operating in the gifts and callings of God with bad character. When people go forth in ministry with character flaws, eventual falling and possible reproach on the ministry can result.

PROPHETS ACTIVATE US

The prophet's anointing carries with it the ability to activate. Prophets have the ability through prophesying not only to impart but also to stir up and ignite ministries and gifts within individuals. The breath of God is released through prophesying, and life is imparted and activated.

The prophet Ezekiel was commanded by the Lord to prophesy to dry bones:

> So I prophesied as He commanded me, and the breath came into them, and they lived and stood up upon their feet, an exceeding great army.
> —EZEKIEL 37:10

These dry bones represented the house of Israel. As Ezekiel prophesied, the bones came together. The prophet has the ability to prophesy people into their right position within the body of Christ.

As Ezekiel prophesied, sinews and flesh came upon the bones. Sinews represent strength, and skin represents form. The necessary components are prophesied into proper form, and then life and strength are added, all through prophetic ministry.

With prophetic activation, local assemblies will have greater strength and proper form. People will come into their right positions. When people are out of position in the local assembly, the result is confusion.

The prophetic ministry can also activate miracles, healings, and signs and wonders within the local assembly. All of the gifts of the Spirit are activated through prophetic ministry.

If there is a lack of anointing within a local assembly, the prophet can activate and bring back to life whatever is dormant and dead. Many individuals have gifts in them that need to be stirred up (activated). If they have not been able to stir up the gifts themselves, their gifts can be activated through prophetic ministry.

Many saints have callings from the womb (Jer. 1:5). There is a particular time when that call is supposed to be activated. The prophet has the ability through the Spirit of God to activate that particular call according to the will of the Spirit of God.

The prophet also has the ability to position people. Many churches are disorganized and the members are not correctly joined together in the spirit. The prophet has the ability to speak order into the house of the Lord.

In short, the prophet has the ability to speak life into a situation. This is activation. This will raise up the army of God. Through prophetic utterances, people are positioned into proper rank. This may come through rebuke, or correction, or by simply prophesying people into their rightful position.

Scripture states that the gifts and callings of God are without repentance (Rom. 11:29). Some people may feel they have lost their gift or that God has taken it back when it simply needs activation because it is dormant. The gift may be dormant because of neglect or blockages.

I often find myself around prophets who can speak into my life and stir up and reactivate the gifts that I have. Prophets have the ability to activate and stir up your gifts too. This will "put sinews and muscles upon you" and make the gift strong.

Activating ministries

> In the church that was in Antioch there were prophets and teachers: Barnabas, Simeon who was called Niger, Lucius of Cyrene, Manaen who had been brought up with Herod the tetrarch, and Saul. As they worshipped the Lord and fasted, the Holy Spirit said, "Set apart for Me Barnabas and Saul for the work to which I have called them." Then after fasting and praying, they laid their hands on them and sent them off.
>
> —Acts 13:1–3

Prophetic ministry activates ministries and sends them forth. For Barnabas and Paul, the call to the apostleship was already present, but it needed to be activated. At a certain time or season it was time for the call to be activated and for the men to be sent forth as apostles. These verses seem to imply that prophetic ministry, through the laying on of hands, was instrumental in the releasing of Paul and Barnabas to begin their ministry to the Gentiles. Although verse 4 states they were sent forth by the Holy Ghost, and the Holy Ghost is the One who calls, anoints, and sends forth ministries, the Holy Ghost uses human channels to accomplish this work. It was important to have prophetic ministry in order to activate and release the ministry gifts of Barnabas and Paul.

Both prophetic impartation and activation are needed when ministry gifts are launched into ministry. Those who do not avail themselves of prophetic ministry will often be released prematurely, without the necessary activation and impartation of anointings and spiritual gifts. The call may be there, but the ability to fulfill it may not.

As we know, Paul and Barnabas were released into a strong apostolic ministry because of the administration of prophets in the church at Antioch. In this hour the Lord is raising up more Antioch churches to release strong ministries into the earth.

PROPHETS CONFIRM US

According to *Webster's*, *confirm* means "to make firm, to strengthen, to give new assurance to, to remove doubt." [2] When something is firm, it is securely or solidly fixed in place. It will be set, definite, and not easily moved or disturbed. When something is confirmed, it will be marked by long continuance and likely to persist. This is the will of God for the saints. The ministry of the prophet has been set in the church by and for the confirmation of the saints.

> Judas and Silas, being prophets also themselves, exhorted the brothers with many words and strengthened them.
>
> —ACTS 15:32

When prophets minister, confirmation will be the result. The saints will be "steadfast, immovable, always abounding in the work of the Lord" (1 Cor. 15:58, NKJV). It was necessary for Judas and Silas to minister confirmation to this particular church because of false teaching. The souls of the saints were being subverted (Acts 15:24), which means they were being overturned or overthrown from their foundation, weakened, or ruined by degrees. They had become destabilized. When saints are unstable, they will not abound in the work of the Lord. After they received prophetic ministry, these churches were established in the faith. They were made firm and strengthened concerning their salvation.

Two or three witnesses

It is a spiritual principle that the truth is established by the confirmation of two or three witnesses.

> This is the third time I am coming to you. "In the mouth of two or three witnesses shall every word be established."
>
> —2 CORINTHIANS 13:1

Prophets can provide another witness. You may have a witness in your spirit concerning a certain matter and yet not be established in the fact that it is from the Lord. The Lord in His mercy has provided prophetic ministry as another witness so that we may be established in the will of God for our lives.

The Word of God tells us to prove all things (1 Thess. 5:21). Anything that is from the Lord can be proven. When the will of God is confirmed by prophetic ministry, there will be assurance and steadfastness instead of wavering and doubting. The testimony of Jesus is the spirit of prophecy (Rev. 19:10). Prophecy is a witness (testimony). This is the very spirit of all prophecy: to give the confirmation and witness of Jesus.

Dissolving of doubts

We find in Scripture this interesting description of Daniel, who was one of the premier prophets:

> Forasmuch as an excellent spirit, and knowledge, and understanding, interpreting of dreams, and shewing of hard sentences, and dissolving of doubts, were found in the same Daniel…
>
> —Daniel 5:12, kjv

Because we more often concentrate our attention on his other qualities, we seldom notice that *Daniel had the ability to dissolve doubts.* Evidently the prophet's anointing will dissolve doubts, causing persons who receive prophetic ministry to walk in a greater degree of faith and assurance. They will have a clearer understanding of the will of God. They will receive confirmation, as I mentioned above, but they will also have doubts removed from their minds.

Daniel was able to remove all doubt and confusion from the king by interpreting his dreams. Saints who struggle with doubts and hesitancy will benefit from anointed prophetic confirmation. Their doubts will disappear, their faith level will be elevated, and they will be able to move forward effectively without hesitation. Prophetic confirmation will destroy double-mindedness and will result in stability instead of instability, making it possible for them to be confirmed unto the end.

> He will strengthen you to the end, so that you may be blameless on the day of our Lord Jesus Christ.
>
> —1 Corinthians 1:8

Spirit-Filled Ordination Services

Ordination is the act of officially investing someone with ministerial or priestly authority. In Acts 6:6 the apostles laid hands upon the first deacons to set them in their offices. This was also an impartation of apostolic anointing that released Stephen and Philip into miracle ministries. In the early church bishops and elders were also ordained in this fashion and set in their respective offices.

After the death of the early apostles the church lost most of its power, and ordination became largely ceremonial. But today the Lord is restoring the reality and power of ordination to set various ministries in the church. Through apostolic and prophetic ministry, anointings can be imparted into those who are being ordained. (See 1 Timothy 4:14.) In the ordination services of our church we call for the prophets to come and prophesy over those who are candidates for ordination. We call this prophetic presbytery. I believe that prophetic presbytery is necessary in this hour to release strong ministry gifts and that as a result ordination services should no longer be merely ceremonial but full of the power and anointing of the Holy Spirit. Allowing the prophets to flow in this administration will launch stronger ministries.

By allowing and encouraging different prophetic administrations, we will see more of the benefits of the Spirit established in the house of the Lord. We cannot become addicted to one type of administration but must receive all that the Lord has for us. In this way we can be filled with all the fullness of God. (See Ephesians 3:19.)

We see that prophets can minister and provide help through revelation, impartation, activation, and confirmation. Through these different administrations prophets can speak and minister to the saints with the authority that is given by grace. God has provided these spiritual helps for the church that we might be changed into the image of Jesus Christ. Thank God for the different functions of prophets. May we release and receive this important ministry and through it draw from the grace of God that has been deposited among us.

CHAPTER 4

MADE BY GOD

*He will sit as a refiner and purifier of silver; he will purify
the sons of Levi, and refine them like gold and silver, and
they will present to the LORD offerings in righteousness.*
—MALACHI 3:3

GOD PUTS PROPHETS through a process of refinement. God purges prophets and develops their character. Prophets have to respond to the dealings of God in their own life before they can effectively deal with the problems in the lives of others. Sometimes as a prophet you will feel as if you are in a furnace. You may find yourself saying, "God, why are You dealing so strongly with me? Why don't You deal with everyone else like this?" Don't give up, prophet. Go through the process.

> The refining pot is for silver and the furnace for gold, but the LORD
> tries the hearts.
>
> —PROVERBS 17:3

LET GOD PURGE YOU

A prophet is a vessel. God purges His vessels. God will take the dross (impurities) out of your life. You have to become the raw material to be a prophetic vessel. Go through the process. Let the fire burn.

> Take away the dross from the silver, and there will come forth a vessel
> for the refiner.
>
> —PROVERBS 25:4

> Take away the dross from the silver, and the smith has material for a
> vessel.
>
> —PROVERBS 25:4, ESV

Prophet, don't allow guilt, shame, and condemnation to prevent you from accepting and walking in your calling. Many prophets struggle with feelings of inadequacy as a result of their past. Isaiah was purged and sent. Allow the Lord to purge you from sins of the past, walk clean before the Lord, and fulfill your call.

And I said: "Woe is me! For I am undone because I am a man of unclean lips, and I dwell in the midst of a people of unclean lips. For my eyes have seen the King, the LORD of Hosts."

—ISAIAH 6:5

Prophets must be faithful.

Moses distinguished himself as a prophet by his faithfulness. Be faithful to the call and commission.

And he said, And my servant Moses is not such, the which is most faithful in all mine house; (Then he said, But my servant Moses is not such a prophet, for he alone is most faithful in all my household;)

—NUMBERS 12:7, WYC

My eyes shall be favorable to the faithful in the land, that they may live with me; he who walks in a blameless manner, he shall serve me

—PSALM 101:6

GOD CHOOSES PROPHETS BY HIS GRACE

But by the grace of God I am what I am. And His grace toward me was not in vain. I labored more abundantly than all of them, yet not I, but the grace of God which was with me.

—1 CORINTHIANS 15:10

Prophets understand grace. They know God's strength is by grace. They understand that they cannot do this in their own strength. Prophets depend on the grace of God (His strength, favor, power, and ability). They understand that without God they can do nothing.

Prophets will find themselves in situations when they have to depend on grace.

I can do nothing of Myself. As I hear, I judge. My judgment is just, because I seek not My own will, but the will of the Father who sent Me.

—JOHN 5:30

Prophets are God's choice, not man's.

God calls all kinds of people to be prophets. The Lord chose the foolish things to confound the things that are wise (1 Cor. 1:27–29). David was an obscure shepherd boy. Amos was not a prophet or a prophet's son. God calls people who would not qualify by the standards of men. Prophets are not determined by men, but by God. God's choice is a challenge and rebuke against the pride of men.

God even calls the rebellious.

> You have ascended on high, You have led captivity captive; You have
> received gifts from people, yes, even from the rebellious, that the
> LORD God might dwell among them.
>
> —PSALM 68:18

Prophets are taught by God.

There are things that you can learn directly from God. This is what happens
to prophets. Prophets know things that are not taught by men. Jesus knew
more than all the religious leaders of His day. They marveled at His knowledge.
Jesus had not attended their schools.

> The people were amazed [marveled] and said, "This man has never
> studied in school. How did he learn so much?"
>
> —JOHN 7:15, EXB

THE HOLY SPIRIT AND PROPHECY

Jesus promised His disciples the gift of the Holy Spirit. His promise was fulfilled
on the Day of Pentecost—and in subsequent "pentecosts" over the centuries.

> And they were all filled with the Holy Spirit, and began to speak in
> other tongues, as the Spirit enabled them to speak.
>
> —ACTS 2:4

The Holy Spirit is also known as the Comforter, and prophecy is one of the
ways He comforts the believer. *Comforter* is the Greek word *parakletos*, which
means "an intercessor, consoler, or advocate." When the Holy Spirit comes,
the results include comfort, strength, and the ability to speak forth the word
of God boldly.

The Holy Spirit "gave the disciples utterance," which in Greek is the word
apophtheggomai, meaning "to enunciate plainly, declare, say, or speak forth." The
first thing that happened when the Holy Spirit came upon the disciples in the
Upper Room on the Day of Pentecost was inspired utterance, which is prophecy.

In other words, the baptism of the Holy Spirit is the doorway into the
prophetic realm. The well-known prophecy of Joel emphasizes the release of
prophecy among the sons, daughters, servants, and handmaidens. The believers
spoke with tongues on the Day of Pentecost, and Peter quoted the prophecy
of Joel to identify what was happening. Those who spoke in tongues were
inspired by the Holy Spirit:

> And it will be that, afterwards, I will pour out My Spirit on all flesh;
> then your sons and your daughters will prophesy, your old men will
> dream dreams, and your young men will see visions. Even on the
> menservants and maidservants in those days I will pour out My Spirit.
>
> —JOEL 2:28–29

Millions of believers worldwide have experienced the baptism of the Holy Spirit with the evidence of speaking in tongues. Many believers have limited their experience to speaking in tongues and have not experienced the blessing of prophecy. The believers in the New Testament church were able to speak in tongues *and* prophesy.

Both prophecy and speaking in tongues are forms of inspired utterance. It is easy to explain: speaking in tongues is inspired utterance in a language that is unknown to the speaker, and prophecy is an inspired utterance in a language that is known to the speaker.

The supernatural power of inspired words

In order to fully understand the power of prophecy, we need a revelation about the power of the tongue. Jesus said that the words He spoke were spirit and life. Words—especially the words that come from God—are like spiritual containers that carry spirit and life.

Words have power for both godly purposes and ungodly purposes. The entire universe came into being through words: "And God said, 'Let there be light,' and there was light" (Gen. 1:3). Words can be used to bless or to curse: "Death and life are in the power of the tongue" (Prov. 18:21).

The Scriptures are filled with verses that emphasize the power of words and the tongue:

> He who speaks truth declares righteousness, but a false witness, deceit. There is one who speaks like the piercings of a sword, but the tongue of the wise promotes health.
>
> —Proverbs 12:17–18, nkjv

> Heaviness in the heart of man makes it droop, but a good word makes it glad.
>
> —Proverbs 12:25

> A wholesome tongue is a tree of life, but perverseness in it crushes the spirit.
>
> —Proverbs 15:4

> A man has joy by the answer of his mouth, and a word spoken in due season, how good it is!
>
> —Proverbs 15:23

> Pleasant words are like a honeycomb, sweetness to the soul and health to the bones.
>
> —Proverbs 16:24, nkjv

> A word fitly spoken is like apples of gold in settings of silver.
>
> —Proverbs 25:11

> ...a soft tongue breaks the bone.
>
> —PROVERBS 25:15

> How forcible are right words!
>
> —JOB 6:25

Right words are forcible. The right word spoken at the right time carries tremendous power and force.

Words cannot exist without speakers, and speakers use their tongues in order to speak. Therefore the Scriptures emphasize the power of the tongue for good as well as for ill:

> Even so, the tongue is a little part of the body and boasts great things. See how great a forest a little fire kindles. The tongue is a fire, a world of evil. The tongue is among the parts of the body, defiling the whole body, and setting the course of nature on fire, and it is set on fire by hell.
>
> All kinds of beasts, and birds, and serpents, and things in the sea are tamed or have been tamed by mankind. But no man can tame the tongue. It is an unruly evil, full of deadly poison.
>
> With it we bless the Lord and Father, and with it we curse men, who are made in the image of God. Out of the same mouth proceed blessing and cursing. My brothers, these things ought not to be so. Does a spring yield at the same opening sweet and bitter water? Can the fig tree, my brothers, bear olives, or a vine, figs? So no spring can yield both salt water and fresh water.
>
> —JAMES 3:5–12

If words are this powerful, just imagine the power of inspired words! Words anointed and charged by the Holy Spirit carry tremendous power. A prophetic word can change your life. Prophecy is powerful because it is the word of the Lord, and no word from God is without power.

> But there is a spirit in man, and the breath of the Almighty gives him understanding.
>
> —JOB 32:8

THE PROPHET'S ANOINTING

The prophet's words are anointed and carry power. When prophets speak, things happen. When prophets speak, things change. When prophets speak, God moves. The word of a prophet is like a fire that burns and a hammer that breaks the rock in pieces.

Open your mouth, prophet, and speak. God will back you up. He will confirm the words of His servants.

Is not My word like fire, says the LORD, and like a hammer that breaks the rock in pieces?

—JEREMIAH 23:29

...who confirms the word of His servant, and performs the counsel of His messengers.

—ISAIAH 44:26

God commands His prophets to prophesy. When they do, there is a noise, a shaking, a coming together. Dead things come to life. Dry bones live again. The prophets' words bring life. They release breath.

So I prophesied as I was commanded. And as I prophesied, there was a noise and shaking. And the bones came together, bone to its bone....So I prophesied as He commanded me, and the breath came into them, and they lived and stood up upon their feet, an exceeding great army.

—EZEKIEL 37:7, 10

Prophets have to prophesy when God is speaking. When God is speaking, who can keep from prophesying? His prophets can't help but prophesy. Who will not prophesy? What prophet can keep quiet? Who can refuse to prophesy? Who can do anything but prophesy? Some may want the prophets to be quiet, but they can't help but prophesy.

The lion has roared; who will not fear? The Lord GOD has spoken; who can but prophesy?

—AMOS 3:8

The word of the Lord will come to prophets, even when people try to lock them up or shut them down.

Now the word of the LORD came unto Jeremiah while he was shut up in the court of the prison.

—JEREMIAH 39:15

Prophets have to have a way to vent and release what God gives them, otherwise they feel like they will burst.

See, my belly is like wine that has no vent; it is ready to burst like new wineskins.

—JOB 32:19

This release can happen in the form of weeping, speaking, writing, singing, dancing, or praying.

The inspiration of the Holy Spirit

God inspires our spirits through the Holy Spirit. The Old Testament prophets spoke by His inspiration. The New Testament prophets spoke by His inspiration. Spirit-filled believers today can also speak by the inspiration of the Holy Spirit.

Those who experience the manifestation of tongues can also prophesy. The Holy Spirit will inspire the believer to do both. The key is yielding to the Holy Spirit and allowing Him to inspire you to speak not only in a tongue that you do not comprehend and have not learned but also in your native language.

We believers can also pray by the inspiration of the Spirit. We can sing by inspiration. We can teach and preach by His inspiration. All results of the Holy Spirit's inspiration are different types of prophetic manifestations in action. We should welcome and cultivate all forms of the Spirit's inspiration.

In the New Testament we are told not to stop inspired utterances: "Do not quench the Spirit. Do not despise prophecies" (1 Thess. 5:19–20). Inspired utterances bring great blessing to the church and to individual believers. There is a tendency to stop or stifle inspired utterances in the church, and this is the reason Paul gave this admonition. When inspired utterances are stifled, the Holy Spirit is not at liberty to act. The Holy Spirit will inspire a person, but He will not force someone to speak. People can decide whether or not to utter an inspired message.

I have been inspired to prophesy to thousands of believers worldwide. I have seen the blessing of inspired utterance, and so can you. Yielding to the Holy Spirit's inspiration will bring countless blessing to those who hear your anointed words.

Words drop like rain

We read this line in a familiar psalm:

> The earth shook, the heavens also dropped at the presence of God...
> —Psalm 68:8, kjv

The heavens "drop" at the presence of God. What does that mean? *Drop* is the Hebrew word *nataph*, meaning "to ooze, to distill gradually, to fall in drops, to speak by inspiration"[1]—in other words, to prophesy.

One of the ways God inspires us is by dropping His word upon us. This usually happens during corporate worship when the presence of God is strong. The word of the Lord falls like rain, and there are usually many in the service who get inspired to speak. Some will be inspired to sing prophetically as God drops a song upon them.

Words bubble up

Naba is the Hebrew word for *prophesy*, which means "to speak or sing by inspiration (in prediction or simple discourse)."[2] The word carries the sense of bubbling or springing up, flowing, pouring out, gushing forth. The word for *prophet* is *nabiy*, which means "an inspired man."[3] The word for *prophetess* is *nebiyah*, which means "an inspired woman, poetess, or prophet's wife."[4] In other words, both men and women can be inspired to flow or bubble up with the words of God in prophetic utterances. The inspiration to prophesy can fall upon us like rain (*nataph*) or bubble up from the inside (*naba*). It is the same Holy Spirit who inspires in both ways, and the result is also the same—inspiration to speak forth the word of the Lord.

Enriched in All Utterance

The Corinthian church was "enriched in all utterance":

> That in every thing ye are enriched by him, in all utterance, and in all knowledge.
>
> —1 Corinthians 1:5, kjv

The Holy Spirit will enrich each one of us in all utterance. When somebody or something has been enriched, it has had something extra added to it. The word carries the idea of wealth or abundance. Because we have been filled with the Holy Spirit, we should abound in utterance. The Holy Spirit is a free Spirit (Ps. 51:12, kjv), which means He is liberal, generous, and magnanimous (willing to share Himself with us). He pours Himself out upon us, and His life flows out from within us. Most often the outpouring of the Holy Spirit is released in an outpouring of prophecy. That is why we are urged not to quench or limit the Holy Spirit by quenching His inspiration.

Inspired utterances are anointed by the Holy Spirit. These words carry tremendous power and authority. Anointed words can bring deliverance, healing, strength, comfort, refreshing, wisdom, and direction.

Inspired utterance has always been a key to breakthrough. It is interesting that the word *nathan* is translated "utter" in Scripture passages such as Joel 2:11 and 3:16, and Psalm 46:6.[5]

> And the Lord shall *utter* his voice before his army: for his camp is very great: for he is strong that executeth his word.
>
> —Joel 2:11, kjv, emphasis added

> The Lord also shall roar out of Zion, and *utter* his voice from Jerusalem.
>
> —Joel 3:16, kjv, emphasis added

> The nations roared; the kingdoms were moved; He *uttered* His voice; the earth melted.
>
> —Psalm 46:6, emphasis added

It is also interesting that Nathan is the name of the prophet who rebuked David after he slept with Bathsheba (2 Sam. 12). Once again, inspired utterance provided the key to the locked door of a human heart. In this case the Holy Spirit inspired the prophet Nathan to tell a parable.

The earth melts when God utters His voice. This means the physical realm is affected by the voice of the Lord, and the physical realm includes men and women, not only because they dwell upon the earth but also because they were taken from the earth at Creation.

Inspired utterances have a dramatic effect upon men and women. Their lives are enriched through the prophetic words that are spoken. Mere human words could not achieve such results. Inspired utterances are not the work of a man but the work of the Holy Spirit.

The Holy Spirit speaks through us, and He puts His word in our mouths.

> The Spirit of the Lord spoke by me, and His word was on my tongue.
> —2 Samuel 23:2

David understood that his utterances were divinely inspired. David would even sing under inspiration while he played on his harp. With His word on your tongue, your tongue can become an instrument of the divine. God desires to release His word by means of your tongue and mine. He has given every believer the gift of the Holy Spirit to accomplish His will.

Prophecy is the result of being filled with the Holy Ghost. Zacharias was dumb and unable to speak until his tongue was loosed through the infilling of the Holy Spirit. Then he not only spoke some words for the first time in months, but he also prophesied:

> His father Zechariah was filled with the Holy Spirit and prophesied, saying…
> —Luke 1:67

Spirit-filled believers and churches *should* prophesy. By virtue of being filled up with the Holy Spirit, we should overflow. *Filled* is the Greek word *pimplēmi*, meaning to "imbue, influence, supply." [6] Spirit-filled believers should speak by the influence of the Holy Spirit because they have been imbued, influenced, and supplied with an abundance of the life of the Spirit of God.

Under the influence of the Holy Spirit we utter words that bring edification, exhortation, and comfort, and there is always an abundant supply of such utterance given to us by the Holy Spirit. (See Ephesians 5:18–19.)

The Prophetic Lifestyle

Cultivating a prophetic life also includes cultivating a hidden life in the Word. Knowing the scriptures enables us to know the character of God, the way He speaks and the parameters He has laid out for prophetic ministry. We can judge prophecy through the standard of the Word and through the fruit of the Spirit knowing that we can discard any words we receive that don't line up with His scripture and the fruit of love, joy, peace, patience, kindness, goodness, faithfulness, gentleness and self-control.

—Patricia Bootsma[7]

Prophets lead unusual lives.

Prophets can find themselves in the most unusual places and circumstances, and wonder, "How did I get here?" Prophet, God has a way of placing you there to release His wisdom and His word. Don't be surprised where you find yourself ministering. God will open doors for you, send you, and place you with people whom you ordinarily would never meet. They need what you have.

> Arise, go to Zarephath, which belongs to Sidon, and live there. I have commanded a widow there to provide for you.
>
> —1 Kings 17:9

Your unusual assignments could have you ministering to presidents, government officials, businessmen, celebrities, widows, and more.

Prophets are often called to speak to power.

Prophets can speak to people of power and those in positions of power. This is because power is so easily abused and misused. Nathan spoke to David. This is an example of speaking to power. Sometimes power does not want to hear what prophets say. Jesus spoke to power when He challenged the religious leaders of His day for their hypocrisy and abuse.

> Ahab said to Elijah, "Have you found me, my enemy?" And he answered, "I have found you, because you have sold yourself to work evil in the sight of the Lord."
>
> —1 Kings 21:20

Prophets are called to speak to political power, economic power, religious power, and so on. Prophets also pray for those in power.

> Power tends to corrupt, and absolute power corrupts absolutely. Great men are almost always bad men.
>
> —Baron Acton[8]

This famous quote addresses the fact that men have a difficult time handling power. Pride tends to corrupt men of power, and this is why we need prophets who will speak to and challenge power.

Moses is the exception. He was a man of great power, but he is called the meekest man of the earth. He never needed a prophet to correct him.

> Now the man Moses was very meek, above all the men which were upon the face of the earth.
>
> —NUMBERS 12:3, KJV

> I will break the pride of your power, and I will make your heaven as iron and your land as bronze.
>
> —LEVITICUS 26:19

Prophets threaten religious position.

The Pharisees hated Jesus because they felt they would lose their place. This was the heart of the matter. They had worked years building their positions, and they were afraid of losing those positions.

> They hated Jesus not because He called them names, but because He threatened their security, prestige and income. He was going to ruin everything they had worked so hard for.
>
> —R. C. SPROUL JR.[9]

> If we leave Him alone like this, everyone will believe in Him, and the Romans will come and take away both our temple and our nation.
>
> —JOHN 11:48

A prophet's gifts will work in the most unusual places.

Joseph's gift worked in the prison and took him to the palace. People need prophets everywhere. Those who need you will find you, or God will send you to them. Your gift will make room for you and bring you before great men (Prov. 18:16).

Prophets have unusual experiences with God (Peniel).

Prophets are not normal, and their experiences are not normal. Prophets are different because they have visitations. Unusual salvations, deliverances, dreams, visions, and divine encounters are the prophet's portion. When a person encounters God, he or she cannot remain the same.

Moses encountered a burning bush. Isaiah saw the Lord in His glory. Ezekiel had visions of God. Daniel had angelic visitations. Jeremiah encountered God at a young age. John was filled with the Holy Ghost from his mother's womb. God appeared to Jacob in a dream.

Prophets are different because they encounter God in unusual ways. Prophets have unusual testimonies. If you tell people some of your experiences, they might think you are crazy and spooky.

God deals with prophets at night.

It is not uncommon for God to deal with prophets in the night. Night visions, prayer in the night, and night meditations are common to many prophets.

When I remember You on my bed, and meditate on You in the night watches.

—Psalm 63:6

I saw in the night visions, and there was one like a Son of Man coming with the clouds of heaven. He came to the Ancient of Days and was presented before Him.

—Daniel 7:13

Then the watchman called: "O Lord, I stand continually on the watchtower in the daytime, and I am stationed at my guard post every night."

—Isaiah 21:8

May I remember my song in the night; may I meditate in my heart; my spirit made a diligent search.

—Psalm 77:6

The prophet's lifestyle is contrary to what they are speaking against.

There is a reason why John the Baptist was in the wilderness and not in Jerusalem, though he was the son of a priest. He could not be where the Establishment was. He could not enjoy its benefits and at the same time "blow the whistle" on the falsity of it. We cannot in our own lifestyle indulge in the very thing that we are condemning before others. Lifestyle is, therefore, remarkably important with regard to the word that is to be proclaimed and probably nothing more betrays whether you are a true or false prophet than this.

—Art Katz[10]

The majority of a prophet's ministry is led in secret.

Most prophets don't have to have platforms, although God may give them one. Prophets don't have to be seen, although God may highlight them. Prophets pray, weep, minister to the Lord, and study in secret. What God shows them in secret, they speak to the world. Prophets love the solitary place. Prophets hate the hype and sensationalism they see on many platforms.

As a prophet's perfect example, even Jesus prayed in secret.

In the morning, rising up a great while before sunrise, He went out and departed to a solitary place. And there He prayed.

—Mark 1:35

But you, when you pray, enter your closet, and when you have shut your door, pray to your Father who is in secret. And your Father who sees in secret will reward you openly.

—Matthew 6:6

Prophets weep in secret.

Prophets weep because of pride and rebellion. They weep when no one is watching. They weep in their closets. They weep in their secret places.

> But if you will not listen to it, my soul will weep in secret places for your pride; and my eyes will weep sorely, and run down with tears, because the flock of the LORD is carried away captive.
>
> —JEREMIAH 13:17

Leaders call prophets secretly.

This is true especially of leaders who are in trouble.

> Then Zedekiah the king sent and took him out; and the king asked him secretly in his house, and said, "Is there any word from the LORD?" And Jeremiah said, "There is!" Then he said, "You shall be delivered into the hand of the king of Babylon."
>
> —JEREMIAH 37:17

> There was a man of the Pharisees named Nicodemus, a ruler of the Jews. He came to Jesus by night and said to Him, "Rabbi, we know that You are a teacher who has come from God. For no one can do these signs that You do unless God is with him."
>
> —JOHN 3:1–2

Prophets are the hidden ones.

Prophets are often hidden from view. They do much of their work in the secret place. The hidden ones are the "secret ones," "the precious ones," "the treasured ones."

> They have given crafty counsel against Your people, and have consulted against Your treasured ones.
>
> —PSALM 83:3

Prophets pray.

Prayer, intercession, supplication, asking, seeking, knocking, pleading, requesting, calling on, crying out, without ceasing, standing in the gap, in the closet, in the secret place, in the spirit, watching, lifting up, agreement, burden, persevering, effectual, fervent, prevailing, wrestling, weeping, laboring, travailing, birthing, groaning—these are what make up the prayer life of a prophet. The prophetess Anna is a picture of an intercessory prophet.

> An important part of the prophet's task is prayer. Because he knows the mind of the Lord, he is in a position to pray effectively. He has a clear picture of what God is doing, so he knows where prayer is needed most. The prophet watches over the word of the Lord and

prays it into being. He must not rest until God has fulfilled His word (Isaiah 62:6).

—Ron McKenzie[11]

Prophetic intercession is a ministry of faith. We do not always know the reason for the prayer burden that the Holy Spirit gives us; neither do we always learn the outcome of our prayers. But we do know that God is faithful. And—that the greatest reward of prophetic intercession is intimacy with the Holy Spirit.

—Helen Calder[12]

The Big Three

He hath shewed thee, O man, what is good; and what doth the Lord require of thee, but to do justly, and to love mercy, and to walk humbly with thy God?

—Micah 6:8, kjv

There are three things the Lord requires of you as His prophet, and these three things are what you and God will contend for throughout your life as a prophet. These three things apply to all believers, and especially prophets. So submit yourself to learn what the Lord requires and be faithful to do and say all He commands, starting and always ending here:

1. Do justly. Treat people fairly. Don't take advantage of the weak. Don't mistreat others. Don't use your power and authority to destroy others. Don't return evil for good. Don't forget or overlook people who helped you. Don't betray your friends. Don't use and misuse others for personal gain. Don't destroy people through slander and backbiting. Protect and defend the innocent. Don't cheat people, but give everyone what is due to them. Issue correct verdicts and judgments against evil and wickedness. Don't favor or excuse the wicked and rebellious.

2. Love mercy. Be kind and compassionate to others. Show lovingkindness. Don't be critical, self-righteous, and condemning. Be forgiving and kind. Help and bless those who are oppressed. Support the weak. Be generous and benevolent. Bless those who curse you.

3. Walk humbly. Don't be vain, proud, rude, and arrogant. Don't look down upon others. Don't be self-promoting. Always be teachable. Be willing to receive correction. Admit when you are wrong, and be quick to apologize. Bow to, worship, and always be reverent of God. Don't think of yourself more highly than you ought to think. Honor and respect those who are greater

than you. Submit and respect those in authority. Don't forget where you came from. Examine yourself.

Maintaining an attitude of humility is essential in the prophetic ministry. Otherwise, elitism creeps in and grows up to characterize prophetic individuals and groups. Experiencing supernatural revelation can be "heady wine," and people too often begin to think of themselves more highly than they ought after having drunk it over a period of time.

—MICHAEL SULLIVANT[13]

PART II

THE PROPHET'S ROLE IN CHURCH AND CULTURE

CHAPTER 5

HOW THE PROPHETS OPERATE TODAY

*He who prophesies speaks to men for their edifi-
cation and exhortation and comfort.*
—1 CORINTHIANS 14:3

I AM NOT TRYING to make every believer a prophet. And yet all of us can prophesy. There are different levels of prophecy. An understanding of the different levels of prophecy will eliminate any confusion.

On the simplest level a prophet is one who speaks words from God that build people up. The verse above in 1 Corinthians 14:3 is the simplest scriptural definition of *prophecy*. Prophetic words edify; they bring edification. *Edify* means "to build up." God desires to "build up" His people through prophecy.

The word *edify* is related to the word *edifice*, which is another word for a building. The church is God's building. His building (His edifice) is built up through prophecy.

How do prophetic words build up the church? By bringing exhortation and comfort to the individual people who make up the church. *Exhortation* is the Greek word *paraklesis*, which means "solace, entreaty, consolation, admonition, or comfort."[1] This word is related to the word *parakletos*, or Comforter, a name for the Holy Spirit.[2] The Holy Spirit uses prophecy to comfort believers and to exhort them to holiness, love, worship, praise, prayer, evangelism, humility, and giving.

Comfort is the Greek noun *paramythia*, which means "consolation."[3] This is a different type of comfort, and it is especially important for believers who are suffering or struggling in their faith.

It is important to note that this simple definition of *prophecy* contains no reference to prediction. This is where many people have erred, believing that *prophecy* is another word for predicting the future. While it is quite possible for prophets to offer prediction when they prophesy, it is not required by definition. Basic prophetic words adhere to the parameters of "edification, exhortation, and comfort."

THREE LEVELS OF PROPHETIC OPERATION

In the rest of this chapter we will be exploring the various levels of prophetic utterance. You will begin to be able to see more options for channeling the flow of your own prophetic inspirations.

1. The spirit of prophecy

The most basic level of prophecy is known as the spirit of prophecy. As we worship God in spirit and in truth, the spirit of prophecy will manifest in our midst, and any believer can yield to this spirit of prophecy, speaking the word of the Lord.

The Lord wants to raise up a prophetic people (Num. 11:29), and the Holy Spirit is a prophetic Spirit (Acts 2:14–18). Therefore the spirit of prophecy causes both men and women, sons and daughters, and "servants and hand-maidens" to prophesy. It provides people with the unction they need in order to speak as the oracles of the Lord, to use the biblical term.

We prophesy according to the proportion of our faith (Rom. 12:6). Our testimony is expressed prophetically:

> I fell at his feet to worship him. But he said to me, "See that you not do that. I am your fellow servant, and of your brothers who hold the testimony of Jesus. Worship God! For the testimony of Jesus is the spirit of prophecy."
>
> —Revelation 19:10

If believers act in faith when the spirit of prophecy is present, they all can prophesy. This does not make each one of them a prophet. Their utterances will be limited to the "testimony of Jesus." They will be speaking forth words of truth, valuable words of truth that are based on the revealed Word of truth in the Bible.

The Word of God testifies of Jesus. The more a person meditates on and knows the Word of God, the easier it will be to prophesy. The Word of God carries with it the spirit of prophecy. Then, as we worship God, the word of the Lord can more easily bubble up in us or fall upon us, and we can prophesy freely.

2. The gift of prophecy

The second level of the prophetic realm is the gift of prophecy (1 Cor. 12:10). This gift can be stirred up:

> Therefore I remind you to stir up the gift of God which is in you through the laying on of my hands.
>
> —2 Timothy 1:6, NKJV

Or a believer can yield to the spirit of prophecy and speak out of the additional strength of this gift as well. The utterances will be stronger than speaking by the spirit of prophecy only because the person is speaking out of a gift.

There are levels of strength of the gift, depending upon the measure of grace received by the person who has the gift. Those who prophesy out of this level will speak words that will bring edification, exhortation, and comfort (1 Cor. 14:3).

We encourage believers who are not called into the office of a prophet to stay within the limit of edification, exhortation, and comfort. Believers who attempt to go beyond their level of grace without additional equipping will bring confusion to the body of Christ. Those who are recognized by the leadership of the assembly as *prophets* are the ones who have the authority to speak beyond the limit of edification, exhortation, and comfort.

3. The office of the prophet

The highest level in the prophetic realm is the office of the prophet.

> God has put these in the church: first apostles, second prophets, third teachers, after that miracles, then gifts of healings, helps, governments, and various tongues.
>
> —1 Corinthians 12:28

The prophets will have the strongest utterances because they speak by the spirit of prophecy, the gift of prophecy, and also out of the strength of the prophet's office. They have the grace to speak messages that go beyond words of edification, exhortation, and comfort.

Prophets prophesy with more authority than other believers who have not been called to the office of the prophet. Their prophecies can carry revelation, direction, correction, confirmation, impartation, and activation. They minister to a wider scope of needs than believers who speak by the spirit of prophecy or the simple gift of prophecy.

The breadth and height of the prophetic reach extends far and wide and to the summit or pinnacle of heaven. The depth and length of the prophetic reach is full and comprehensive, complete and thorough. The Lord desires His church to walk in the breadth, length, depth, and height of the prophetic realm, and He installs men and women in the office of the prophet to make this possible. The prophet has the anointing by grace to minister and speak in higher, wider, and deeper ways.

I believe that prophets should minister under authority and be recognized by the leadership of their local body of Christ because the Lord desires that all things be done decently and in order.

WHERE GRACE DOES ABOUND

When it comes to the breadth and depth of your prophetic anointing, you are only limited by the amount of grace you have received from the Lord. Paul made this clear in his letter to the local church in Rome:

> For as we have many members in one body, but all the members do not have the same function, so we, being many, are one body in Christ, and individually members of one another. *Having then gifts differing according to the grace that is given to us, let us use them: if prophecy, let us prophesy in proportion to our faith*; or ministry, let

us use it in our ministering; he who teaches, in teaching; he who exhorts, in exhortation; he who gives, with liberality; he who leads, with diligence; he who shows mercy, with cheerfulness.

—ROMANS 12:4–8, NKJV, EMPHASIS ADDED

Every believer should operate in the prophetic realm in one or more of these prophetic levels. But our levels of grace differ. When the spirit of prophecy is strong in the local assembly, more believers will be able to operate in the different levels of prophecy.

You must discern your measure of grace and operate within its boundaries. All believers can prophesy, but all will not be able to operate in the highest level of the prophetic anointing—the office of the prophet. It is the highest and strongest level, and it will usher God's people into a greater degree of glory. It is this higher degree of the prophetic anointing that we will discuss at more length in this book.

Until the church begins to understand and walk in all the levels of prophecy—including this highest level, the office of the prophet—we will not see the greatest results and manifestations of the Holy Spirit in our midst. Jesus died, rose again, and sent the Holy Spirit so that we, God's people, might be perfected and matured into His image. Powerful prophetic utterances provide part of the direction for that maturing and perfecting process.

We should not settle for anything less than the fullest of what Jesus has provided for us. As we learn how to flow in the spirit of prophecy and the gift of prophecy, we will also learn how to walk in and receive from the ministry of the prophet. This is a grace gift to the body of Christ.

I cannot overemphasize the importance of prophecy. Churches should excel in it:

So, seeing that you are zealous of spiritual gifts, seek that you may excel to the edifying of the church.

—1 CORINTHIANS 14:12

The prophetic level of your local church should not be mediocre, average, or subpar. People need to be activated and trained to flow in the spirit of prophecy. We must take time to teach in this area and make room for its operation. It will not happen by accident. We should have a strategy to raise the level of operation of the prophetic anointing within our local church.

PROPHETIC ADMINISTRATIONS

Administer means "to manage or supervise the execution, use, or conduct of."[4] It also means "to minister or serve." Scripture tells us that "there are differences of administrations, but the same Lord" (1 Cor. 12:5). In the context of prophecy there are different ways to minister the prophetic anointing.

As I detailed above, I have divided the prophetic anointing into three levels: (1) the spirit of prophecy, (2) the gift of prophecy, and (3) the office of the prophet. All represent administrations of the prophetic anointing with further specific administrations falling under the realm of the office of a prophet. Because the prophet has grace and authority to go beyond these first two levels, prophets can administer the prophetic anointing through rebuke, correction, direction, impartation, activation, confirmation, and revelation. Prophets can also minister help, healing, miracles, and deliverance. We will be examining each of these in turn in this chapter and the next.

Did you know that there is an administration of healing that can come through prophets? I have seen people receive healing through prophetic utterances and the laying on of hands. I also have seen devils come out of people as they receive prophecy; this is an administration of deliverance through the prophetic anointing.

Elijah and Elisha both raised the dead and performed miracles of healing and provision. John the Baptist did no miracles, yet he was definitely a prophet of the Most High. (See John 10:41.) There is no record of Daniel performing miracles, yet he was strong in visions, dreams, and understanding.

All were prophets, but they flowed in different administrations. Moses was a prophet who was strong in administration and deliverance. Ezekiel and Zechariah were visionary prophets. Prophets are different depending on the measure of grace and giftings of the Holy Spirit. The prophet's office cannot be limited to one specific type or mode. Although there are certain characteristics and similarities we can look for to identify true prophets, there are also differences.

Some prophets are stronger in healing and miracles while others are stronger in visions and dreams. Some prophets are stronger in activation and impartation while others are stronger in confirmation. The prophetess is an administration of the prophetic anointing through a handmaiden of the Lord.

These different administrations or applications of prophecy reach different people. What one administration can't reach, another can. Every administration has a time and purpose (Eccles. 3:1). It is important to acknowledge and receive all the different administrations of each office as they are expressed in the local church. Together they comprise the Lord's body on the earth today.

Helpers

Prophets are helpers of a specific kind. Haggai and Zechariah were prophets sent by God to *help* Zerubbabel and Joshua rebuild the temple and reestablish the priesthood:

> Now the prophets, Haggai and Zechariah the son of Iddo, prophesied to the Jews that were in Judah and Jerusalem in the name of the God of Israel who was over them. Then Zerubbabel the son of Shealtiel and Joshua the son of Jozadak rose up and began to build the house

of God which is at Jerusalem, *and the prophets of God were with them, helping them.*

—EZRA 5:1–2, EMPHASIS ADDED

In general, prophets help build the house of the Lord. The people had felt it was not time to build the house of the Lord (Hag. 1:2). They felt this way because of the difficult conditions under which they were trying to build it. They had just returned from seventy years of captivity in Babylon. They were busy building their own houses and returning to the land (v. 4). There was also considerable opposition to the work from their adversaries. The people of the land were trying to weaken the hands of the people of Judah, troubling them in the building process (Ezra 4:4). As a result, the work of building the temple was badly hindered. The prophets came to help with the work and to reverse the opposition.

We should note here one of the major differences between Old Testament prophetic ministry and New Testament prophetic ministry. Old Testament saints depended more upon the prophets because they did not have the infilling of the Spirit as we do. New Testament ministry confirms what the Spirit of God is leading us to do. Remember, we are led by the Spirit of God, not by prophets.

However, even though we are filled with the Spirit, we still need confirmation and prophetic ministry. Spirit-filled believers still need edification, exhortation, and comfort. We still need the witnesses the Lord has provided to be established in the will of God, which will cause us to be confirmed unto the end.

Worshippers and musicians

Another administration of the prophet's anointing is through music. There are prophets who function as psalmists and minstrels. David is a good example of a man who had this administration, and he is called the sweet psalmist of Israel (2 Sam. 23:1). David understood the importance of music in stirring up and maintaining the corporate flow of God's Spirit. The strength of the spirit of prophecy in our midst will always be determined by our level of worship. (See Revelation 19:10.)

I believe that everyone who leads worship or plays instruments in the house of the Lord should flow to some degree under a prophetic anointing. Look how David organized the worship leaders:

> Then David and the officers of the army also set apart for the service some of the sons of Asaph, and of Heman, and of Jeduthun, those who prophesied with lyres, harps, and cymbals.
>
> —1 CHRONICLES 25:1

All may not be prophets, but the spirit of prophecy can be strong enough in our churches whereby everyone can enter into the prophetic flow.

Psalmists and musicians who are prophets will sing and play instruments under strong prophetic anointing. This can bring impartation, activation, direction, confirmation, and revelation just as prophesying without music can. It is a different administration of the anointing. The Spirit of the Lord will use the vehicle of song and music to impart and establish gifts and anointings in the local assembly.

Revelation flows through this administration. Divine secrets are revealed as we flow in prophetic singing and music. "I will incline my ear to a parable; I will expound my riddle with a harp" (Ps. 49:4). Parables are the mysteries of God, and yet all of them do not remain mysteries because it has been given unto us to know the mysteries of the kingdom (Matt. 13:11). I have found that congregations who flow in the worship/music administration of the prophetic anointing walk in a greater degree of revelation.

It is no wonder that the enemy fights music in the house of the Lord. Many pastors have a difficult time establishing the music department. I have seen churches struggle in this area more often than not. The enemy tries to bring confusion in this area of ministry. The enemy desires to block the flow of revelation that would come through prophetic music.

Prophets make great praise and worship leaders. Some prophets have the misconception that praise and worship is beneath them. They say, "Give me the pulpit, because I am a prophet." But I say that the prophets should return to praise and worship. Not all prophets can flow in this administration. Some can't carry a tune in a bucket. But there are prophets who are definitely called to this area. We need to receive this administration into our local assemblies.

The company of prophets under Samuel prophesied with instruments and music (1 Sam. 10:5). So do not be surprised to see many prophets being trained in church music departments, where they will develop a listening ear and the sensitivity they need to hear the voice of the Lord accurately through music.

A return to prophetic worship

We need more than musicians. We need prophet musicians who release the sound of heaven on earth. We can learn from biblical examples of prophet musicians.

- Heman, King David's seer—Heman was a musician and a seer. We need more than musicians. We need prophet (seer) musicians. "All these were the sons of Heman, the king's seer, according to the words of God, to exalt him, for God gave fourteen sons and three daughters to Heman" (1 Chron. 25:5).

- John and Jesus, singing prophets—John and Jesus ministered to Israel in different ways. (See Matthew 11:17.) Prophetic ministry is like a song. John came singing a dirge (a song of mourning). Jesus came playing a wedding song. Israel did not respond to either, and prophetic music requires a response.

Prophets release a sound and a song. We should be asking, "What are the prophets singing and playing?"

- Miriam and David, dancing prophets—Both Miriam (Exod. 15:20) and David (2 Sam. 6:14) expressed themselves in the dance. Prophets are expressive, and the dance is one of the most powerful ways to express God's power, victory, love, and mercy. (See Luke 7:32.)

PROPHETIC WORSHIP

Worship is one of the areas that will be greatly impacted when the prophetic is activated.

> And he set the Levites at the house of the LORD with cymbals, harps, and lyres according to the commandment of David, and Gad the seer of the king, and Nathan the prophet. For the commandment came from the LORD through His prophets.
>
> —2 CHRONICLES 29:25

Notice that Israel's worship was established by prophets. Hezekiah reestablished this worship based on the commandment of David, Gad, and Nathan. There is a strong connection between worship and the prophetic.

Prophets should be instrumental in worship. They should be involved as musicians, singers, seers, and dancers. David established worship on Mt. Zion with the prophetic families of Asaph, Heman, and Jeduthun (1 Chron. 25). Heman was the king's seer. The prophetic level in Israel at the time was extremely high because of the ministry of Samuel and the school of the prophets.

Music was evidently used in training emerging prophets. Saul met a company of prophets who were playing instruments (1 Sam. 10). Elisha called for a minstrel, and then began to prophesy. Music is very important in worship and also in training prophetic people.

Anointed minstrels help release the prophetic flow and keep it strong in an assembly. The secrets of God are opened upon the harp.

> I will incline mine ear to a parable: I will open my dark saying upon the harp.
>
> —PSALM 49:4, KJV

Minstrels should be Spirit-filled, skillful, and consecrated. They need to work with the singers and dancers in bringing forth the song of the Lord. We need prophet musicians as a part of the worship team. If the members of the worship team are not prophets, they need to be activated in the prophetic to some degree. Prophetic people are sensitive to the word of the Lord. The word of the Lord can be spoken or sung.

David, a worshipper, was also a prophet. He was the sweet psalmist of Israel.

> Now these be the last words of David. David the son of Jesse said, and the man who was raised up on high, the anointed of the God of Jacob, and the sweet psalmist of Israel, said,
>   The Spirit of the LORD spake by me, and his word was in my tongue.
>   The God of Israel said, the Rock of Israel spake to me, He that ruleth over men must be just, ruling in the fear of God.
>   —2 SAMUEL 23:1–3, KJV

Sweet is the Hebrew word *na`iym* meaning "pleasant, delightful, sweet, lovely, agreeable, delightful, lovely, beautiful (physical), singing, sweetly sounding, or musical."[5]

David was a singing prophet; he was a musical prophet.

Musical prophets bring great blessing and refreshing to the church. They should be identified and released. They are an important part of true worship. They release the word of the Lord in song. Habakkuk released the word upon Shigionoth.

Habakkuk 3:1 says, "A prayer of Habakkuk the prophet on Shigionoth." The word *Shigionoth* is a Hebrew word that refers to a song or rambling poem.[6] The World English Bible says, "A prayer of Habbakuk, the prophet, set to victorious music."

Prophesy simply means "to speak or sing by inspiration." This is often spontaneous and comes as the anointing flows from within, or rests upon. The musician can play, pray, and sing by inspiration. We are inspired people. Inspiration is powerful when released in worship.

The first place we see the word *prophet* in the Bible (Gen. 20:7) is when it is used to describe Abraham. He is called an "inspired man," a prophet, one who speaks or sings by inspiration. Inspiration is the result of the breath of God. Moses desired that all of God's people were prophetic (Num. 11:29).

THE PROPHETIC ANOINTING IS A WEAPON AGAINST SATANIC OPPOSITION

Satanic opposition will come when men rise up to build the house of God. Many local assemblies are stifled and hindered because of evil spirits opposing the work. The prophetic anointing gives discernment as to the source of problems that we may encounter. Prophets have the ability to discern and identify the spirits that are hindering a person or a ministry.

In the time of the temple rebuilding the people of the Lord, unaware of the satanic nature of the opposition, left off building the house of the Lord. The leaders, Zerubbabel and Joshua, became discouraged. The house of the Lord lay waste (Hag. 1:4).

The people and the leaders needed prophetic help, so the Lord sent Haggai and Zechariah to help them finish the work. First, there was rebuke for not continuing the work in spite of the opposition. Rebuke is unpleasant but sometimes necessary in building the house of the Lord. Prophets have the anointing and authority to rebuke when necessary. Rebuke can be part of the exhortation function of prophecy.

I have seen local assemblies being hindered by satanic opposition. The result was the people stopped using their faith and became apathetic concerning the work of the Lord. I have witnessed prophets minister in rebuke with the result being a complete transformation in the people. Repentance and obedience resulted, and the work of the Lord prospered.

Destroying satanic mountains

The opposition to the rebuilding of the temple and reestablishing of the priesthood was satanic. In a vision the prophet Zechariah saw Satan standing to oppose this work:

> Then he showed me Joshua, the high priest, standing before the angel of the LORD, and Satan standing at his right hand to accuse him. And the LORD said to Satan, "The LORD rebuke you, Satan! The LORD who has chosen Jerusalem rebukes you! Is this not a burning brand taken out of the fire?"
>
> —ZECHARIAH 3:1–2

Haggai and Zechariah did not just rebuke the people and Satan, but they also exhorted the people and the leadership to complete the work. Zechariah gave the word of the Lord to Zerubbabel, the governor and overseer in charge of the work:

> And he said to me: "This is the word of the LORD to Zerubbabel, saying: Not by might nor by power, but by My Spirit, says the LORD of Hosts. Who are you, O great mountain? Before Zerubbabel you will be made level ground, and he will bring out the top stone amidst shouting of 'Grace! Grace to the stone!'"
>
> —ZECHARIAH 4:6–7

The satanic opposition to this work was a mountain to Zerubbabel. He could not get past it in his own strength. The prophet encouraged him to depend upon the Spirit of the Lord to overcome this mountain. The mountain would fall before Zerubbabel because of the grace of God upon him, and then the work would be completed.

Satanic opposition to the work of the Lord can appear to be a mountain. Many leaders need prophetic ministry to destroy and get past the mountain of opposition they face. The Lord has commanded many leaders to build, and opposition as large as a mountain has blocked their way. Obstacles do not mean a leader is not obeying the Lord. Many leaders become discouraged and need prophetic help. Prophets can minister strength and encouragement to God's leaders, enabling them to complete the work of the Lord.

Sometimes the mountain is financial. Sometimes opposition can come from people within the congregation. The word of the Lord from the prophets will help destroy these mountains. It is no wonder Satan hates prophets and tries to alienate them from leadership, especially from pastors. Satan knows that the anointing upon the prophet will destroy the mountains he places in the way to hinder the work of the Lord. I have witnessed congregations and leaders turned around and brought into victory through prophetic ministry. Mountains are destroyed and the work prospers.

PROPHETS HELP TO REBUILD AFTER OPPOSITION

Haggai prophesied strength into the leadership and into people:

> Yet now be strong, O Zerubbabel, says the LORD, and be strong, O Joshua, son of Jehozadak, the high priest. Be strong all you people of the land, says the LORD. Work, for I am with you, says the LORD of Hosts.
> —HAGGAI 2:4

The word they received from the prophet gave them the strength they needed to build the Lord's house. It takes strength to defeat the powers of darkness and build the house of the Lord. The prophet brings strength and confirmation. Without this strength the people will become weary and often faint. The weak hands need to be strengthened, and the feeble knees confirmed (Isa. 35:3).

> The rebuilding by the elders of the Jews prospered through the prophesying of Haggai the prophet and Zechariah the son of Iddo. And they built, and finished it, according to the decree of the God of Israel.
> —EZRA 6:14

The elders represent leadership. As the leaders hearkened unto the voice of the prophets, they prospered and finished the work. The prophets were not sent to be in charge of the work as coleaders. The leaders were the ones in charge of the work. The prophets were sent to *help* the leadership. If the leaders listened to the prophets, they would succeed; if they refused, they would fail. True prophetic ministry is not sent to control and dominate leadership but to help it. Prophets can be in leadership positions in local assemblies, and there are many pastors who are also prophets. However, if a prophet is not a pastor, he will be sent to help a pastor. Prophets are sent to help discern direction, to build, and to bless the work of the Lord, not to control and dictate decisions.

Believe in the LORD your God, and you will be supported. Believe His prophets, and you will succeed.

—2 CHRONICLES 20:20

Quite simply, the work of the Lord prospers through prophecy. Your life will prosper through prophecy as well. Since a lack of prosperity and blessing is often the result of evil spirits, we need prophets to break and destroy demonic kingdoms through prophecy.

Just as Ezekiel prophesied to the dry bones, and skin and sinews came upon them, giving form and strength to an exceeding great army (Ezek. 37:8–10), so too strength is imparted into people when prophets prophesy. The result will be stronger churches, stronger leaders, stronger anointings, stronger praise, stronger giving, and stronger evangelism. People can be prophesied out of weakness into strength. If pastors want to have strong churches, they must allow prophets to minister and to prophesy freely. Local churches will then become strong enough to break through all opposition and to prosper.

OTHER WAYS PROPHETS OPERATE WITHIN THE LOCAL CHURCH

As we've already seen, prophets do much more than prophesy. They also pray, intercede, discern, weep, worship, sing, declare, announce, pronounce, renounce, decree, build, break, uproot, warn, correct, renew, revive, restore, reform, counsel, help, assist, strengthen, see, expose, preach, teach, disciple, train, release, equip, impart, activate, stir up, break down, tear down, plant, water, send, guard, protect, watch, prepare, open, close, gather, sound the alarm, blow the trumpet, stand in the gap, bring conviction, bring change, release judgment, enlighten, labor, plow, confirm, direct, uncover, dream, have visions, dance, edify, comfort, repair, heal, deliver, loose, bind, evangelize, shepherd, establish, set, unstop, charge, challenge, perfect, equip, ordain, and encourage.

Let's take a look at another specific role a prophet may operate through.

Prophets as scribes or writers

They write down their dreams, visions, prophetic words, and insights. They love journaling (keeping a personal record of occurrences, experiences, and reflections kept on a regular basis—a diary).

Therefore I send you prophets, and wise men, and scribes. Some of them you will kill and crucify, and some you will scourge in your synagogues and persecute them from city to city.

—MATTHEW 23:34

The scribal prophet is not limited to writing, but he or she can release the word through audio, video, print, and other media. Prophets have a desire to record what God is saying.

> Scribal prophets are not simply prophets who write and record personal prophecy, or the occasional prophetic word. They are actually vessels that God uses fully as His prophets (in every sense of the word); but who also have a burning passion rooted inside them to record, watch over, release and teach the messages of heaven entrusted to them under a specific directive. (Read Ezekiel 9 and Ezekiel 10 in full.)
> —Theresa Harvard Johnson[7]

If you know that you are a scribal prophet, then I encourage you to go back and read the things you wrote down years ago, and you might be shocked at what the Lord has done to bring those words to pass. Some of you have journals that you have written over the years. God is faithful.

Consider also that scribes are also persecuted because religious systems of control hate scribes. This is because their writings challenge these systems. Truth and revelation can be imparted and released through writing. Writing has always been a powerful tool of reformation.

How Prophets Operate With Other Ministry Gifts

Prophets are essential to the life of any church body, but they are complementary to the other four ministry gifts—pastor, apostle, teacher, and evangelist. How do they function together? What is God's plan for how prophets support other church leaders?

Prophets and pastors

Prophets sometimes clash with pastors. Some pastors have a hard time dealing with prophets. Pastors need to be prophetic as well. Prophetic pastors will be better able to embrace prophets and prophetic people. One of the worst things that can happen to a prophet is to be shut down by pastors.

Controlling pastors don't like prophets. This is because control and domination are a form of witchcraft, and prophets can smell it out.

But these pastors should beware: when a church or denomination loses its prophets (they depart, get put out, or get shut down), it will begin to decline spiritually. Sometimes it is unnoticeable at first, but eventually the presence of God departs and it becomes a monument instead of a movement.

Now the boy Samuel was ministering to the LORD before Eli. And the word of the LORD was rare in those days. There was no vision coming forth.

—1 SAMUEL 3:1

Prophets and apostles

Prophets like being with apostles, and apostles like being with prophets. These two ministries are linked together in the New Testament. Prophets stir apostles, and apostles stir prophets. These ministries complement and strengthen each other. They both tend to be persecuted and misunderstood, and it seems as if they understand each other.

Prophets should be apostolic, and apostles should be prophetic.

Therefore also the wisdom of God said, "I will send them prophets and apostles, and some of them they will kill and persecute."

—LUKE 11:49

Many apostolic leaders are married to prophetic spouses.

Apostles and prophets work together. They complement and balance each other. Apostles tend to deal with structure and order, while prophets are more spontaneous. Apostles can become too rigid and need prophets to help them stay flexible and spontaneous. Prophets can be too spontaneous and need the order and structure of the apostle. These ministries can impart into each other and both be more balanced as a result.

Prophets and apostles are similar in their functions.

Many of the prophets in the Old Testament did what we would consider apostolic today. Many apostles today are doing what the Old Testament would consider prophetic. Jesus said He would send (which is the Greek word *apostolos*) prophets and apostles (Luke 11:49). Prophets therefore are sent (*apostolos*).

Prophets should be apostolic, that is, "sent ones." They should be sent with power and authority to establish and build.

Prophets and apostles work well together.

The apostle breaks and establishes new ground, biblical purpose, and order in enemy territory; and prophets bring fire, passion, and a continual sense of urgency into the faith communities of those entities established by apostles.[8]

The apostle needs the prophet to keep the fire burning in what has been pioneered and established.

Prophets and apostles working together results in synergy.

"Synergy is the interaction or cooperation of two or more organizations, substances, or other agents to produce a combined effect greater than the sum of their separate effects."[9] Apostolic leaders need prophetic input (both verbally and in anointing), or their churches will lack a fundamental ingredient needed to keep momentum. Prophets help release energy and enthusiasm.

Prophets and apostles want to see Christ formed in believers.

Prophets desire the image of Christ to be seen in the saints. This is the travail (labor, hardship, birthing...) of the prophet. This is also the desire and labor of apostles.

> My dear children, I am suffering the pains of giving birth to you all over again—and this will go on until the Messiah takes shape in you.
> —GALATIANS 4:19, CJB

Neither prophets nor apostles like to see men receive the glory when all glory goes to God. There is nothing wrong with honoring men. There is nothing wrong with supporting leaders. We are just not to glory in them. *Glory* means "to boast." Apostles and prophets will challenge "boasting in men." It is all about Christ and His working through us. It is in Him that we live and move and have our being. No one person is greater than another. All the men and women God sends belong to us all.

> So let no one exult proudly concerning men [boasting of having this or that man as a leader], for all things are yours.
> —1 CORINTHIANS 3:21, AMPC

When apostles and prophets get together, it is important that they keep a sober perspective of themselves and each other. God is not looking for super prophets and apostles. You don't have to be an "elite" or "super" prophet to hear and speak for the Lord. Don't compare yourselves with others. Many have elevated these ministries to a level where people feel they can never arrive. There were hundreds of prophets in Israel whose names are never mentioned in the Bible. Be humble. Be confident in the call of God on your life. Be you.

Prophets and evangelists

Together prophets and evangelists make sure the fire never goes out. The fire of prayer, worship, and evangelism must never go out. This fire must burn from generation to generation.

> A perpetual fire shall be kept burning on the altar. It shall never go out.
> —LEVITICUS 6:13

Prophets and teachers

These ministries work together to build the church. Prophets and teachers complement each other. Prophets need teachers to help with instruction. Teachers need prophets to help with inspiration. These two working together balance each other and strengthen each other. They also provide an atmosphere for apostolic release (Acts 13:1–5).

> In the church that was in Antioch there were prophets and teachers: Barnabas, Simeon who was called Niger, Lucius of Cyrene, Manaen who had been brought up with Herod the tetrarch, and Saul.
>
> —Acts 13:1

Prophets and other prophets

Prophets are not out of control when they minister. Prophets are disciplined people who respect order (prophets hate disorder and confusion). Prophets know how to work with and minister with others, especially other prophets.

Prophets are the hardest on each other. Prophets know other prophets. Prophets can discern when something is wrong with another prophet.

> Let two or three prophets speak, and let the others judge.
>
> —1 Corinthians 14:29

> The spirits of the prophets are subject to the prophets.
>
> —1 Corinthians 14:32

> The spirits of prophets are under the control of [subject to] the prophets themselves [unlike in pagan religions, where a spirit would seize control of a speaker, causing frenzy, mania or ecstasy].
>
> —1 Corinthians 14:32, exb (See also 1 Kings 18:28)

Prophetic operation is one of the most important functions in the life of a church and in the lives of believers individually. Without seers, visionaries, and ones who hear from and speak for God, there would be no life, and the church would be left scrambling in darkness. Let's take a look now at the office of a prophet and see how this higher level of prophetic function benefits the people of God.

CHAPTER 6

The Office of the Prophet

God has put these in the church: first apostles, second prophets, third teachers, after that miracles, then gifts of healings, helps, governments, and various tongues.

—1 Corinthians 12:28

T HE CHURCH IS a prophetic community. God has set prophets in the church because they are important to the health and strength of the local assembly.

Carrying tremendous authority and having the capacity to bring great blessing to those who receive their ministry, prophets should function under the new-covenant law, under which they are accepted as bearers of one of the ministry gifts established by God to perfect believers. (See Ephesians 4:11–12.) No longer should prophets have to function under the old-covenant mind-set of rejection, persecution, and exile. Prophets need to be integrated into the fabric of the life of a healthy church.

Prophetic Authority

Jeremiah gives a picture of the authority of a prophet:

> See, I have this day set you over the nations and over the kingdoms, to root out and to pull down, and to destroy and to throw down, to build and to plant.
>
> —Jeremiah 1:10

This is true not only for Old Testament prophets but also for present-day prophets. When prophets speak, the utterances that come from their mouths are charged with the anointing and power of God. They carry divine authority. This authority is given to prophets by the grace of God, and it is given for two reasons:

1. For the destruction of Satan's kingdom
2. For the establishment of the kingdom of God

In this chapter we will be exploring the specific ways in which prophets function to tear down the kingdom of darkness and bring in the kingdom of God's light. The kingdom of darkness produces sin, rebellion, sickness, and poverty, but the kingdom of God is righteousness, peace, and joy in the Holy Ghost (Rom. 14:17).

All ministry gifts are called to and responsible for establishing righteousness, peace, and joy in the Holy Ghost, but the authority of the prophets enables them to root out, pull down, destroy, and throw down the works of the devil. Prophets also have the authority to build and plant the kingdom of God. Although the end result of coming against Satan's kingdom is to make room for the kingdom of God, it often seems like twice as much emphasis is given to destroying the kingdom of darkness as opposed to building up the kingdom of God.

Those who operate in the prophetic anointing seem to find themselves being thrown into warfare frequently and being in direct conflict with the powers of darkness. The prophetic anointing is often *confrontational*. An example of this confrontational anointing is Elijah, who challenged and confronted the powers of idolatry on Mount Carmel. Because of the prophet's office he was able to pull down the stronghold of Baal that ruled Israel. As a result of Elijah's ministry, eventual judgment came upon the house of Ahab.

Through the utterances of prophets, evil spirits are rooted out of their dwelling places. Those who have the office of the prophet speak with more authority than believers who prophesy by the spirit of prophecy or by the simple gift of prophecy. The words of the prophets are like an ax laid at the root of the trees (Luke 3:9). By their divinely inspired words, every tree that does not bear fruit is cut down and cast into the fire. In the midst of true prophetic ministry, only what is fruitful and productive to the kingdom will stand.

Pulling down strongholds

> For the weapons of our warfare are not carnal, but mighty through
> God to the pulling down of strongholds.
> —2 Corinthians 10:4

Jeremiah the prophet was given authority over kingdoms and nations. Prophets have authority over demonic kingdoms. Satan sets up demonic strongholds in individuals, families, churches, cities, and nations. The prophet's anointing is a spiritual weapon in the hand of the Lord to pull down strongholds.

I have seen deliverance come through prophesying to individuals, families, and local assemblies. I have seen people weeping and broken after receiving prophetic utterances. Prophets usually carry a strong deliverance anointing. As a result, the ministry of the prophet provides deliverance and the pulling down of strongholds.

> By a prophet the LORD brought Israel up from Egypt, and by a
> prophet he was preserved.
>
> —HOSEA 12:13

The prophet has the responsibility to minister the word of God just as much as he or she prophesies by the Spirit of God. This combined anointing provides the ability to bring deliverance to God's people in a unique way. I have witnessed pastors struggle with strongholds in local assemblies that they were unable to pull down. The pastor's anointing is important, but it may take a different anointing to pull down certain strongholds. This does not elevate the prophet above the pastor in the local assembly, for we are all laborers together with God. However, pastors need to discern the importance of the prophet's anointing to the pulling down of strongholds.

Rooting out evil

> But He answered, "Every plant which My heavenly Father has not
> planted will be uprooted."
>
> —MATTHEW 15:13

Jesus was referring to the religious leaders of that day. His ministry was causing them to be offended, and because they were offended, an uprooting was taking place in the spirit. When people are uprooted through prophetic ministry, they will often be offended. Eventually the entire system of religion in Judah and Jerusalem was uprooted and the Jewish people were scattered.

The enemy had planted tares among the wheat. (See Matthew 13.) The enemy can plant certain people in local assemblies to cause confusion and to harm the work of the Lord. Prophets are the ones who have the anointing to root them out.

If the troublemakers are rooted out without the anointing, damage can result. This is why the Lord told His servants not to attempt to gather the tares, lest while gathering the tares, they "pull up also the wheat with them" (Matt. 13:29).

Rooting out a spirit or demonic influence is not something that can be done in the flesh. A spirit or demonic influence must be rooted out in the power of the Spirit of God.

> His confidence will be rooted out of his tent, and it will bring him to
> the king of terrors.
>
> —JOB 18:14

There are times when the prophet is unaware in the natural of what is being accomplished in the spirit. The actual rooting out may not occur until after the prophet has departed the scene, sometimes even years later. What is taking place in the natural may be the result of what has happened in the spirit years ago. What we see in the natural is only a reflection of what is taking place, or what has already taken place, in the spirit.

Destroying the works of the devil

True prophets are able to destroy the works of the devil. Many people, including pastors, fear prophetic ministry because it is so powerful. However, the righteous pastor should not be afraid, for true prophetic ministry will only destroy what is of the devil; it will never destroy what is of the Lord. True prophetic ministry will establish the things of the Spirit while destroying the things of the devil.

Unfortunately much of what goes on in local assemblies is fleshly and even sometimes demonic. The prophet's ministry will destroy what is fleshly and demonic and establish holiness and purity in the house of the Lord. Prophets have a hatred for what God hates (Ps. 139:21–22). This is why prophets will often be criticized for not being more "tolerant."

The prophetic gift leaves no room for compromise. In fact, a compromising prophet will soon lose his or her effectiveness and eventually will be judged by the Lord. This is not to say that prophets have the right to be offensive or to minister in the flesh. Prophets must minister in the Spirit at all times. A prophet who tries to minister in the flesh will end up destroying and damaging that which is of the Lord instead of that which is of the devil. It is the same with any ministry gift. To minister in any way in the flesh causes reproach and damage.

True prophets will always have love and compassion for people but a corresponding hatred and intolerance for the works of the devil. Do not mistake hatred and intolerance for the works of the devil for being hard or judgmental, which is a fleshly response. We must discern between the operation of the flesh and the administration of the Holy Spirit. Without proper discernment and understanding we will misjudge prophets and reject them, thus depriving the body of Christ of a very important ministry gift.

Throwing down idolatry

> It shall come to pass that as I have watched over them to pluck up,
> and to break down, and to throw down, and to destroy, and to afflict,
> so I will watch over them, to build, and to plant, says the LORD.
> —JEREMIAH 31:28

The nation of Israel was commanded to enter Canaan and throw down the altars of the heathen. They were supposed to root out the nation of Canaan for their iniquity. Israel had to dispossess the Canaanites before they could enter and possess the Promised Land. Notice that before building and planting come rooting out and throwing down. This is an unpleasant part of ministry, but it is necessary nonetheless.

The prophet's anointing is like this; it is one of confrontation and warfare. First come confrontation and warfare; then come building and planting. Many a prophet has pulled back from confronting evil because of soulish fear and intimidation. Warfare is unpleasant to the soul. However, if a prophet allows the anointing to change him or her "into another man" (1 Sam. 10:6), the strength of the anointing will prevail over the drawing back of one's soul and cause one to be able to rise up and throw down the altars of sin (Hosea 8:11).

Often, in ministry, prophets will not understand why that which they are ministering is going in a certain direction. In the spirit prophets may encounter rebellion, control, witchcraft, and pride in an assembly without knowing in the natural anything about what is going on in the congregation. Sometimes the direction is the total opposite of where they started ministering in the Word. The anointing and leading of the Holy Spirit will cause prophets to hit areas of sin and rebellion in the spirit without knowledge in the natural.

Authority to Build

Besides destroying, uprooting, pulling down, and throwing down the works of the devil, the prophet also builds up the body of Christ. This is their ministry of edification, exhortation, and comfort. Prophets have a strong hatred for the works of the devil, but they also have a genuine love and compassion for God's people, and the saints will be built up and edified through true prophetic ministry. When the church is built up in this way, the gates of hell will not be able to prevail against it.

We always need to remember that the purpose of tearing down strongholds is to build up the kingdom of God. Spiritual warfare is not an end but rather a means to an end. Those who have been called to prophetic ministry must always keep their focus on the goal, which is to build up the church.

It is possible to lose focus. There is no guarantee of pure motives. If the prophets lose focus, they end up doing considerable damage to the work of the Lord. Sometimes prophets develop what I refer to as a "blasting" mentality. They just want to blast everything that is not like God.

Remember, John the Baptist's mission was to prepare a people for the coming of the Lord. He spoke against wickedness and sin, but he also announced the arrival of the kingdom of God. In the same way, prophets must concern themselves not only with the works of the enemy but also with the needs of the people. They must balance their ministry with love and compassion, and they must avoid ministering in a harsh, critical, or bitter spirit. They have a responsibility to minister the word in love. They have a responsibility to build up the Lord's house.

Planted to flourish

> Those that are planted in the house of the LORD shall flourish in the courts of our God.
>
> —PSALM 92:13

When people are exposed to true prophetic ministry, they will be *planted* in the house of the Lord. Those who are planted will flourish in every way. *Planted* means "rooted and grounded." People in prophetic ministry can uproot what the enemy has planted, and they can plant in local assemblies what has been ordained by the Lord.

In local churches I have witnessed people coming with a hesitancy to be planted. They may waver, and they may not be dependable to help in the work of the Lord. Through the prophet's anointing a prophet can minister strength and certainty to such hesitant saints and establish them in the house of the Lord.

We don't need more church members who are not rooted and planted. We need saints who are planted in the house by the Lord. Those who are planted will develop strong roots, and they will be like trees planted by the rivers of living water. The planting of the Lord will be fruitful Christians who will be steadfast, unmovable, and always abounding in the work of the Lord (1 Cor. 15:58). As we receive prophetic ministry, we will become trees of righteousness, the planting of the Lord (Isa. 61:3).

I am firmly convinced that one of the reasons we don't have more fruitful Christians in our local assemblies is because of the lack of true prophetic ministry. I have been ministering and telling people for years that it takes the anointing to perfect the saints. Each ministry gift carries a distinct anointing. Each ministry gift has a divine ability to build the church. Prophets have an anointing and ability to build and to plant. Without this anointing there will be areas where the saints are not built up and things they are not planted in.

To summarize, prophets have the authority from God to *root out*, to *pull down*, to *destroy*, to *throw down*, to *build*, and to *plant*. These will be the identifiable results of the word of the Lord that comes out of the mouths of the prophets.

GETTING IN THE FLOW

Prophets must never use their authority to control or abuse God's people. Control and domination are forms of witchcraft. To insure against the abuse of their authority, prophets must work to develop godly character, and they must walk in humility.

Prophets can also work together in teams. Teams help keep prophets balanced, and teamwork provides a healthy barrier against pride, isolation, and exclusiveness. We have many recognized prophets in our local assembly, and they understand that teamwork is the way to go.

We need to be connected with people who flow strongly in prophetic ministry. When you move in the prophetic, a whole new realm of authority and spiritual ability opens up to you. You can move in prophetic music, which includes playing prophetically, singing prophetic songs, and singing new songs. You need to be able to get in the flow.

> He sends out His word and melts them; He causes His wind to blow and the waters flow.
>
> —Psalm 147:18

When you are in the flow, you will prophesy not only to other saints. You will also begin prophesying unto God and unto principalities and powers. You can prophesy to devils and kingdoms in the spirit realm. This is how the tearing down of strongholds happens. The prophet Jeremiah was anointed of God to prophesy to kingdoms and nations. He had authority to tear down kingdoms and to exercise rule over nations.

According to 1 Corinthians 2:10, the Spirit searches the deep things of God. The twelfth verse goes on to say that we have been given the Spirit of God that we might know the things that are freely given to us of God. So prophesying to God is speaking to Him out of your spirit according to the depths of revelation that the Spirit of God has given you.

God already knows what He is going to do. The problem comes when God has to have someone on the earth fulfill His plan. There can be things in the heavenlies that God wants to do. God knows about it, for He has decreed it. Jesus, the Holy Ghost, and the angels are all aware of it. All heaven is in one accord, but it is different when God tries to get it established in the realm of the earth.

When you begin to prophesy out of your spirit, that is God flowing out of you. Whatever is bound in heaven is bound on the earth. Whatever God establishes in heaven and makes to flow out of us on the earth is exactly what is going to be established in the earth's realm.

One of the prayers we pray goes like this: "Your kingdom come; Your will be done on earth, as it is in heaven" (Matt. 6:10). It is the God in heaven who is in you, speaking out of you on the earth, joining heaven to the earth. He desires to fulfill His plan in the earth's realm that we might walk and live in His will. We are not trying to be God. We are just His instruments. We know that without God we can do nothing.

Most of us have never really understood the authority that we have in the prophetic realm. We think we are very different from the great prophets of old who walked in tremendous authority. Joshua had the authority to stop the heavenly motion, to stop the moon and the sun. Moses walked in enough authority to open a pathway in the Red Sea. These men of God knew how to flow in the prophetic realm.

Most of God's people, most churches, don't know how to flow in that type of authority. That is why we sit around twiddling our thumbs, waiting for God to perform everything automatically. Just imagine Moses standing on the shore of the Red Sea, with the Egyptian army bearing down on the Israelites, just "waiting on God to do something." That would have been the end of the story right then and there; they all would have died. Many times God is waiting on us to flow with Him. His anointing, initiative, and power are there for us, but since most of us have not been taught how, we do not know how to flow in the prophetic. I have found that often, in a conference, it is very difficult to break through in prophetic songs because there are so many religious people in the service who don't know how to flow prophetically. When I get up to prophesy or to give a message in tongues, they are jumping, singing, and clapping because they have never been taught how to flow in the anointing. Their actions are not wrong, but they are misplaced, and they throw off the entire service. The whole church needs to learn how to flow with the anointing.

> Behold, how good and how pleasant it is for brothers to dwell together in unity!
>
> —Psalm 133:1

Anointing flows from the head down

If you want a prophetic church, you must have prophetic leadership because the anointing always flows from the head down. In the Book of Psalms the Bible reports that when Aaron was anointed, the oil flowed from his head all the way down to the skirts of his garments. The anointing always flows down. It doesn't flow up.

If the leadership of a local assembly does not flow in the prophetic anointing, then the people are not going to flow in prophecy. If the leadership does not flow in miracles, the congregation will not flow in miracles. That is why it is futile for people who get a hold of something at a conference to think they are going to take it back and transform their churches with it. Unless they are church leaders themselves, they will be trying to get the anointing to flow upward.

I don't care how much you know about deliverance or prophecy; if you try to introduce it into your church instead of the leaders doing it, you are going to end up getting hurt and disappointed. You will waste years trying to create a spiritual move in that church, but it will not work because you do not have the authority—unless you get into a prophetic realm of praying and you pray it in.

You have to get into the authority in the spirit world in order to bring things into manifestation in your local church. God will then put it on the heart of your pastor, and it will flow down under the authority of that pastor. Any other move in a church is a rebellious uprising, and God cannot bless it.

> And the LORD came down in a cloud, and spoke to him, and took of the Spirit that was on him, and gave it to the seventy elders, and when the Spirit rested on them, they prophesied, but did not do it again.
>
> —NUMBERS 11:25

God wants a prophetic people, and He is looking for people who will flow in miracles. But you will never flow in miracles in advance of your leadership. When your leadership begins to flow in miracles, that anointing will flow down upon everyone under their authority. It always works that way.

That's why you can go to some churches, and if the leadership is not flowing in the prophetic, chances are there is not going to be much prophesying, no matter how much you want to flow in the prophetic. There are not going to be very many new songs birthed, even though you personally may be able to flow in that anointing.

I know you can minister to laypeople all day long, but unless the leadership is ahead of them, the church is not going to be effective to the degree that God desires. It is because the leaders are keeping the people out of that realm. Remember, you just cannot go beyond your leadership.

For this reason, my heart is set on those in leadership. This is why I try to reach pastors and leaders. It is so important to minister to them first. Whether or not you are a leader, pray for church leadership. God is raising up prophetic leaders, people of authority, people who will be able to flow in miracles. They are going to minister, and when they do, the anointing is going to come down upon the people of God to the extent that they follow their leaders into different realms of the Spirit of God.

CHAPTER 7

Decently and in Order— Prophetic Protocol

Therefore, brothers, eagerly desire to prophesy, and do not forbid speaking in tongues. Let all things be done decently and in order.
—1 Corinthians 14:40

GOD HAS AN unlimited number of thoughts concerning His people, and prophets have been given the gift to know God's thoughts and to share them. There are two main avenues through which God reveals His thoughts to His people: personal and corporate prophecy. In order for people to benefit from one or both of these avenues, it is important for prophets to proceed with their ministry according to the protocol outlined in the Word.

PROTOCOL FOR PERSONAL PROPHETIC MINISTRY

I have received hundreds of prophetic words in my lifetime. These words have brought greater clarity to my life concerning my destiny. These words have encouraged me in times of discouragement. These words have imparted strength and gifts to my life. I highly value personal prophecy, and I desire that every believer benefit from receiving the word of the Lord.

God is a personal God, and every person has a destiny in His plan. He wants each of us to choose to hear from Him. In our church we have developed prophetic teams to meet the needs of many believers who desire to receive words of personal prophecy. In particular, every new member and new believer has the opportunity to receive personal prophecy. Many individuals request personal prophecy, so we have built our church to meet this need. Is it right to seek personal prophetic words, or should a person wait until such words are given only by the unction of the Holy Spirit?

I have prophesied over thousands of people with no initial unction simply because they requested ministry. I have found that as I begin to speak in faith, the unction will increase. In fact, some of the strongest prophecies I have ever received have come even though I had no initial unction.

Prophecy can be stirred up through faith. Sometimes there is an unction to prophesy that needs no stirring, but you should know that it can be stirred up if necessary. All of the gifts can be stirred up. Teaching and preaching can be stirred up. Tongues can be stirred up. Prophecy can also be stirred up through faith and an act of the will. If you ask, you will receive:

> Ask and it will be given to you; seek and you will find; knock and it will be opened to you. For everyone who asks receives, and he who seeks finds, and to him who knocks, it will be opened.
>
> What man is there among you who, if his son asks for bread, will give him a stone? Or if he asks for a fish, will he give him a snake? If you then, being evil, know how to give good gifts to your children, how much more will your Father who is in heaven give good things to those who ask Him!
>
> —MATTHEW 7:7–11

As you become more fluent in prophetic utterance, your opportunities to minister to others will increase. People will come to you with expectations—some good and some bad. Since prophecy is about building up the body of Christ, here are ways that you can edify those who come to draw from your anointing.

Let them seek a rhema word.

Seeking a rhema word, sometimes called a "now word," is not a new concept. We all want to be included in what God is doing right now. *Rhema* is a personal prophetic word from the Lord that is not something you simply read from the Word of the Lord in the Bible. There are plenty of church leaders who discourage people from seeking a word from a person with a prophetic anointing. Ministers have warned against personal prophetic ministry in their teaching because they have seen abuses. Too much deception and error have occurred in the name of "personal prophecy."

As a result, some ministers teach their people that all they need is the Bible, the Word (logos) of God. They teach their people, "If you just study the Word, you will get all of the answers that you need. Christians should never go to a service expecting someone to give them a word [rhema] from God." Consequently many people go for years without ever getting a word from God because they have been taught to be suspicious of the supernatural flow of personal prophecy.

I understand the reasons for warning people in this way, and I know the dangers of being deceived. However, the Lord has shown me some things concerning the prophetic anointing, and I believe that it is a mistake to "throw the baby out with the bathwater." For starters, we can see in the Old Testament that people went to the prophets of God often to get the word of the Lord. They did not yet have the unction of the Holy Ghost in their own lives as we do under the new covenant, so they sought out the prophets who did have the unction. Now, even though God can speak to us individually, there are still times when we need to hear from God through the avenue of prophecy. We need to hear God's word for our lives through another saint. When we receive such a word, we will know for ourselves how prophecy operates, and we will be able to judge the word of the Lord by the Spirit of truth.

Let them ask, "What is God's will for my life?"

During my years of service as a pastor, many people have come to me with questions concerning knowing the will of God for their lives. You may have had questions about this as well. As your prophetic gift becomes known in your local body, people may come to you with this question. Do not discourage them. Minister to them. As I have said, as you begin to open your mouth, God will fill it.

They may ask you, "How do I really know whether this is my will or God's will?" What I always tell people is that the will of God is following the desires of your heart.

They may respond to that by saying, "Well, pastor, how do I know whether it is my desire or God's desire? How can I tell the difference between the desires I have and those that God gives me?" My answer to that is, "If your heart is pure and you really desire to do the will of God, you don't have to worry about your desires being wrong."

> To the pure, all things are pure. But to those who are defiled and unbelieving, nothing is pure. Even their minds and consciences are defiled.
>
> —Titus 1:15

The only time believers have to be concerned about their desires being wrong is when they are in rebellion, disobedience, lust, or some other type of sin. Then they have to be careful that they don't confuse their desires with God's desires. People in a sinful spiritual state will twist or pervert God's desires. Encourage the people you minister to that as long as they are pure, sincere, and open before God, they can trust their desires because their heart is open to receive the desires of God rather than their own.

Let them know that prophecy will flow according to their faith.

To my surprise, in one service nearly every person in the building received a prophetic word from the Lord, even though there did not seem to be any real supernatural unction to prophesy. What happened is that I simply stirred up the gift of God that is in me. Now I know that I can lay hands upon people and prophesy to them in faith. Now I know how that gift operates, and I can flow in it. Since every person in that building needed to hear from God, I had the ability to stir up the gift of God and to prophesy out of my gift to each one of them.

A few years ago I probably would have discouraged that type of prophesying.

I very likely would have said, "If there is no supernatural unction to prophesy, if the Spirit of God doesn't really just come upon me, then I am not going to try to prophesy to everyone in the building." I also would have said, "These people should not be coming to church expecting to hear a word from God."

I have since found that you should always expect to hear from God, especially in church. Too often it is religious tradition that keeps us away from receiving God's best.

> We have diverse gifts according to the grace that is given to us: if prophecy, according to the proportion of faith.
>
> —ROMANS 12:6

Let them know that they need to beware of "itching ears."

> For the time will come when people will not endure sound doctrine, but they will gather to themselves teachers in accordance with their own desires, having itching ears.
>
> —2 TIMOTHY 4:3

There is such a thing as itching ears, which means that sometimes it may be necessary to teach the person you are ministering to that getting a word from God does not excuse them from praying and seeking Him for themselves. Prophecy is not for lazy people who do not want to pray and seek God, who would rather have someone prophesy to them.

But then there are people who are genuinely and sincerely seeking God. They want to know: "Is there a word from the Lord on this situation?" They think, "We don't want to make decisions on our own. We do not want to operate out of our own minds. We want to hear from God because we know if we get the mind of God on the matter, whatever we do is going to be the right thing."

Do minister to these people without any hesitancy. Because of their faith, the Lord will reveal the answers they seek.

Let them know that it is OK to be cautious of false prophets.

I know there are false prophets. However, let us not forget that before there can be a counterfeit of something, there must first be a genuine thing.

There are some people who want to prophesy to you for the sake of monetary reward. They have a prophetic gift, but their purpose in prophesying is to take advantage of God's people financially. They can even be accurate in the spirit because they are prophesying out of a genuine gift. But their characters are flawed to the point that they will take advantage of God's people. Fears and financial pressures can drive people to resort to these tactics.

But this is not who you are, prophet. You operate with humility, integrity, and high accountability to the Spirit of God and the other prophets around you.

If this comes up during ministry, encourage the person to take any fears about false prophets to the Lord. Tell them to ask God to keep them pure of heart so that they are able to discern a false prophet. Give them the Word on this that they will know prophets—true or false—by their fruit (Matt. 7:16, 20; Luke 6:44). Encourage them not to let the existence of counterfeit prophecy deter them from receiving the real thing. That would be like deciding not to pay for purchases with dollar bills because they heard people manufacture counterfeit ones.

Let them know they need to be open to receive.

There have been many times when I went to a meeting confused about the specifics concerning the will of God for my life. I just did not know how to accomplish what I felt He was telling me to do. I needed to hear God speak to my situation. But because the sermon was "general" in nature, an all-purpose good message, I would leave in the same state in which I came, and I would not have an opportunity to receive prophetic ministry, which is what I needed most.

It wasn't until I started seeking a rhema word from God that I got the direction I needed for my life. This is important for believers to know when they want personal ministry. If they open up their hearts to the word of the Lord through personal prophecy and go to local assemblies where believers flow accurately in the prophetic gift, they will get the direction they need for their lives. Thank God for the gift of prophecy.

THIRTEEN KEYS FOR MINISTERING PERSONAL PROPHECY

1. Always prophesy in love. Love the people you minister to. Love is the motivation behind prophecy (1 Cor. 14:1). Do not prophesy out of bitterness, hurt, or anger. Love always seeks to edify. Love is not rude. Love is not harsh or condemning. Be sensitive to the person you are ministering to. Be polite.

2. Prophesy according to your proportion of faith (Rom. 12:6). Do not copy others. Be yourself. God wants us all to be originals, not copies. We lose our own God-given individuality and uniqueness when we copy others. Strive to do your best and to be yourself.

3. Avoid being too demonstrative, dramatic, theatrical, or showy when ministering prophetically.

4. When ministering to a person of the opposite sex, do not lay your hands on any area of the person's body that could be considered sensitive. If you must touch, lay your hands gently on the head or on the shoulder. You may ask another person of the same sex as the recipient to place a hand on the person for the purpose of impartation and healing.

5. Do not allow people to worship you! Stay humble when people give

praise and good reports about the ministry they received from you. Remember to worship Jesus. The testimony of Jesus is the spirit of prophecy.

6. Don't be a prophetic "lone ranger." Learn to minister with others. We only know in part and prophesy in part. Submitting to others is a way to avoid pride. Prefer others when ministering. Do not be a prophetic "hog." Give others a chance to minister. Don't take up all the time. Learn to be a team player. A good follower makes a good leader.

7. Eliminate excessive hand motions, which distract the ministry recipient. This includes motions such as pointing, waving, and making fists. Also avoid rocking the person back and forth. Do not speak in tongues excessively while ministering prophetically. We can generally speak in tongues while beginning to get into the flow, but afterward stay with the known words of prophecy.

8. Never release a prophetic word that is contrary to the written Word of God. It is important for prophetic people to be students of the Word. Study to show yourself approved.

9. Know your strengths and limitations. Some people are stronger in certain areas of the prophetic than others. Do not attempt to go beyond your measure of grace. We are not in a competition; we are not trying to outdo others.

10. Remember, the spirit of the prophet is subject to the prophet (1 Cor. 14:32). God does not give us something we cannot control. You should always have rule over your spirit (Prov. 25:28). Never allow things to get out of control.

11. Do not be repetitious while prophesying. This often happens when people speak too long. Stop when the Holy Spirit stops.

12. Use a recording device when possible. This will give the recipient the ability to write the prophecy down and review it. This avoids allowing the recipient to report that the minister said something he or she did not say, and it makes it possible for the prophecy to be judged by the leadership.

13. Speak in the first person. This may take time and practice to get accustomed to, but you are the voice of the Lord on the earth. This will result in a deeper flow prophetically.

Protocol for Corporate Prophecy in the Local Church

Corporate prophecy is important to build strong local assemblies. God edifies, exhorts, and comforts local churches through corporate prophecy. Paul wrote to the assembly at Corinth to give them proper instruction concerning prophecy:

He who speaks in an unknown tongue edifies himself, but he who prophesies edifies the church. I desire that you all speak in tongues, but even more that you prophesy. For greater is he who prophesies than he who speaks in tongues, unless he interprets, so that the church may receive edification.

—1 Corinthians 14:4–5

Paul was writing because as an apostle, he had a concern for the well-being of the local church. He desired to see the church built up and edified in every way, and that would include through prophecy.

Although today there seems to be much emphasis on personal prophecy, it is important for local churches to allow prophets to speak to the entire congregation as well. This is one of the ways God desires to bless and build up the local body of Christ. Churches that allow the voice of the Lord to be heard will be blessed.

It is important to give proper instruction to the local body of believers so that prophets will be able to flow in prophecy in an orderly manner. Otherwise, confusion will result.

Perhaps the biggest misconception people have about the prophetic ministry is that prophecy should be ministered in a judgmental or condemning tone of voice, as a rebuke. While some prophecies may in fact speak of judgment, this tone should be reserved for the mature prophets who function in the office of the prophet and for those who are recognized elders in the assembly. There are times when God wants to bring a word of correction to an assembly, but the majority of prophecies given to the corporate body should be given for edification, exhortation, and comfort.

Decently and in order

In the apostle Paul's first letter to the church in the city of Corinth, he gave them advice about how corporate prophecy should be delivered:

Let two or three prophets speak, and let the others judge. If anything is revealed to another that sits by, let the first keep silent. For you may all prophesy one by one, that all may learn and all may be encouraged. The spirits of the prophets are subject to the prophets. For God is not the author of confusion, but of peace, as in all churches of the saints....

If anyone thinks himself to be a prophet or spiritual, let him acknowledge that what I am writing you is a command of the Lord....

Therefore, brothers, eagerly desire to prophesy, and do not forbid speaking in tongues. Let all things be done decently and in order.

—1 Corinthians 14:29–33, 37, 39–40

Paul's basic assumption was that corporate prophecy would happen on a regular basis. Therefore it needed to be regulated so that it would contribute to edification rather than to confusion.

The early church did not have microphones or sound systems, and it appears that at times too many prophets, caught up in the spirit of prophecy, were interrupting each other in an effort to be heard. In our day and age, with the large size of many of our churches as well as the concern for maturity in those who utter prophetic words in front of the entire assembly, it is necessary to add some more advice.

For example, someone who wants to prophesy might be required to come to one of the leaders to request a microphone. What other considerations should be addressed?

Music, worship, and prophecy

As we gather together in worship, we should expect to hear the word of the Lord. Prophecy can be spoken—or it can be sung:

> What is it then? I will pray with the spirit, and I will pray with the understanding. I will sing with the spirit, and I will sing with the understanding.
>
> —1 Corinthians 14:15

As I mentioned earlier in the book, the primary Hebrew word for *prophecy* is *naba*, meaning "to prophesy, to speak or sing by inspiration, to boil up, to gush forth, and to praise God while under divine influence."

Worship can cause the spirit of prophecy to be released (Rev. 19:10). As worship arises, you will see new songs and prophetic words begin to "gush forth" as the spirit of prophecy becomes strong in the assembly.

Besides being important to initiate a strong prophetic flow, music is very important to maintain it. Musicians help set the tone and atmosphere for worship. In addition, musicians can prophesy with their instruments. All of the musicians in the tabernacle of David were prophetic:

> Then David and the officers of the army also set apart for the service *some* of the sons of Asaph, and of Heman, and of Jeduthun, those who prophesied with lyres, harps, and cymbals. The number of those who did the work according to their service was:
>
> From the sons of Asaph: Zakkur, Joseph, Nethaniah, and Asarelah, the sons of Asaph under the guidance of Asaph, who prophesied according to the decree of the king.
>
> For Jeduthun, the sons of Jeduthun: Gedaliah, Zeri, Jeshaiah, Hashabiah, and Mattithiah, six, under the guidance of their father Jeduthun, who prophesied with the lyre in giving thanks and praise to the Lord.

For Heman, the sons of Heman: Bukkiah, Mattaniah, Uzziel, Shubael and Jerimoth, Hananiah, Hanani, Eliathah, Giddalti, and Romamti-Ezer, Joshbekashah, Mallothi, Hothir, Mahazioth. All these were the sons of Heman, the king's seer, according to the words of God, to exalt him, for God gave fourteen sons and three daughters to Heman.

—1 Chronicles 25:1–5

Have a submissive and teachable spirit

As they minister spiritual gifts, it is extremely important for all of the saints in the local assembly to truly maintain a submissive and teachable spirit toward their pastor and their local leadership. The pastors and other leaders have been given the responsibility to be shepherds for both the people in the body and for those who are ministering in their gifts.

Input and correction given by those in authority should be eagerly received by saints, who should desire to manifest their ministry in a way that will complement the philosophy of the local church. No prophetic team member should ever assume that he or she does not need to receive direction or correction from the pastor. (See Proverbs 12:15.)

We are all humans who are fallible and subject to error, so at some point in time while ministering, every one of us will make mistakes. Sometimes we will be aware that we have erred, but not always. Therefore it is important to decide beforehand to be open and willing to be corrected by those over us. It is equally important for those who have been set over the congregation to exercise their authority not to shrink back from issuing rebukes if necessary.

When you make a mistake in the content or delivery of a public prophetic word, it is at these times in particular that your pastor can save your life. Remember that you are a member of a prophetic team, not a lone ranger, and that each one of us is only going to receive a partial revelation. At the same time, your pastor is responsible for the overall vision and the many functions of the local church.

If someone has a gift of prophecy, or even holds the office of the prophet in the local church, that never means that the person can supersede his or her local pastor.

Do not go too long

A common complaint among pastors is that many people go too long when they prophesy or minister spiritual gifts in the church. Prophets deliver elaborate words—as long as whole sermons at times.

While it is true that prophesying is like preaching, in the sense that both have truth to present, it is equally true that a complicated or too-lengthy presentation can be dull or can deaden the effect of that truth.

Most congregational prophecies can be given in one minute or less—two minutes at the most. Anything longer will become extremely wearisome for others, and it will be problematic for the pastor, who is responsible for the order, schedule, and flow of the service. Those who prophesy should endeavor to present any revelation as clearly and concisely as possible.

Along the same line, a person should not feel that he or she should prophesy at every single service, since this may limit others from ministering their gifts and may even give the impression that this particular individual is trying to monopolize the prophetic or spiritual ministry of the church. Neither long-windedness nor frequency of prophesying should indicate higher giftedness in or honor for the speaker.

Flow with the order of the service

It should be obvious that prophecy is not appropriate during any part of the service when attention needs to be focused on something, in particular during the preaching, the announcements, or the altar call, when a prophetic word would be seen as an interruption. Normally the time to flow in the gifts of the Spirit is during the worship part of the service. During the brief lull between choruses, prophets can be ready to speak. The leaders should expect and encourage manifestations of the Spirit through prophecy at this time.

When saints minister during the right time of the service, their ministry should complement the flow of the service and not contradict and change the order of the service.

For example, if the congregation is involved in exuberant and demonstrative high praises of God, it would be inappropriate to share a word about being quiet and silent before the Lord.

We believe that while God might share a key word with an individual saint that would change the order of the service, that responsibility would normally be given to the pastor and those appointed in leadership and therefore should be directed through them.

If a pastor is readily accessible during the worship service, you may share your revelation privately and allow that pastor to determine if the timing is right to share it. If not, do not be offended! You will have given what you feel God has shared with you, and it now will be in the hands of those God has appointed over the service.

A PROPHECY TO THE CHURCH

The following examples of corporate prophecies released over our local assembly are edifying, exhortative, and comforting:

> The Spirit of God would have me to say that the signs and wonders recorded in the Bible are real. They happened. They are not fairy tales. The power of God is real. The miracles of God are real. The anointing of God is real.
>
> Behold, as it has been prophesied in times past, changes are

coming. The spiritual climate is changing. Prophecies are going forth and changing the atmosphere. The Word of God that is going forth prophetically in this hour is changing the seasons. You will see a new move of the Spirit of God in the land. You will see God working with His mighty hand. You will see healings and miracles take place. You will see people coming, saying, "Oh, this is new."

But I want you to know, My people, that in this day and hour, you must rise up in Holy Ghost power. You must not draw back. You must not be afraid to go forth. Know this, My people, that the time is ripe and the season is now for the miracles of God to come forth.

Out of your belly the rivers of living waters will flow. Yes, they will flow, and they will flow, and they will flow. And then people will begin to know the power of God, and they will begin to know the miracles of God.

Yes, I prophesy signs and wonders into the church. I prophesy the miracles of God into the church and into our cities. Yes, I proclaim that people will see the glory of God. They will believe, and many will come from the north, and from the south, and from the east, and from the west. They will come, and they will enter into a new phase of ministry and praise and glorifying the name of God. Yes, they will come because you will rise up, just as Moses did with his rod. You will speak forth into the earth. You will call down the fire of God. You will call forth the miracles of God with the authority I have given you.

Yes, the name of Jesus and the power of the Holy Ghost is in you, and you can use the rod and the authority to begin to command the signs and the wonders to come, even as Moses did when he went into Egypt. He was afraid, but I told him, "I will be with you." I gave him signs and wonders.

Yes, God is going to even give the church signs and wonders. As you receive the signs and wonders in your own lives, you will believe just as Moses did. You will go into Egypt. And you will use the rod and the authority I have given you to proclaim the miracles of God, bring My people out of bondage, and see them set free from the pharaoh, from the taskmaster, from slavery, from cruelty, and from bondage.

Yes, many will come out of churches where they are bound and pharaohs have ruled them. Pharaohs have controlled them. Pharaohs have made slaves of many of My people. Yes, they will come out, but they won't come out until the miracles and the signs and wonders come. Yes, the miracles and the signs and the wonders will open the way for them to come out. They will come out with a mighty hand. They will come out with rejoicing. They will come out of Egypt and out of bondage. They will come through the Red Sea. Yes, they will receive the glory and the power, and the cloud and the fire.

They will go on to Canaan land, and they will go in. They will challenge the giants, they will pull down the strongholds, and they will possess their possessions, says the Spirit of God.

———————

There is nothing—no man, no devil—that can keep My people bound. For whom the Son sets free is free indeed!

As I said in My Word, I have given you the authority and the liberty in the Spirit to be free and to be not again entangled with the yoke of bondage. But to be free that you might go into the land, challenge the giants, pull down the strongholds, receive your inheritance, walk in the blessings, and get into the land flowing with milk and honey, yes, a land of prosperity and a land that is blessed and fruitful. Yes, it's coming, says the Spirit of God, but the signs and the wonders must come. Yes, the prophetic flow must be strong.

As I put My prophetic anointing upon Moses and upon the elders in that day, I am putting My prophetic anointing upon the leadership of My church. There will be strong prophets of God that will come up, and there will be men who will flow strongly in the prophetic. Yes, and they will train My people how to be prophets and how to flow in the prophetic. They will release the people of God to flow in the supernatural realm. They will prophesy in their homes, and they will prophesy on their jobs, and they will prophesy in the streets, and they will prophesy in the church.

The prophetic word that goes forth out of their mouths will be like a fire. It will be like a hammer that breaks the rocks in pieces. Yes, the principalities and powers, they will bow. And they will know that you are the people of God with a prophetic flow. They will come down from the high places in the land. Yes, they will see. They will see God's hand. Yes, they will tremble, and they will shake at the power of God.

When you go forth and you speak the word of the Lord, they will obey. And they will come down because the Word is like a sword. So look up, My people, and know that I am in your midst. I am there to deliver you and set you free and raise you up and thrust you into a new realm.

You will know that it is the hand of God. It is the hand of God. It is the hand of God upon the people of God in this hour to bring the people out of darkness into the marvelous light, that they might shout and dance and leap for joy, that they will know pain and sorrow no more. They will be a people prepared by the Lord to do the works of God. Then I will call them home in glory to be My bride, says the Spirit of the living God.

Protocol for Women in Prophetic Ministry

Philip the evangelist…had four virgin daughters who prophesied.
—Acts 21:8–9

I am often asked about the role of women in prophetic ministry. Can a woman function in the role of a prophet? The answer is yes, women can function in the office of a prophet as well as a prophetic believer. It is the Lord's desire that we all hear from Him and speak His word to bring edification to all who hear. Women have special prophetic expressions that are specific and essential to the body of Christ. Read what Bible scholar and theologian Stanley Horton has to say on this topic:

> Some have misinterpreted 1 Corinthians 14:34…to mean that women should not minister in the vocal gifts. However, Paul had already said in verse 31, "you can all prophesy in turn so that everyone may be instructed and encouraged." In the context…Paul "suggests that another type of interruption should be avoided. Women (who were usually uneducated in that day) were asking questions in an improper manner and thus contributing to the confusion. They were told to hold their questions and ask their husbands at home. This should be applied to both men and women in matters that custom considers unbecoming. But Paul is in no sense trying to hinder women from prophesying, speaking in tongues, singing, or otherwise contributing to the worship."[1]

Here are some examples from my own ministry experience and from the Bible of women prophets and the benefits they bring to the prophetic ministry.

Prophetic wives

There are many pastors who have prophetic wives. Some pastors want their wives to be first ladies who simply look good and smile. Some pastors do not receive the gift that God has placed in their wives and do not allow them or release them to minister. This is shameful and needs to stop. Don't allow religion and tradition to keep women locked up in a box. God did not give women the Holy Ghost to sit down, be quiet, and be stopped and ignored. Pastors like this will end up in trouble because they reject the gift that God has placed in their lives to help.

The Jael anointing

This is a prophetic word God gave me for women using the example of Jael driving a nail through the head of Sisera.

> Then Jael the wife of Heber took a tent peg and a hammer in her hand and went quietly to him, for he was fast asleep and tired. She drove the tent peg into his temple, and it went down into the ground, so he died.
>
> —Judges 4:21

Hit the nail on the head means "to get to the precise point; to do or say something exactly right; to be accurate; to hit the mark; to detect and expose (a lie, scandal, etc.)." Prophetic women, get ready to "hit the nail on the head." Your prophetic utterances will "hit the mark."

The daughters of Zelophehad

Just as we speak about the sons of God inheriting spiritual gifts, the daughters of God also have an inheritance. His daughters have an inheritance in the prophetic ministry to actively and boldly prophesy. Apostolic fathers release and bless daughters. See this revealed here in the story of Zelophehad and his daughters:

> Then came near the daughters of Zelophehad, the son of Hepher, the son of Gilead, the son of Makir, the son of Manasseh, of the families of Manasseh the son of Joseph, and these are the names of his daughters: Mahlah, Noah, Hoglah, Milkah, and Tirzah. They stood before Moses, and before Eleazar the priest, and before the leaders and all the assembly by the door of the tent of meeting, saying, "Our father died in the wilderness, and he was not in the company of them that gathered against the LORD, in the company of Korah, but died in his own sin and had no sons. Why should the name of our father diminish from among his family, because he has no son? Give to us a possession among the brothers of our father."
>
> Moses brought their case before the LORD. The LORD spoke to Moses, saying: The daughters of Zelophehad speak right. You will certainly give them an inheritance among their father's brothers, and you will cause the inheritance of their father to pass on to them.
>
> —Numbers 27:1–7

Philip's daughters

Philip had four daughters who prophesied (Acts 21:9). The prophet Joel said the daughters would prophesy (Joel 2:28). There were a number of women in the Upper Room (Acts 1:14). The release of the Holy Spirit on the Day of Pentecost opened the door for women to be involved in the prophetic ministry in an unprecedented way. Women are now released to prophesy in numbers that are greater than ever before.

"In the last days it shall be," says God, "that I will pour out My Spirit on all flesh; your sons and your daughters shall prophesy, your young men shall see visions, and your old men shall dream dreams."

—ACTS 2:17

Miriam

Miriam, the sister of Moses, was a prophet. She led the women in dancing to celebrate God's victory over Pharaoh. She is also recognized as being sent along with Moses and Aaron to bring Israel out of Egypt. She therefore played a prominent role in Israel's deliverance from bondage.

Miriam the prophetess, the sister of Aaron, took a timbrel in her hand, and all the women went out after her with timbrels and with dancing.

—EXODUS 15:20

For I have brought you up from the land of Egypt, and from the house of slaves I have redeemed you; and I sent before you Moses, Aaron, and Miriam.

—MICAH 6:4

Huldah

Huldah was a prophet who was recognized by King Josiah. When the king discovered the Book of the Law, he rent his clothes and sent men to Huldah to inquire of the Lord. Huldah was the keeper of the king's wardrobe and spoke the word of the Lord to the king about the coming judgment upon Israel. She stated that it would not happen in his day because he had humbled himself.

"Go and seek the LORD on my behalf and on the behalf of the remnant in Israel and Judah concerning what is written in the book that was found, for the wrath of the LORD that is poured out on us is great because our fathers have not kept the word of the LORD, to do everything that is written in this book."

So Hilkiah and those with the king went to Huldah the prophetess, the wife of Shallum the son of Tokhath, son of Hasrah, who kept the wardrobe. She lived in Jerusalem in the Second Quarter, and they spoke to her about this.

And she said to them, "So says the LORD God of Israel: Speak to the man who sent you all to Me."

—2 CHRONICLES 34:21–23

Deborah

Deborah was a prophetess, a judge, and a mother in Israel. She was a national prophet and judge who was recognized throughout Israel. Israel came to her to settle disputes. Prophets can help settle disputes. Deborah's role as a mother represented her love and compassion for Israel. Mothers can be prophets.

Now Deborah, the wife of Lappidoth, was a prophetess. She judged Israel at that time.

—JUDGES 4:4

Village life ceased. It ceased until I, Deborah, arose; I arose like a mother in Israel.

—JUDGES 5:7

Isaiah's wife

The major prophet Isaiah considered his wife to be a prophetess. This shows that both a husband and wife can be prophets. This will make a strong prophetic team.

So I went in to the prophetess, and she conceived and bore a son. Then the LORD said to me, Call his name Maher-Shalal-Hash-Baz.

—ISAIAH 8:3

Anna

Anna was a praying and fasting prophet. She spoke to all those who were looking for redemption and the coming Messiah. By her prayer and fasting she helped prepare the way for the Lord to come. She prayed and fasted in the temple and did not depart from the house of God. Anna is a picture of the intercessory prophet.

And there was Anna a prophetess, a daughter of Phanuel, of the tribe of Asher. She was of a great age and had lived with her husband seven years from her virginity. And she was a widow of about eighty-four years of age who did not depart from the temple, but served God with fasting and prayer night and day. Coming at that moment she gave thanks to the Lord and spoke of Him to all those who looked for the redemption of Jerusalem.

—LUKE 2:36–38

There is an order to everything that God does. He is not haphazard, confused, or lost, and His prophetic people shouldn't be either. The Bible says we should excel in prophecy, meaning our ministering in this area should be done with excellence. To help us excel, the next several chapters are going to break down specific functions of the prophet's ministry—those that bring the biggest rewards to the kingdom and to the world.

CHAPTER 8

Prophets Protect

*And by a prophet the LORD brought Israel up from
Egypt, and by a prophet he was preserved.*
—HOSEA 12:13

THE CHURCH HAS often assumed that pastors are the spiritual guardians of the church while neglecting the ministry of prophets. However, the church was never intended to function with only pastors serving as protectors of the people. Prophets also have been set in the church to help fulfill this important role (1 Cor. 12:28). Churches that ignore this aspect of the prophetic ministry will not be able to withstand the attacks of hell in the last days.

Hosea 12:13 reveals to us that one of the major functions of the prophet's ministry is preservation. Israel was delivered from Egypt through the ministry of the prophet Moses, and then Israel was preserved through the intercession of Moses (Num. 14:11–20).

The word *preserve* means "to keep from harm, damage, danger, or evil." It also means "to protect or to save." In Hebrew, the root word is *shamar*. *Shamar* means "to hedge about (as with thorns), to guard, to protect, to watch, and to keep."[1] The word *shamar* is first used in Scripture in Genesis 2:15, where Adam is told to keep (*shamar*) the garden. It is also mentioned in Genesis 4:9, where Cain asks God if he is his brother's keeper (*shamar*).

THE SHAMAR PROPHET

This word *shamar* emphasizes the protective element of the prophet's mantle. The preserving and guarding aspect of the prophet's ministry is needed in every local church. Many well-meaning pastors have suffered unnecessarily due to the lack of understanding this aspect of the ministry of the prophet. The *shamar* aspect of the prophet's ministry is one of the most important ones, and it will benefit the church greatly.

The local church is kept safe through prophetic intercession, prophetic discernment, prophetic praise, prophetic preaching, prophetic teaching, and prophetic worship. This is how the church is best defended. Without a revelation of the *shamar* aspect of the prophetic ministry, a local church will suffer from many attacks that can be averted.

Each church should identify, develop, and train the *shamar* prophets who have been set in their assembly by God. A revelation of the importance of the ministry of *shamar* prophets is vital to the success and long-term health of every church. Because the role of *shamar* prophets is so important, I will devote most of this chapter and the next one to an explanation of how they can help pastors of churches protect and defend their flocks.

Watchman

Shamar means "to guard, to keep, to be a watchman." It can refer to guarding a flock, the heart, the mind, a nation, or a city from outside attack or ungodly influences. It is used in reference to keeping (guarding) the gates or entries to cities. Each local church needs a prophetic guard. This is not one prophet but a company of prophets who help guard the church from the invasion of the enemy. Churches that develop the prophetic ministry will have the advantage of being protected through prophetic intercession and the shamar aspect of the prophetic ministry.

Guard means a number of things. It can mean "to protect, to watch over, to stand guard over, to police, to secure, to defend, to shield, to shelter, to screen, to cover, to cloak, to preserve, to save, to conserve, to supervise, to keep under surveillance or control, to keep under guard, to govern, to restrain, to suppress, to keep watch, to be alert, or to take care." Synonyms for *guard* include protector, defender, guardian, custodian, watchman, sentinel, sentry, patrol, and garrison. These words help us visualize and define the shamar aspect of the prophetic ministry.

The shamar components of the prophetic mantle pertain to the prophet's role as a guardian tending to the flock over which he or she has care. It applies to the guardian function of the office, the aspect of prophetic ministry that makes a person like a sentinel or a protector. To shamar a people is to work prophetically, to encircle the people or the church with a divine wall or hedge of protection—or to reseal the gap in the hedge through which the devil has broken in with satanic assaults, attacks, and warfare.

Look at these examples from the Bible that use the word *shamar*:

> Except the LORD build the house, those who build labor in vain; except the LORD guards the city, the watchman stays awake in vain.
> —PSALM 127:1

> My soul waits for the Lord, more than watchmen for the morning, more than watchmen for the morning.
> —PSALM 130:6

I have set watchmen on your walls, O Jerusalem, who shall never hold their peace day nor night. You who remind the LORD, do not keep silent.

—ISAIAH 62:6

The watchmen found me, as they went about the city. "Have you seen him whom my soul loves?"

—SONG OF SONGS 3:3

We can see that watchmen duties in the church are accomplished through the prayer, intercessions, and petitions of the prophet on behalf of the local body of believers. Such a guard would consist of the prayer team, the special intercessors, dedicated psalmists, seers, and subordinate prophets. It is the word *shamar* that emphasizes the status of prophets as spiritual guards, warriors, supernatural enforcers, and keepers of the churches of God. Without the help of the watchmen, pastors cannot take care of their flocks. As a result, the people of God become open prey to the enemy forces:

My people have been lost sheep. Their shepherds have caused them to go astray; they have turned them away on the mountains. They have gone from mountain to hill and have forgotten their resting place. All who found them have devoured them, and their adversaries said, "We are not guilty."

—JEREMIAH 50:6–7

Building a hedge of protection

Additionally the word *shamar* identifies a prophet who encircles (or surrounds) to retain and attend to, as one does a garden. The prophet's spiritual authority acts as a fence or garrison around an assigned congregation to shield it from harm, attack, or demonic trespass. Protection from trespassers, as meant here, includes protection from the spoilage, destruction, invasion, and threats that result from spiritual and human trespassers in the church.

Behold, He who guards [*shamar*] Israel shall neither slumber nor sleep. The LORD is your guardian [*shamar*]; the LORD is your shade at your right hand. The sun shall not harm you during the day, nor the moon during the night. The LORD shall protect [*shamar*] you from all evil; He shall preserve [*shamar*] your soul. The LORD shall preserve [*shamar*] your going out and your coming in from now and for evermore.

—PSALM 121:4–8

We can see from these verses that God shamars His people. God loves His people and protects them. The shamar aspect of the prophet's ministry is a part of the nature of God. God never slumbers or sleeps. He is always alert. God shamars us from evil. God shamars our souls (our minds, wills, and emotions).

God shamars our going out and coming in (our travels). It is the nature of God to protect. Protection from God is a part of our covenant with Him, and shamar prophets are therefore a practical part of the working out of our covenant relationship with God.

Role and position

There are times when heretical types or wayward renegades join a church to sow seeds of destruction in it. The watchful eye of the resident prophet can spot these people and bring spiritual discomfort on them so they are ill at ease among the flock and quickly leave.

Some leaders look at prophets as translocal ministries only; in their view only the pastor's role is stationary. Of course, it is always a blessing to bring prophets in from the outside to minister to a congregation. But this does not replace prophets who are stationed in the house, shamar prophets who are a part of the local church, just as a pastor is.

Prophets need an understanding of their role and position in the local church. Having a revelation of the shamar aspect of their prophet's mantle will help them to fulfill their ministries more fully.

The shamar aspect of the prophet's ministry can also be seen in the life of Samuel:

> So the Philistines were subdued, and they did not again come into the territory of Israel. And *the hand of the LORD was against the Philistines all the days of Samuel.*
>
> —1 SAMUEL 7:13, EMPHASIS ADDED

The Philistines were subdued and could not enter the coasts of Israel as long as Samuel was alive. This gives us a good picture of the power of a prophet's presence.

The enemy hates the prophet because the prophet's presence thwarts his advances. This is why he has done everything in his power to keep prophets from being recognized and operational in the church, and his efforts are often visible if we look for self-limiting unbelief, fear, or tradition.

ENEMIES OF THE CHURCH

We can rejoice that we live in a day when we are currently seeing the restoration of the prophetic ministry and a corresponding release of revelation and understanding concerning this ministry.

Shamar prophets help guard the church against:

- Accusation
- Apathy
- Backbiting

- Backsliding
- Betrayal
- Carnality
- Compromise
- Confusion
- Control
- Covetousness
- Death
- Deception
- Destruction
- Disorder
- Division
- Doctrines of devils
- False prophets, apostles, and teachers
- False teaching
- Financial attacks
- Gossip
- Greed
- Idolatry
- Immorality
- Jealousy
- Jezebel
- Legalism
- Lukewarmness
- Pride
- Rebellion
- Sickness
- Slander
- Slothfulness
- Strife
- Treachery
- Witchcraft

In addition to identifying these potential enemies, shamar prophets ought to seek God so that they can develop strategies to resist, expel, and overcome them in the power of the Holy Ghost. These strategies can include prayer, fasting, worshipping, teaching, preaching, correcting, and outright expelling. In other words, prophets should do more than cry, "Thus saith the Lord." That will not be adequate. As a defense, it is insufficient. Shamar prophets are a part of the covenant community and have a vested interest in the health of the flock. They are not outsiders looking in. They must love the church. They must experience the joy of victory and the grief of the enemies' attacks on the saints they love. Jeremiah wept for Israel because he was a part of Israel and suffered with Israel. Prophets must understand that God has "set" them in the church, which means that they have been appointed, established, or positioned in this role.

Shamar prophets help protect the preaching, teaching, evangelism, worship, and intercession of the local church. They help identify and confront religious spirits, occult spirits, and spirits of sin, pride, rebellion, and witchcraft.

Shamar prophets are the spiritual immune system of a local church. They help fight off spiritual disease that is Satan's effort to undermine the health of the church. Shamar prophets are needed for the overall health of the church.

Shamar prophets help to protect the vision of the church. They also help to confirm the vision of the church. They help ward off Satan's attack on the vision of the church. They must share a divine jealousy for the health of the church and the purposes of God for the church. (See 2 Corinthians 11.)

Common holes in church defense

Sometimes it is not enough to talk only about what "should be." Often we only become convinced of a need when we look at the compelling needs around us. In a local assembly problems such as the following reveal the gaping holes in the defenses of the church. Without an operational shamar anointing, these problems are all too common:

- Accidents
- Apathy
- Attacks on the pastor and the family
- Backsliding
- Broken relationships
- Church splits
- Confusion
- Conspiracies
- Control and domination
- Divorces and separations
- Failures in leadership

- False brethren
- False prophets, false teachers, and false apostles
- False teaching, error, or heresy
- Family problems
- Financial setbacks
- Hindrances, blockages, or obstructions
- Immorality
- Infighting and division
- Loss of anointing
- Manipulation
- Occultists
- People leaving the church
- Premature deaths
- Satanists
- Stagnation
- Unexplainable sicknesses and illnesses
- Warlocks
- Witches
- Wolves entering the flock

There are certain spirits that attack congregations. These spirits seem to specialize in undermining the body of Christ in every locality. Over time the church has given them biblical names to better identify them and resist them. Here are five demonic powers prophets must protect the church from.

1. Idolatry and Witchcraft

> But I have a few things against you: You permit that woman Jezebel, who calls herself a prophetess, to teach and seduce My servants to commit sexual immorality and eat food sacrificed to idols.
> —Revelation 2:20

The prophet Elijah warred against Jezebel. God raised up Elijah during the time Jezebel was destroying the nation through idolatry and witchcraft. The Jezebel spirit will always seek to destroy and hinder the development of the prophetic ministry in a church. Jezebel will attempt to kill true prophets. The Jezebel spirit operates through members of a congregation. The Jezebel spirit is responsible for false prophecies. This spirit operates through divination, control, manipulation, and domination. Jezebel is also responsible for false teaching and sexual impurity.

Jezebel spirits have destroyed many congregations. Many leaders have fallen victim to Jezebel because Jezebel loves to be in a position of leadership. The spirit will gain influence by inciting slander and gossip to harm the ordained leaders of the church. Jezebel hates ordained leadership and will do everything possible to destroy it or control it. (Athaliah, the daughter of Jezebel, attempted to kill the royal seed [2 Kings 11:1].)

Jim Goll has stated that "a Jezebel spirit stirs up fear, flight, and discouragement, often prompting a spiritual leader to flee his or her appointed place just as Elijah did. Every year hundreds of spiritual marketplace and governmental leaders resign because of debilitating discouragement, confusion, depression, loss of vision, despair, disorientation, withdrawal, a sense of worthlessness, defeat, burnout, physical illness, financial insufficiency, character assassination, moral failure, and an almost infinite variety of other factors. In many cases, this maligning control spirit is responsible." [2]

The Jezebel spirit hates prophets because they are her greatest threat. Jezebel will attempt to cut off intercession. Jezebel will attack the prayer ministry of a church. In the biblical event Jezebel was able to gain power and influence over Israel through her marriage to King Ahab. Marriage is a covenant, and this marriage covenant gave Jezebel the legal right to enter Israel, bringing with her all of her idolatry, witchcraft, and whoredom.

This should warn us that leaders must be very careful whom they enter into covenant with. One wrong covenant can open the door for a Jezebel.

Prophets walk in discernment and can detect Jezebel. Even before a Jezebel spirit is evident to them, prophets should pray for the leaders of the church. They must provide a prayer covering to prevent Jezebel from gaining influence.

Just as Ahab's wife Jezebel was notorious for being very manipulative, so is the Jezebel spirit. Prophets can discern and expose subtle manipulation through teaching, false prophecy, and flattery. The influence of the Jezebel spirit will always be seen in false teaching and efforts to control decisions. It may also involve witchcraft, seduction, and sexual sin. Obviously, a church cannot remain healthy with the influence of a seducing Jezebel spirit. This spirit seduces believers, leading them astray, misleading them.

The Jezebel spirit causes churches to be guided more by the flesh than by the Spirit. The spirit of Jezebel draws the whole church away from purity and interferes with true worship. When a Jezebel spirit is present, spirits of perversion, adultery, immorality, and fornication will run rampant in a body of people. Slander and gossip are the marks of this spirit.

Churches under the influence of a Jezebel spirit will go astray in their doctrine. Dangerous false teaching and heresy will affect the lifestyles of the saints, and even once-strong assemblies will find themselves in a broken-down, weakened condition. The Jezebel spirit is like a black widow spider, which is deadly and will even eat its mate. (The name *Jezebel* means "unhusbanded.")

John Paul Jackson states, "No church is too great, too healthy, or too pure to be exempted from an attack by a Jezebel spirit. In fact, the greater the church, the greater the assurance that those with a Jezebel spirit will seek to gain influence and power—unless the pastor, the leadership team, the intercessors, and prophetically gifted individuals exercise their responsibility and withstand this spiritual attack."[3]

2. Betrayal and Treachery

> Absalom would go early and stand beside the way into the gate....So Absalom stole the hearts of the men of Israel....Now the conspiracy was strong, for the number of people with Absalom was continually growing.
> —2 Samuel 15:2, 6, 12

Absalom rebelled against his father, David, and tried to seize the kingdom. In other words, he was disloyal to his father, and he acted out of pride, vanity, rebellion, and bitterness.

Therefore an Absalom spirit represents betrayal and treachery. Many leaders have suffered betrayal and treachery from other leaders who have Absalom spirits, resulting in splits and defections. Prophets need to be on guard against this spirit that seeks to divide and separate churches.

Absalom turned the hearts of the people away from David, who was the rightful king. Absalom tried to usurp his authority by gaining followers. Even Ahithophel, David's wisest counselor, joined the rebellion. In a similar way, many leaders have suffered betrayal from people with Absalom spirits.

The Absalom spirit can be stopped through prophetic intercession. It is interesting to note that Absalom stood by "the way of the gate" to seduce the people into becoming his followers. This proves the importance of having prophetic intercession at the gates of the church. (We will talk more about this in the next chapter.)

David almost lost his throne to Absalom. He had to flee Jerusalem for his life. He had been unaware of what Absalom was doing beforehand. Absalom planned a conspiracy against his father, David. He planned and acted together secretly with others who were not happy with the way things were going under David's leadership. The conspiracy continued to gain strength as the number of people increased who went to Absalom's side. An Absalom spirit will attempt to get as many people on its side—against leadership—as possible. Subtle and cunning, an Absalom spirit will carry out its rebellion secretly. Ambitious, subtle, and crafty, this spirit will go after the father figure or leader. Sometimes the Absalom spirit will attack the spiritual sons and daughters of a leader. The Absalom spirit is like a serpent, sliding in between people to attack them.

Many leaders have fallen victim to ungodly conspiracies perpetrated by other leaders in the church. These hidden plots came as a surprise. Too often, even when leaders try to recover, it is too late. Hidden conspiracies have not been exposed soon enough.

The shamar anointing is designed to see hidden conspiracies and expose them before it is too late.

3. Rebellion

> Now Korah the son of Izhar, the son of Kohath, the son of Levi, and Dathan and Abiram the sons of Eliab, and On the son of Peleth, sons of Reuben, took men, and they rose up before Moses and men of the children of Israel, two hundred and fifty chiefs of the assembly, famous in the assembly, well-known men. They assembled against Moses and against Aaron.
>
> —Numbers 16:1–3

Korah also represents rebellion, although he was more open and defiant than Absalom. Korah openly challenged the leadership of Moses and Aaron. Korah accused Moses of exalting himself above the other leaders. The insinuation was that he was holding the other leaders down. Whereas the Jezebel spirit seems to work primarily through women, the Korah spirit seems to work primarily through men.

As we know, rebellion is as the sin of witchcraft (1 Sam. 15:23). Witchcraft operates through all three of these evil spirits: Jezebel, Absalom, and Korah. If unchecked, witchcraft can blind and seduce many believers in a congregation.

The Korah spirit will cause a leader to exalt himself in the midst of the congregation, disregarding God's appointed leadership. The Korah spirit is bold and brazen, not afraid to speak openly against leadership. This spirit accuses leaders of being self-appointed instead of God appointed.

The devil hates God's ordained leaders, and he will attempt to slander, pull down, accuse, and overthrow those who have been ordained to be leaders. The Korah spirit is one of those spirits that attempt to exalt a person to challenge true leadership. The Korah spirit hates apostolic and prophetic leadership.

Prophets must stand alongside the leadership of the church against the spirit of Korah, which will appear as a spirit of revolt, a refusal to submit to established authority.

4. Constriction of the Flow of the Spirit

> On one occasion, as we went to the place of prayer, a servant girl possessed with a spirit of divination [python] met us.
>
> —Acts 16:16

The word *python* is translated here as divination, and a python is a constrictor snake. Pythons kill their victims by squeezing the breath out of them, and the breath represents the spirit of a person. Python spirits attempt to choke the life out of churches. This can include choking the life out of the praise and worship and the prophetic ministry. Python spirits also attempt to squeeze the prayer life out of the church. (Remember, the damsel possessed with the spirit of python met the apostles as they were going to prayer.)

People with python spirits will attempt to stop or constrict the move of the Holy Spirit in the church. The evil spirit will try to curtail the new life that the Spirit of God brings. This spirit convinces leaders to draw back from the gifts of the Spirit and a move of the Holy Ghost. When any spirit attempts to stop the flow of the Holy Spirit or pervert it, we call it "witchcraft."

The noticeable characteristics of a church that is affected by a python spirit can include a lack of prophecy and other manifestations of the Holy Spirit, prayerlessness, tiredness and spiritual lethargy, lack of fervent praise and worship, and lack of development of ministries. False gifts and manifestations can occur instead of genuine manifestations of the Holy Spirit. Churches should experience a continual flow and anointing of the Holy Spirit. Something is seriously wrong when the spiritual life is getting choked out of the church.

Prophets are sensitive to the operations of the Holy Spirit, and they have the ability to sense when something is wrong. They not only sense something is wrong, but they can also identify the problem. Prophetic intercession can stop witchcraft and divination from entering and affecting the spiritual flow of a congregation.

5. Pride

> In that day the LORD with His fierce and great and strong sword shall punish Leviathan the fleeing serpent, even Leviathan the twisted serpent; and He shall slay the dragon that is in the sea.
>
> —Isaiah 27:1

Leviathan is the king over all the children of pride. The Leviathan spirit, represented by a crocodile or a large sea serpent, attacks leaders, causing them to become arrogant and puffed up. We are aware that God resists the proud but gives grace to the humble (1 Pet. 5:5) and that humility is a prerequisite for accessing the grace of God.

The most extensive reference to Leviathan is found in chapter 41 of the Book of Job. Accordingly, the characteristics of the Leviathan spirit include prayerlessness (Job 41:3), harsh words (v. 3), covenant breaking (v. 4), an inability to serve others (v. 4), no breath (or spirit, or air; v. 16), stubbornness (or being stiff-necked; v. 24), hardness of heart (v. 24), and, above all, pride (v. 34). Pride opens the door for destruction (Prov. 16:18).

Ministries can become proud through knowledge and success (1 Cor. 8:1), but this is the opposite of humility, which is the key to honor and success. A lack of humility will open the doors for spirits of pride, arrogance, haughtiness, and self-exaltation. These are dangerous spirits that must be identified and driven out and away from the assembly.

STRATEGIC TARGETS FOR PROPHETIC INTERCESSION

Prophetic intercession—divinely inspired prayers that target evil influences and take them out—is one of the primary functions of a shamar prophet.

Each area of a church should be covered by the prophet's intercession. This includes the following:

- The pastor (apostle, set man)
- The elders (presbytery, bishops)
- The prophets and prophetic teams, intercessors
- The praise and worship teams (minstrels and psalmists)
- The deacons
- The pastors (shepherds)
- The teachers (doctors, instructors)
- The evangelists and evangelistic teams
- The helps ministry
- The administrators (governments)
- The dance teams
- The youth ministry
- The children's ministry
- The business ministry
- The finances
- The missions (nations)
- The media outreach (television and radio)
- The new believers
- The new members
- Married couples
- Singles
- Men and women
- Widows

- Families

Prophetic intercession also includes prayer for the release of:

- Church growth
- Deliverance
- Evangelism
- Favor
- Gifts of the Holy Spirit
- Glory
- Healing
- Holiness
- Humility
- Love
- Miracles
- Peace
- Property
- Prophecy
- Prophetic worship
- Prosperity
- Protecting angels
- Revelation
- Salvation
- Signs and wonders
- Strength
- Unity
- Wisdom

We will continue this discussion of prophetic protection in the next chapter.

CHAPTER 9

PROPHETS WATCH

Go, set a watchman, let him declare what he seeth.
—ISAIAH 21:6, KJV

I N THE BIBLE watchmen were positioned at the outer defenses (the wall of a city or the hedge fence of a field) or in a raised outlook or tower that overlooked the territory that needed to be watched. A watchman is one who stands guard. Ancient cities had watchmen stationed on the walls. Their responsibility was to sound a warning if an enemy approached. (See 2 Kings 9:17; Ezekiel 33:2–3.) The Israelites also posted watchmen to serve as sentinels over their vineyards and fields, especially during harvest. Their responsibility was to guard the produce from animals and thieves. In a similar way, Israel's prophets saw themselves as watchmen, warning the nation of God's approaching judgment if the people did not repent.

Today, one way of identifying their position and role is to say that the watchmen guard the *gates*—of a local church and more. If you read Scripture with the word *gates* in mind, you begin to see this connection everywhere. For example, consider the following passages from the Old Testament:

> Your choicest valleys shall be full of chariots, and the horsemen shall set themselves in array at the *gate*.
> —ISAIAH 22:7, EMPHASIS ADDED

> For He has strengthened the bars of your *gates*; He has blessed your children within you. He makes peace in your borders, and fills you with the finest of the wheat.
> —PSALM 147:13–14, EMPHASIS ADDED

> …warfare was at the city *gates*…
> —JUDGES 5:8, EMPHASIS ADDED

Then Daniel requested of the king, and he set Shadrach, Meshach, and Abednego, over the affairs of the province of Babylon: but Daniel sat in the *gate* of the king.
—DANIEL 2:49, KJV, EMPHASIS ADDED

Gates are entry points, and they need to be strengthened in order to keep the enemy out and to keep the people and all that they possess safe. The prophet's ministry helps strengthen the gates so that the children will be blessed and peace will be within the church. With the benefit of the protection of the prophetic ministry, the church will be filled with the finest of the wheat (prosperity).

People who serve in the office of the prophet need to have an understanding of gates and entry points in their churches, their cities, their regions, and their nations. Having a revelation of gates and their importance will help prophets defend these entry points from invasion by the enemy. When prophets gain a clearer understanding of their role and position in the church, a revelation of the shamar aspect of the prophet's mantle, they will be better able to fulfill their ministries.

Praise is a gate.

Praise is a gate (Isa. 60:18). That is why the enemy often attempts to attack and infiltrate the praise and worship of a church. He attacks praise leaders, minstrels, and psalmists. Prophets must help protect this gate through inter-cession. (See Psalm 118:19–20.)

Prophets can speak with the enemies in the gate (Ps. 127:5). *Speak* is the Hebrew word *dabar*, which can mean "to command, to subdue, or to warn."[1] To be as effective as possible as watchmen at the gates of the church, it is impor-tant that prophets, those who sit in the gate, keep themselves from speaking evil against the leadership of the church. (See Psalm 69:12.)

Prophets in leadership

If the enemy is victorious in the gates, the church is in trouble. This is why prophets must be a part of the leadership of the local church. They have been set into the church "second" by God:

> God has put these in the church: first apostles, second prophets, third teachers, after that miracles, then gifts of healings, helps, governments, and various tongues.
>
> —1 Corinthians 12:28

Prophets should be a part of the music ministry, the youth ministry, the children's ministry, the presbytery, and the overall ministry of a church. Each ministry represents a specific gate, and each gate of a church needs prophetic intercession. Prophets will intercede and stop the enemy at the gates. They will go to war against demons in the gates where they have been stationed.

The warfare will always be at the gates because that is where the defenders clash with the invading enemies. The enemies "set themselves in array" at the gate. That is where demons launch their attacks. This is why we need prophets standing watch at the gates.

Not only are prophets assigned by God to the numerous gates of a local church, but there are also "gateway churches" (in other words, apostolic churches) that are the key to a region or territory. These gateway churches need highly qualified prophets to keep the enemy out. Strong prophetic intercession is a must if the gates are to be protected.

Preventing destruction

A church will lose its protection if the gates are destroyed. The destruction of a gate results in unwanted things entering in. Demons can enter a church and establish strongholds if the gates are open. A destroyed gate means that nothing can be closed. "In the city desolation is left, and the gate is stricken with destruction" (Isa. 24:12, NKJV).

The gate represents a place of authority, and the enemy wants to unseat that authority so that he can plunder the inhabitants and usurp the authority for himself. The inhabitants cannot effectively counter the enemy's advance unless their defenses are coordinated by someone with the proper authority to do so. The prophet has the spiritual authority to stand at the gate and challenge the enemy. When demons attack the gates and attempt to destroy them, they cannot get past the prophets who stand strong at the gates, alert and well fortified with the anointing of God.

Rebuke in the gates

The gate is a place where the enemy can be rebuked. *Rebuke* means "to force back." A rebuke is a sharp reprimand. A reprimand is a severe or formal rebuke by a person in authority.

Demons need to be rebuked. They need to be beaten back. Prophetic intercession rebukes the enemy, and it takes place in the gates, the very centers of traffic and business in every area of the kingdom of God. Spirits of witchcraft, lust, rebellion, deception, pride, Jezebel, religion, and carnality must be rebuked in the gates. This will prevent them from entering in and destroying the church.

Needless to say, demonic spirits do not yield quietly to rebuke. They will resist and struggle. They hate the gatekeepers, the prophetic watchmen who interfere with their evil plans:

> They hate him that rebuketh in the gate.
>
> —Amos 5:10, KJV

A word of prevention

Often a prophet will be able to warn a leader about an encroaching enemy, and the warning will prevent a disaster. Sometimes the best defense is simple prevention.

> But Elisha, the prophet that is in Israel, telleth the king of Israel the words that thou speakest in thy bedchamber.
>
> —2 Kings 6:12, KJV

Elisha was able to warn the king and prevent him from being ambushed. The prophet's ministry is preventive. It is better to prevent something from happening than having to react to it after it happens.

The vineyard of God

Besides being like a walled city with gates at intervals in the protective wall, the church is God's vineyard.

The church is a divine institution ordained by God and hated by the enemy. The church is the Israel of God, and He Himself has set up its defenses:

> Now will I sing to my wellbeloved a song of my beloved touching his vineyard. My wellbeloved hath a vineyard in a very fruitful hill: And he *fenced it*, and gathered out the stones thereof, and planted it with the choicest vine, and *built a tower* in the midst of it, and also made a winepress therein.
>
> —ISAIAH 5:1–2, KJV, EMPHASIS ADDED

Israel is God's vineyard, and so is the church. The result of the planting of the Lord should be fruitfulness. We have been ordained to bring forth fruit and for the fruit to remain (John 15:16). But the enemy wants to destroy the fruit of churches and ministries. Therefore the local church needs prophets to prevent the fruit from being destroyed.

It is unwise to plant a vineyard without a fence. A fence provides a protective barrier for the vineyard. A tower is a place for the watchman. The Lord hedges His vineyard. He places a tower in the midst. These are both pictures of the prophet's ministry in the church. The hedge and the tower are necessary to keep the enemy out.

Vineyards need watchmen too, just as cities do. It is just a different picture of what local churches need—towers and watchmen and gatekeepers to protect the life of God's people.

Now, the enemy plots to destroy the tree with its fruit. He spends all of his effort devising devices:

> I knew not that they had devised devices against me, saying, Let us destroy the tree with the fruit thereof.
>
> —JEREMIAH 11:19, KJV

Devise is the Hebrew word *chashab*, meaning "to plait or to weave." Another word for it is *impenetrate*, which is related to the word *impenetrable*.[2] Something that is impenetrable cannot be solved or understood. *Plait* means "to braid or interweave," and *interweave* means "to connect closely or intricately." In other words, the enemy sets up intricate plans against the church. It takes a prophet's anointing to unweave these plots.

The Prophet's Ward

My lord, I stand continually upon the watchtower in the daytime, and I am set *in my ward* whole nights.

—Isaiah 21:8, kjv, emphasis added

Ward is an interesting word. In Hebrew it is the word *mishmereth*, meaning "watch, the sentry, the post, preservation, office, ordinance, a safeguard."[3] It is from the root word *mishmar*, meaning "a guard."[4]

The prophet Isaiah was set in his ward. *Set* is the word *natsab*, meaning "to station, a pillar."[5] Since a ward is a means of defense or protection and *ward* is the root of the word *warden*, and since a warden is a person who guards or has charge of something, prophets are spiritual wardens. They have been set into particular assigned positions, and they help guard and protect the house of the Lord from the enemy. Many local churches have been defenseless against the enemy because they do not have prophets stationed in their wards.

Not only must local churches have prophetic wards established to preserve the church from the attacks of the devil, but also the prophets must station themselves in their respective wards like spiritual superintendents. They must watch and pray to fortify the church, protecting the church from spiritual infiltration.

The prophet was set in his ward whole nights. I believe this can be a reference to all-night prayer being an effective way of preventing the enemy from infiltrating the church.

Prophets are appointed and set in their wards by God. They are responsible to take their place as watchmen and protect the church. They must stand continually upon the watchtower. They must be faithful to their assigned posts. They cannot vacate their wards. They must understand their importance to the safety and protection of the church.

They must set themselves in a posture of prayer and intercession. They must not move from their set position. Satan will attempt to cause prophets to move out of their places. He will attempt to discourage them and prevent them from taking their places in the watchtower in the first place. For their part, prophets must take on an attitude of being unmovable. They must accept their assignments, stand in their assigned places, and fulfill their ministries.

Prophets should ask, "Where is my ward?" and when they find out, they will know that God has placed them there. They must have a revelation of their assigned position. Then they must set themselves in that place and *watch*, operating as spiritual wardens to protect those over whom they have been given charge. Prophets have been assigned as spiritual wardens in many situations, from local churches, to cities, to regions, to nations.

Seeing and saying

After watchmen have been set, they are responsible to declare what they see:

For thus hath the Lord said unto me, Go, set a watchman, let him declare what he seeth.

—Isaiah 21:6, kjv

Shamar prophets, or watchmen prophets, have been set or put into their proper or designated places, *and these are the places* in which they will have the strongest ability to see with spiritual vision. They will be able to see with spiritual eyes that can penetrate the impenetrable. They will be able to see what others cannot see. And they will be able to *say* what they see.

They will make declarations and reveal hidden things. They will pray decisive prayers that will keep their set charge, whether it be a ministry, a church, a city, a region, or a nation, safe and flourishing.

In the Old Testament prophets were called seers, and they are still seers today. Every local church needs seer watchmen.

From earliest times watchman prophets have helped prevent the enemy from destroying the people of God and their property. Many things can be prevented through the watchman prophet's ministry. It is the will of God that many things be prevented. Everything that happens is not necessarily the will of God. Prophets help us prevent things that are not the will of God.

Synonyms for *prevent* include obstruct, hinder, hamper, block, impede, interrupt, interfere, stop, put a stop to, halt, check, arrest, abort, frustrate, thwart, foil, restrain, hold back, oppose, prohibit, neutralize, and turn aside. These words help us better understand and visualize how a watchman watches.

There are three Hebrew words for *watching* or *watchman*: tsaphah, shamar, and natsar. *Tsaphah* means "to lean forward, to peer into the distance, to observe, to await, to behold, to espy, to wait for, to keep the watch." [6] *Shamar*, which we have already discussed at length, means "to hedge about (as with thorns), to guard, to protect, to attend to, to be circumspect, to take heed of, to look narrowly, to observe, to preserve, to regard, to reserve or save, to lie in wait, to be a watchman." *Natsar* means "to guard (in a good sense or a bad one), to conceal, to besiege, to keep, to observe, to preserve, to be a watcher." [7] Each of these words provides insight into the function of the watchman. As the watchman peers into the distance, receiving forewarning from God, he speaks forth the word that can bring preservation, change, protection, and effective strategy.

As a watchman myself, I have often seen the enemy's strategies and, at times, received specific insight. I could *see* very clearly what the enemy looked like in ways ranging from the exact name of an evil spirit to specific strategic responses in spiritual warfare methods that we were to use in battle. I have also had a watchman's eye to see and understand the times and seasons of God, which influence the nature of our responses. I have watched and warned when the enemy was on the move, when we as a ministry may have been out of

God's spiritual position, or when it was right to rise up and lay hold of a new season of release and blessing lest we miss what God was doing in our midst.

MAKE THE WATCH STRONG

When Nehemiah came to help the Israelites who were returning to rebuild Jerusalem, adversaries also came to oppose him. What did Nehemiah do? He set up a watch against them:

> ...and conspired all of them together to come and to fight against Jerusalem, and to hinder it. Nevertheless we made our prayer unto our God, and set a watch against them day and night, because of them.
> —NEHEMIAH 4:8–9, KJV

Nehemiah is a picture of the apostolic ministry because apostles are builders. Whenever God is building or rebuilding something, opposition to the building process is to be expected. The only way to overcome the opposition is to set a watch against them, and that watch needs to be diligent day and night. Apostles need prophets who will assist them in building by watching and praying, seeing and announcing what they see. Apostles and prophets should work together in the building of the church.

> Also I set watchmen over you, saying, Hearken to the sound of the trumpet.
> —JEREMIAH 6:17, KJV

Because the watchmen of the Old Testament blew a trumpet to warn of coming danger, the trumpet has become symbolic of the voice of the prophet. The shamar watchmen whom the Lord sets over His people have the authority to sound the trumpet. With the warning sound of the trumpet (the prophet's voice), the people will rally. The enemy's plans can be thwarted when the people respond to the sound of the trumpet. To ignore the trumpet is to invite danger.

> Make the watch strong, set up the watchmen.
> —JEREMIAH 51:12, KJV

We need to set the watchmen (the prophets) in place. No city in ancient times could be defended without a strong watch. In the same way no church can be defended without a strong watch.

> All believers are commanded to watch: All the people shall keep the watch of the LORD.
> —2 CHRONICLES 23:6, KJV

All believers, however, are not called to be watchmen. Watchmen are the prophetic intercessors who have a special grace to shamar the church, to keep it safe. Watchmen have the grace and discernment to see clearly the approach of the enemy, to sound the trumpet, and to rally the rest of the people to battle in prayer and action.

The word of the Lord can stir us to intercession:

> But if they be prophets, and if the word of the LORD be with them, let them now make intercession to the LORD of hosts.
> —JEREMIAH 27:18, KJV

The false prophets of Israel had no burden for intercession. They were not concerned about protecting the people. They were blind to the danger approaching. They were not fulfilling a shamar function.

The prophet's primary charge, if you recall, is to stand in the gap and make up the hedge for God's people on the earth. This responsibility is where many of Israel's prophets failed.

> And the word of the LORD came unto me, saying, Son of man, prophesy against the prophets of Israel that prophesy, and say thou unto them that prophesy out of their own hearts, Hear ye the word of the LORD; thus saith the Lord GOD; Woe unto the foolish prophets, that follow their own spirit, and have seen nothing!
>
> O Israel, thy prophets are like the foxes in the deserts. Ye have not gone up into the gaps, neither made up the hedge for the house of Israel to stand in the battle in the day of the LORD.
>
> They have seen vanity and lying divination, saying, The LORD saith: and the LORD hath not sent them: and they have made others to hope that they would confirm the word. Have ye not seen a vain vision, and have ye not spoken a lying divination, whereas ye say, The LORD saith it; albeit I have not spoken?
>
> Therefore thus saith the Lord GOD; Because ye have spoken vanity, and seen lies, therefore, behold, I am against you, saith the Lord GOD. And mine hand shall be upon the prophets that see vanity, and that divine lies: they shall not be in the assembly of my people, neither shall they be written in the writing of the house of Israel, neither shall they enter into the land of Israel; and ye shall know that I am the Lord GOD. Because, even because they have seduced my people, saying, Peace; and there was no peace; and one built up a wall, and, lo, others daubed it with untempered morter.
> —EZEKIEL 13:1–10, KJV

Ezekiel was told to lay siege against the city of Jerusalem by means of a prophetic act:

> Thou also, son of man, take thee a tile, and lay it before thee, and pourtray upon it the city, even Jerusalem:

> And lay siege against it, and build a fort against it, and cast a mount against it; set the camp also against it, and set battering rams against it round about.
>
> —Ezekiel 4:1–2, kjv

This prophetic act demonstrated and released the siege of the Babylonians upon Jerusalem. It is not too much to say that this is a picture of the warfare aspect of any prophet's ministry.

Prophets have the ability to attack strongholds and to war against the powers of hell. They lay siege. They build forts against the enemy. They cast mounts and set a camp and set battering rams against the strongholds of the enemy.

They also discover strategies that God wants them to employ against powerful enemies. It is a type of siege warfare.

Elisha instructed the king to dig the valley full of ditches:

> And he said, Thus saith the Lord, Make this valley full of ditches.
>
> —2 Kings 3:16, kjv

The Moabites saw the ditches filled with water and thought they were full of blood. The enemy was confused and thought the Israelites had smitten each other, so they felt emboldened to come right in to the camp of Israel—where they were smitten themselves and defeated.

Elisha gave the king a prophetic strategy to defeat the enemy. In the same way, prophets give strategies to the church so that the people of God can overcome the attacks of the enemy.

Prophets are a vital part of spiritual warfare. Without prophets in the gates, the church cannot be victorious.

CHAPTER 10

PROPHETS RELEASE MIRACLES, HEALING, AND DELIVERANCE

They shall prophesy. And I will show wonders in heaven above and signs on the earth below.
—ACTS 2:18–19

I FIRMLY BELIEVE THAT one of the ways miracles are birthed is through prophecy. We thought that prophecy was just someone coming up and telling us some uplifting things about ourselves or prophesying some information to us about the future. Of course that is a part of the prophetic flow, but I am finding out that there is a much greater manifestation of the prophetic flow. Prophecy is much more powerful than we think.

I am finding out that the prophetic flow opens up the spirit realm for the glory of God to manifest itself in our midst.

> "In the last days it shall be," says God, "that I will pour out My Spirit on all flesh; your sons and your daughters shall prophesy, your young men shall see visions, and your old men shall dream dreams. Even on My menservants and maidservants I will pour out My Spirit in those days; and they shall prophesy. And I will show wonders in heaven above and signs on the earth below: blood, and fire, and vapor of smoke. The sun shall be turned into darkness, and the moon into blood, before that great and glorious day of the Lord comes. And whoever calls on the name of the Lord shall be saved."
> —ACTS 2:17–21

Notice that signs and wonders follow prophecy. We prophesy, and then God begins to show signs and wonders. As soon as the people of God begin to prophesy, "Thus saith God..." things will begin to happen in the spirit realm with manifestations of signs and wonders in the natural realm. Prophecy is one of the keys to opening up the spirit realm.

Moses was a prophet of God. He had the prophetic anointing when he went into Egypt, and he performed signs and wonders. Moses is a type of the church because the church is responsible for going into Egypt (a type of the world) to deliver the people out of bondage. I believe God is going to raise up modern-day "Moseses" (modern-day prophets) who will go in with signs and wonders and cause the devil to let God's people go.

I want to see the signs and wonders. I am tired of just talking about them. I believe that one way we are going to see them is through prophetic utterances, because the prophets of God and the prophecies that they will deliver will open the way for the signs and wonders to come. I have read the second chapter of Acts many times before, but never until recently did I make the connection between prophecy and miracles.

What I am saying is that we should expect signs and wonders to follow the prophets. When the prophets prophesy into the spirit realm and the anointing of God comes upon them, they will begin to activate the miracles of God. Supernatural occurrences will begin to happen in the spirit realm through prophetic utterances.

What kinds of signs and wonders and miracles should we expect to see? I believe we should expect to see all kinds—*financial miracles, healing miracles, miracles of deliverance, supernatural signs and wonders*—in the heavens and on the earth. These things will take place, and they will confound unbelievers. The prophets of God are going to prophesy those things into manifestation. This is why it is so important to know, if we want signs and wonders in our churches, we have to be prophetic churches.

PROPHETS SET THE ATMOSPHERE
FOR DELIVERANCE

Before God does anything supernatural on a major scale, prophetic utterances must go forth. Because some spiritual climates are not conducive to miracles, we need a prophetic culture to make changes in the spiritual atmosphere of a place.

Jesus went into His hometown and could do no mighty works there because of their unbelief. The spiritual climate of that town was not conducive to miracles:

> He could not do any miracles there, except that He laid His hands on a few sick people and healed them. And He was amazed because of their unbelief. Then He went to the surrounding villages, teaching.
> —MARK 6:5–6

Even though He was the Son of God with the power and anointing of God without measure, when He went to Nazareth, He could not do any mighty works. In other words, the spirit of unbelief was strong in that city. Jesus laid hands on only a few sick people and healed them, but He could not do any mighty works.

Most churches and cities have a spiritual climate that is not conducive to the miracle-working power of God. Too many spirits of religion, tradition, unbelief, doubt, sin, perversion, darkness, and other spirits are holding the people back.

God always wants to minister to people. The problem is not that He is not ready; it's the people who are not ready. To get the spiritual climate to change, something needs to break.

When God went to bring Israel out of Egypt, they were not ready to just come straight out. God had to send ten plagues for the purpose of breaking something up first:

> Moses said, "Thus says the LORD, 'About midnight I will go out into the midst of Egypt, and all the firstborn in the land of Egypt shall die, from the firstborn of Pharaoh who sits on his throne, even to the firstborn of the maidservant that is behind the mill, as well as all the firstborn of beasts. Then there shall be a great cry throughout all the land of Egypt, such as there has never been, nor shall ever be again.'"
> —EXODUS 11:4–6

Many times something has to be broken in the spirit realm before God can accomplish what He desires to do. You may wonder why God could not just go in and bring the children of Israel out. It is because something had to be broken in the spirit realm before God's people could come out. This is the case in many instances. Something has to be broken in the realm of the spirit before God can bring people out of a particular area of bondage into a new area of liberty.

Some people never come out of certain areas of bondage because something has not been broken in the spirit realm and dealt with by the power of God. Until the power of God breaks that thing in the spirit realm, those people will remain in bondage.

LET MY PEOPLE GO

Satan is never going to let the people go willingly. It is not his nature to do so. Satan is never going to allow a person to just go free. He will hold them. We see this when every time Moses would go to Pharaoh and say, "Let my people go," Pharaoh would harden his heart. He had to be forced to let the people go. Something had to be broken before he would let them go.

There are many people bound by religion and tradition. Those spirits are not going to let them go just because they ask them to, no matter how much of a man or woman of God they are. If I were to say, "OK, devils, just let the people go, would you, please? We want to go and serve God. We are tired of being in bondage," I do not think the devil would say, "OK, you can have them, Eckhardt."

No way! You have to break that stronghold in the spirit.

God sent Moses into Israel with the rod of authority of God to command the plagues, signs, and wonders in order to break that bondage in the spirit. Moses was a prophet.

In the same way in our time God is raising up people with a prophetic anointing to break things in the spirit. Then God can move. This is why God wants to raise up strong prophetic churches. These churches will arise in the spirit and prophesy. The glory will come. The anointing will go forth and break the powers of darkness in the heavenly realm and open the way for signs, wonders, and deliverance.

When Prophets Lay Hands

> Now when the sun was setting, all those who had anyone sick with various diseases brought them to Him. And He laid His hands on every one of them and healed them. And demons came out of many, crying out, "You are the Christ, the Son of God!" But He rebuked them and did not permit them to speak, because they knew that He was the Christ.
>
> —Luke 4:40–41

From the above verse, notice that when the anointing flows through the hands into the bodies of those oppressed by the devil, it heals them. It also stirs up demons and drives them out.

God anointed Jesus of Nazareth with the Holy Ghost and power to heal those who were oppressed of the devil (Acts 10:38). Sickness is an oppression of the devil. It is no wonder that the demons reacted as Jesus ministered through the laying on of His hands. Demons hate the laying on of hands. They do not want you to lay your hands on sick people and drive them out.

Some have been taught to never lay hands on demonized people, but this is not the teaching of Jesus. He laid His hands upon people who had demons and drove them out. I am not advocating that believers look for everyone who is demonized to lay hands upon, but I am saying that you should not fear laying hands upon people to drive out demons. All deliverances do not require the laying on of hands, but it is a valid administration of the ministry of deliverance.

Releasing virtue

If a believer is filled with the power of the Holy Ghost, he or she is filled with *virtue*. Sometimes the word *dunamis* is translated as *power* and at other times as *virtue*. Virtue and power (*dunamis*) are the same. When the woman with the issue of blood touched the hem of the garment of Jesus, He perceived virtue (*dunamis*) had gone out of Him. Healing virtue can flow into the bodies of the sick through the laying on of hands.

This virtue can be used to heal the sick and drive out evil spirits. Spirit-filled believers can lay hands on the sick and expect to transfer virtue into their bodies. This virtue will drive out sickness and disease, which are the works of the devil.

The disciples were told by Jesus, "Ye shall receive power [*dunamis*, virtue], after that the Holy Ghost is come upon you" (Acts 1:8). Spirit-filled believers are walking reservoirs of the healing anointing. You carry with you the virtue of Christ. The Lord desires to release His virtue into the earth through the laying on of your hands. That is how it worked for Paul, even in unusual situations:

> It happened that the father of Publius lay sick with a fever and dysentery. Paul visited him and, placing his hands on him, prayed and healed him.
>
> —Acts 28:8

Paul started a healing meeting on the island of Malta (also called Melita) through the laying on of his hands. "When this happened, the rest of the island who had diseases also came and were healed" (Acts 28:9). He was illustrating the prediction in the Gospels: "They will lay hands on the sick, and they will recover" (Mark 16:18).

There was enough healing virtue in the hands of Paul to heal every sick person on that island. No wonder the devil hated him, and no wonder demons hate and fight the doctrine of the laying on of hands. They do not want believers to know the power and virtue that is released through the laying on of hands. They want to hide the truth from you because the laying on of hands is the *foundation* of releasing the power of God into the earth.

This is a sign that should follow every believer. Every believer should be able to lay hands on the sick and expect them to recover. This is different from the presbytery laying on hands to equip through impartation. Every believer is not a part of the presbytery. The Holy Ghost honors the laying on of hands by the presbytery when it comes to separating ministry gifts, and every believer cannot lay hands upon ministers to release them the way the presbytery can. But every believer can lay hands upon people to receive the Holy Ghost for healing and deliverance. This is an honor God has given to all His saints.

Binding and loosing

Jesus loosed the woman from a spirit of infirmity through the laying on of hands:

> He was teaching in one of the synagogues on the Sabbath. And there was a woman who had a spirit of infirmity for eighteen years and was bent over and could not straighten herself up. When Jesus saw her, He called her and said to her, "Woman, you are loosed from your infirmity."
>
> Then He laid His hands on her, and immediately she was made straight and glorified God.
>
> —Luke 13:10–13

There was an immediate, instantaneous healing. Thus, we have the power of loosing and the laying on of hands. Loosing people is a manifestation of deliverance. The church has been given the power of binding and loosing. One of the ways we can operate in loosing is through the laying on of hands.

The connection between healing and deliverance

The woman in this passage received her healing through deliverance. There are some people who will not be healed until evil spirits are cast out. There is a fine line between healing and deliverance. These two ministries often overlap. The laying on of hands is effective in both cases. Once the evil spirit is cast out, the damage done to that part of the body can then be healed. In many cases spirits of death and destruction will also need to be cast out, along with a spirit of infirmity. Unforgiveness and bitterness also need to be renounced, in most cases, before healing and deliverance through laying on of hands can be effective.

Working in unison with the laying on of hands is a *command* to every believer. Believers need to understand the subjects of authority and power in addition to the laying on of hands.

The understanding of the power of laying on of hands when coupled with prophecy will help believers release deliverance, healing, promotion, and blessing. We often lay hands on people when we prophesy. I have seen people healed and delivered through prophecy and the laying on of hands. I have personally received tremendous impartation through prophecy with the laying on of hands.

It is not necessary to lay on hands when prophesying, but the two combined are powerful ways to impart and release blessings.

No Prophets, No Miracles

We used to think that a prophet was someone who just walked around and knew everything about you. This is not true. I flow in the prophetic, and I barely know anything about anyone. Usually I only receive revelation about people when I lay my hands on them. That's the way my gift works. I very seldom just look at a person and know things about them.

Even through their natural discernment, anybody can look at people and tell that they have made mistakes. You do not need a dream or a vision for that. If a man is walking down the street looking wild and crazy, talking to himself, fighting and swinging his fists in the air, you do not need an anointing from heaven to see that he has a problem.

The main purpose of prophetic ministry is not to reveal secrets. It is to prophesy with such an anointing that you blast through the heavenlies and break the powers of darkness. Prophecy opens the door for the glory of God to come. Prophecy really paves the way for the Word of God to be ministered.

Prophetic ministry also paves the way for miracles. Prophecy makes it possible for a change to come in the lives of people. The prophetic worship that goes forth in the praise service even before the speaker ministers creates a change in the spiritual atmosphere. A flow of glory begins to come. By the time the speaker gets up to minister the Word of God and build the faith of the people, the place is already so filled with the glory of God that the next step is to enter right in to miracles, signs, and wonders. You've probably seen it yourself. That's why many times God has to bring the prophetic flow first before the miracles occur.

Read the Bible with this in mind. Seldom will you find miracles in the Bible where there were no prophets. Read in the Book of Judges where the angel of the Lord came to Gideon and said, "O mighty man of valor…" and Gideon replied, "Well, where are all His miracles?" (See Judges 6:12–13.)

If we read about miracles in the Bible and wonder why we do not see very many of them today, we do not need to wonder any longer. It is because we don't have very many prophets flowing in the prophetic anointing and bringing in the glory of God. We do not have very many prophets prophesying miracles into manifestation.

God always tells His servants, the prophets, before He does anything (Amos 3:7). You can enter a city that is so bound by demons and so locked up by devils, with principalities and powers so strong, that you are unable to start a move of God in that city. You need the prophets to come and prophesy the mind and will of God in that place.

Some pastors don't have any miracles in their churches, and yet they rebuke their people for attending a service that does. They tell their members, "No, don't go over there. There are a lot of false prophets in the land."

I'll tell you what, pastor; why don't you get your whole church together, go down there with them, and determine whether that person is of God or not. If he is of God, then release them to attend. If he is not, then go ahead and warn your people. If people get off track, the pastor has the right to correct them. Some people do need to be corrected, but please do not kill the hunger and the desire that people have to flow in the supernatural and the glory of God. Don't kill it. Guide them, admonish them, and encourage them to go after the glory of God, because it is by the glory of God that they will experience change.

This is the reason we encourage people to come out and witness the miracles, signs, wonders, healings, and prophetic flow of the Spirit of God. Many pastors don't like it. They say, "You are taking my members."

Well, they need to come to a place like our church because those pastors are hindering their people from flowing in the Holy Spirit. They are standing in the way of God's glory.

The Scripture says that He "manifested His glory." Miracles are a manifestation of the glory of God. It is the glory of God that changes you. Miracles will change you because they introduce you to the life-changing glory of God. The apostle Peter is an example.

The Bible says that Jesus called Peter and his brother and told them to follow Him and He would make them fishers of men (Matt. 4:19; Mark 1:17). There is another account that says that Jesus told Peter to cast his net "for a catch":

> When He had finished speaking, He said to Simon, "Launch out into the deep and let down your nets for a catch."
>
> Simon answered Him, "Master, we have worked all night and have caught nothing. But at Your word I will let down the net."
>
> When they had done this, they caught a great number of fish, and their net was tearing. So they signaled to their partners in the other boat to come and help them. And they came and filled both boats, so that they began to sink.
>
> When Simon Peter saw it, he fell down at Jesus' knees, saying, "Depart from me, for I am a sinful man, O Lord." For he and all who were with him were astonished at the catch of fish which they had taken, and so were James and John, the sons of Zebedee, who were partners with Simon.
>
> Then Jesus said to Simon, "Do not fear. From now on you will catch men." So when they had brought their boats to land, they left everything and followed Him.
>
> —Luke 5:4–11

When Peter drew his net, the catch was so great, it was miraculous! Upon seeing this, Peter fell at Jesus's feet and said, "Depart from me, Lord, for I am a sinful man." That miracle broke Peter and changed his life.

One of the reasons we have a lot of weak ministries and not a lot of strong ministries being birthed into the earth is because too many of them have not been birthed through miracles.

Peter's ministry was birthed through a miracle. When that net broke, and he fell at the feet of Jesus and said, "Lord, depart from me," the Lord said, "Fear not, Peter; from now on, you will catch men." In other words, "This is your ministry, Peter."

Miracles are so much more than just, "Well, we had a miracle." Miracles can change people, and miracles can birth strong ministries into the earth. How many of you reading this book would like to see strong apostles, strong prophets, strong evangelists, strong pastors, and strong teachers?

I am not talking about some little weak preacher who does not walk in any supernatural ability and says he has been called by God. I am talking about strong ministries that change churches, cities, and nations. I am not talking about someone with ordination papers. Anyone can study to be a preacher, get ordination papers, and still be weak. I am talking about anointed ministries of God.

The glory of God is going to be orchestrated through the prophetic flow. The prophetic flow is going to bring in the glory. When the glory comes, miracles are going to follow. Healings are going to follow. We are going to prophesy things that are going to be established in the spirit realm. We are going to see the miracles of God come forth. We are going to see lives changed by the supernatural power of God!

CHAPTER 11

PROPHETS CONFIRM AND IMPART SPIRITUAL GIFTS

For I long to see you, that I may impart unto you some spir-
itual gift, to the end ye may be established.
—ROMANS 1:11, KJV

I N ORDER TO better understand God's power through the laying on of hands, we must understand the subject of impartation. The word *impart* is taken from the Greek word *metadidomi*, meaning "to give over or to share."[1] When something is imparted, it has been conveyed from one person to another.

The apostle Paul had a desire to impart unto the saints "some spiritual gift." In the Weymouth translation of this passage, it reads, "For I am longing to see you, in order to convey to you some spiritual help, so that you may be strengthened."[2]

Therefore what Paul was imparting was meant to be of spiritual help to the saints. Spiritual impartations are given to help us fulfill the will of God for our lives. This is a part of equipping. We become equipped to do the work of the ministry through impartation.

ESTABLISHED AND STRENGTHENED

The result of impartation is establishment. In some translations, "to the end ye may be established" is translated "to strengthen you" or "and so give you fresh strength." Thus the believer is equipped *with fresh strength* as a result of impartation.

One important channel by which this equipping of fresh strength is imparted is through the laying on of hands. We know that Timothy received a spiritual gift through the laying on of hands by Paul. This is impartation from one ministry gift to another. Timothy was strengthened and equipped for his ministry as a result of impartation.

Impartation can also come through association. In this way there will be a transference of anointing from or to the people you associate with. With or without an accompanying laying on of hands, we can receive through impartation from the ministries we submit to and associate with.

There are, I believe, divine relationships ordained by the Lord before the foundation of the world. There are certain people the Lord has predestined for you to link up with in the Spirit. They will have the spiritual deposits you need. You can receive an extra measure of these deposits through the laying on of hands.

It is the will of God that the church operate in all of the gifts and anointing it needs as we await the return of our Lord. It is not the will of God for us to lack any necessary gift.

Paul wrote to the local church in Corinth:

> I thank my God always on your behalf for the grace of God which has been given to you through Jesus Christ. By Him you are enriched in everything, in all speech and in all knowledge, even as the testimony of Christ was confirmed in you, so that you are not lacking in any gift while waiting for the revelation of our Lord Jesus Christ. He will strengthen you to the end, so that you may be blameless on the day of our Lord Jesus Christ.
>
> —1 Corinthians 1:4–8

God has given us the means to obtain all we need. He is ready and willing to gift and equip us with all the spiritual grace we need to complete our commission: *to preach the gospel to all nations and make disciples of all men* (Matt. 28:19).

If we are lacking in spiritual power, it is not the Lord's fault. He has provided everything we need, but we must take advantage of it. This is why it is so important to understand the teaching and wisdom about the laying on of hands. The laying on of hands is a primary channel through which we can receive the spiritual gifts we need as we work and wait for the coming of the Lord.

Strong, not weak

There is really no excuse for so much weakness in the body of Christ. I am so tired of weak Christians and weak churches. A weak and spiritually anemic church is the result of a lack of spiritual gifts. Far too many churches are deficient in spiritual gifts because they do not know how to release God's power through the laying on of hands. When you are deficient in spiritual gifts, you will not be the able ministers of the New Testament that the Word talks about.

The Word tells us to be strong in the Lord and in the power of His might. We are to be strengthened with might by God's Spirit in the inner man. It takes spiritual strength to cast out devils, heal the sick, raise the dead, and reach the lost. Without the gifting and equipping that come through impartation, the church becomes traditional and ceremonial. Many have a form of godliness but deny the power thereof. The kingdom of God is not in word but in power! There is too much preaching of the letter of the law without the power and demonstration of the Holy Spirit.

If you associate with strength, you will become strong. You become like the people you associate with. Don't allow yourself to become weak by linking up with the wrong kind of believer. It is important to associate with strong ministries and receive impartation through the laying on of hands. You need to associate with strong churches and strong ministries. If you associate yourself with weakness, you will become weak.

You must find your own company and fellowship there. You must find a New Testament church that believes in and practices the doctrine of the laying on of hands. You need strong apostles and prophets to lay hands upon you and impart spiritual gifts and strength. Then you will be able to rise up and be the strong believer the Lord expects you to be.

IMPARTATION OF SPIRITUAL GIFTS

Beyond the gifting and equipping that every believer needs to do the works of Jesus, there is special gifting needed for the fivefold ministry. Not everyone is called into the ministry of apostle, prophet, evangelist, pastor, or teacher. There is gifting and equipping that will come at the time of separation for a specific ministry. This gifting and equipping can be received through prophetic presbytery:

> Do not neglect the gift that is in you, which was given to you by prophecy, with the laying on of hands by the elders.
> —1 TIMOTHY 4:14

The *presbytery* is the group of ruling elders in a local church or a group of local churches. Elders need to flow in prophecy along with the laying on of hands. This is one of the ways Timothy received gifting and equipping for his call into the ministry. This is a biblical pattern for ordination.

At the time of ordination those being ordained need to have prophetic utterances spoken over them, with the laying on of hands for the impartation of spiritual gifts. Each ministry has a prophetic destiny that needs to be revealed and activated through the *prophetic presbytery*. The laying on of hands imparts the spiritual gifts needed to fulfill the call. As a result, the person or group receives the word of the Lord concerning their life and ministry plus the power and ability needed to fulfill it. It happens through the laying on of hands.

When ministry gifts do not receive this kind of ministry, they often lack the prophetic direction and spiritual ability necessary to fulfill their call. The laying on of hands has become ceremonial and traditional in some churches, lacking the power it had in the early church to gift and equip ministers. The Lord desires to restore to the church the prophetic presbytery, with the laying on of hands, in its fullness. When you receive gifting and equipping, you will become able ministers of the New Testament.

Divine pattern

If we desire to have Bible results, we must begin to do things the Bible way. The early church left us a divine pattern to follow. If we follow this pattern, we will begin to see supernatural results:

> Therefore I remind you to stir up the gift of God, which is in you by the laying on of my hands.
>
> —2 Timothy 1:6

Paul is reminding Timothy to stir up the gift he received through the laying on of hands. One translation says, "...to fan the flame of that special grace."[3] The gift of God can be referred to as special grace. This gifting and equipping go beyond the gift of the Holy Ghost, which is available to all believers and is known as "common grace." Special grace is needed to fulfill a special call into the ministry.

Paul warned Timothy not to neglect the gift but rather to stir it up. The gifts of God must be continually stirred up by faith. A person can receive gifts through the laying on of hands and not operate in them because of spiritual neglect. The recipient of special grace through the laying on of hands has a responsibility that comes with the gift. This is in line with the charge often given when hands are laid upon an individual to ordain him or her to the service that God has indicated.

The charge is a solemn responsibility the recipient must keep. Unto whom much is given, much is required (Luke 12:48). Don't be too anxious to receive impartation through the laying on of hands unless you are committed to use what you receive.

The gifts received in this way are what I call spiritual deposits. The Lord desires to make spiritual deposits in all of us. He wants us to use these deposits to be a blessing to others. In essence, the Lord expects returns on His deposits. Just as we expect interest on bank deposits, the Lord expects interest on the gifts He deposits into us.

The Lord equips us with gifts, and He expects us to do something with what He has given us. He has equipped us to do the works of Jesus. He expects apostles, prophets, evangelists, pastors, and teachers to take seriously their responsibility to perfect the saints and build up the body of Christ.

Every believer needs to ask himself or herself this question: Am I equipped to do what the Lord has called me to do? If you are not, then how can you fulfill your call?

Is the laying on of hands for gifting and equipping strong enough in our local assemblies? Is there enough teaching on this subject for the saints to function effectively in ministry? If not, how can we become better equipped to do what the Lord has called us to do?

Every local church should lay hands upon people to receive the Holy Ghost. Every believer needs to be baptized with the Holy Ghost. All believers need to be equipped to do the works of Jesus. Every local church should have elders who flow strongly in the laying on of hands. Without these means of equipping and strengthening, the local church cannot even accomplish the minimum of what God established it for. The saints need the spiritual strength that is released through the laying on of hands.

These things will become stronger in our assemblies if we teach and emphasize their importance. The things of God operate and are received by faith. Faith comes by hearing the Word of God. As we teach the Word of God in this area, the leadership will be able to release gifts, and the saints will be able to receive gifts through the laying on of hands.

Once this truth is taught, received, and practiced, the saints will be gifted and equipped. Gifting and equipping won't just happen, but we must teach about and practice the laying on of hands. It will change a local church. Our churches will be full of the gifts of the Spirit. We will see stronger anointings come forth in our churches.

Don't draw back from teaching and practicing the laying on of hands. Prophetic prayer with the laying on of hands is foundational for equipping the saints to perform the will of God. When you lay hands on people, do it in faith. Expect the Lord to move through the laying on of hands.

Separating and Releasing

The first purpose for the laying on of hands is promotion and exaltation, which includes the impartation of wisdom and honor. The laying on of hands imparts blessing to the person being prayed for. The laying on of hands, together with prophetic, prayerful declarations, also releases gifts and equips people to fulfill their callings.

A third purpose for the laying on of hands is to *separate and release* ministry gifts into the earth. Barnabas and Paul were separated and released into their apostolic ministries through the laying on of hands:

> As they worshipped the Lord and fasted, the Holy Spirit said, "Set apart for Me Barnabas and Saul for the work to which I have called them." Then after fasting and praying, they laid their hands on them and sent them off. So, being sent out by the Holy Spirit...
>
> —Acts 13:2–4

In this case it was accompanied by prayer and fasting. Again, we see the principle that when the Lord desires to release His power into the earth, He often does it through the laying on of hands.

There are several points I want to emphasize in these verses. Number one is the Holy Ghost said that they should "separate" Barnabas and Saul. Barnabas and Saul were now to be *separated* to the ministry that they had been previously called to. The Holy Ghost had already called them to be apostles, but they had not yet been separated to that call. There is a time period between calling and separation called *preparation*. That period of time was now finished. The laying on of hands was for their separation to their ministry.

There is a time for calling, a time for preparation, and a time for separation. The *calling* is sovereign, and it comes by the Holy Ghost. The preparation for the call depends upon the individual's willingness to pray, study, and develop the character of Christ. There are different periods of preparation for different people. For some it is longer than others. Patience is required until the time of separation to the actual ministry. The Holy Ghost knows the time of separation. Just because a person has a call does not mean that he or she is ready to function in that capacity. The call is only the beginning, followed by preparation, then separation.

The gifting and equipping for ministry can also come at the time of separation for ministry. In other words, you can receive the grace you need to fulfill your call at the time of separation through the laying on of hands.

People often go into ministry *prematurely*, without the necessary equipping and separation that are accomplished through the laying on of hands. This is one reason why so many ministry gifts are weak and ineffective. It is not because they have not been called, but because they have not been properly equipped and separated. *Separation has to be done in proper spiritual timing.* It should not be done prematurely, but rather it should always be done by the leading of the Holy Ghost.

Notice also that the apostles did not leave the church at Antioch without first receiving the blessing of the leaders of the church. The Holy Ghost honors submission to the presbytery that comes through the laying on of hands. After Paul and Barnabas were released to minister, they remained accountable to the leaders of the church at Antioch. They reported to this church after their missionary journeys. They were submitted and accountable to the ones who had laid hands upon them.

Barnabas and Saul had to be separated from the local church to travel as apostles. They had to be released by the church. They were not *sent forth* by the Holy Ghost until they were *sent away* through laying on of hands by the presbytery. Even though the Holy Ghost is divine, He works through men. This is one of the ways the Holy Ghost separates and releases ministry gifts into the earth.

We see here the authority that is given to the local church by the Lord. The Lord honors and recognizes this authority because it comes from Him. That authority to separate and release ministry gifts is released through the laying on of hands.

Based on this biblical pattern seen in the church at Antioch, there are several questions to ask if you feel called into the ministry:

1. First, do you have the necessary preparation (training, study, wisdom, character) to be separated to the call?
2. Do you have the necessary gifting and equipping to fulfill the call? (This will often come at the time of separation.)
3. Is it the right time for separation to that call?

Remember, the calling is sovereign and comes from God through the Holy Ghost, but the preparation is dependent upon your response to the call. You have a part in the preparation by studying, praying, and developing the character of Christ, and this will take different amounts of time for different people.

The gifting, equipping, and separation can be done through laying on of hands after the calling and preparation have been established, but the separation depends on Spirit-led timing. In turn, gifting, equipping, and separation will hinge on how well developed the church is in the area of prophetic presbytery. The body of Christ as a whole needs more mature prophets so that this process can function according to the biblical pattern.

RELEASING HELPS

Deacons were released to serve through the laying on of hands by the apostles:

> ...whom they presented before the apostles. And when they had prayed, they placed their hands on them.
>
> —ACTS 6:6

The result was "the word of God spread, and the number of the disciples grew rapidly in Jerusalem" (v. 7). Deacons were set in the church, thus freeing up the apostles to give themselves to prayer and the ministry of the Word. Thus the laying on of hands is also a channel to release the helps ministry in the church.

In this case the Holy Ghost did not separate them; the church separated the seven men who were full of the Holy Ghost and wisdom, and the church set them before the apostles. The apostles gave their approval to the selection through the laying on of hands.

Later the apostle Paul gave a list of qualifications for deacons. (See 1 Timothy 3:10.) He wrote that they must first be proved before the laying on of hands to set them in the church, releasing them to serve. Just as ministers need to be released to minister in their call, deacons also need to be released to serve through the laying on of hands.

As I have already indicated, the reason that many churches do not have the ability to gift, equip, and separate people properly into their callings is because they have no prophetic presbytery. The elders (presbytery) of the local church must be able to flow prophetically and be established in a foundational understanding of the laying on of hands in order to release people into every calling necessary for healthy, strong church life.

After people have been gifted, equipped, and separated through the laying on of hands, they can then be released. Prophecy, prayer, and fasting should accompany the laying on of hands to release all of the grace and power needed for effective ministry.

CHECKS AND BALANCES

Here is a piece of advice from Paul to Timothy:

> Do not lay hands suddenly on anyone.
> —1 TIMOTHY 5:22

I believe this verse applies to specific ordination, but it is also a general principle to be followed by the church. The word *suddenly* has to do with spiritual timing. We should not proceed in haste, but rather we should be led by the Holy Ghost as to the proper time to lay hands on people to ordain and separate them.

The Holy Ghost knows the call, character, and preparation of every believer. He knows the proper time to tell us when to lay hands upon people for equipping, gifting, and separation. Laying on hands prematurely can be harmful for the believer and also for the church. I cannot emphasize enough the importance of being sensitive to the Holy Ghost in the area of the laying on of hands.

In a general sense this is also a warning to the church concerning the laying on of hands without using discernment first. This is especially true because of the possibility of transference of spirits. There is such a thing as a dangerous transference of spirits. Just as Joshua received a spirit of wisdom from Moses through the laying on of hands, a person can also receive the wrong spirit from a wrong-spirited minister who lays hands on him or her. Paul warned the Corinthians about receiving "another" spirit (2 Cor. 11:4). In the Old Testament the sins of the people were symbolically transferred to the scapegoat by the laying on of hands (Lev. 16:21). The Lord does not want you to be a scapegoat for somebody else.

There are two extremes to avoid as a believer: first, being so afraid of an evil transference that you become paranoid of anyone laying hands upon you, or you laying hands upon anyone; second, allowing everyone to lay hands upon you, or you laying your hands upon everyone. "Lay hands suddenly on no man" gives us a balance. It does not tell us not to lay hands on people, but rather *not to do it too hastily.*

Just don't be too quick to lay hands on people or to allow people to lay hands on you. Allow yourself to be led by the Holy Ghost. Don't walk in fear, but walk in faith; keep yourself covered by the blood of Jesus. The laying on of hands is a powerful thing; do not misuse it.

CHAPTER 12

Prophets Engage Culture

A prophetic voice will not... be silent in the face of bigotry or prejudice or false pride, and will not compromise faithfulness for practical ends no matter how noble those ends may be in themselves. A truly prophetic voice is one that will sweep away all the trappings of religion and simply ask, "What does God require?" and answer simply, "do justice, love mercy, walk humbly with God." Or simply "love God, love others." A prophetic voice is one that will settle for nothing less than holiness of heart and life as the result of faithful obedience to the voice of God. In a real sense, a prophetic voice even today is the voice of God.

—Dennis Bratcher[1]

P ROPHETS HAVE A fierce loyalty to God and a love for justice (just behavior or treatment of others, especially the poor and disadvantaged). There is nothing wrong with you if injustice and the mistreatment of others grieve and anger you. This is the way you are configured by God.

> None calleth for justice, nor any pleadeth for truth: they trust in vanity, and speak lies; they conceive mischief, and bring forth iniquity.
> —Isaiah 59:4, kjv

> To do justice and judgment is more acceptable to the Lord than sacrifice.
> —Proverbs 21:3, kjv

PROPHETS DEFEND THE CAUSE OF THE POOR, NEEDY, AND FATHERLESS

It is the nature of a prophet to defend the poor and needy. Prophets hate injustice and will defend those who are being treated unfairly.

> How long will ye judge unjustly, and accept the persons of the wicked? Selah. Defend the poor and fatherless: do justice to the afflicted and needy. Deliver the poor and needy: rid them out of the hand of the wicked.
>
> —Psalm 82:2–4, kjv

Prophets Cry Out for Justice, Fairness, and Equity

Righteousness can be translated as justice, fairness, and equity. The prophets hated religion and sacrifice without justice and fairness.

> But let justice and fairness flow like a river that never runs dry.
> —Amos 5:24, cev

> But let judgment run down as waters, and righteousness as a mighty stream.
> —Amos 5:24, kjv

> Then shalt thou understand righteousness, and judgment, and equity; yea, every good path.
> —Proverbs 2:9, kjv

Justice was a major theme of the Old Testament prophets. They equated justice with righteousness. You cannot be unjust and righteous at the same time. Synonyms for *justice* include equitability, equitableness, evenhandedness, fair-mindedness, fairness, impartiality, goodness, righteousness, virtue, honor, integrity, and uprightness.

The opposite words for justice include bias, favor, favoritism, nonobjectivity, one-sidedness, partiality, partisanship, and prejudice.

Prophets Will Not Allow the Powerful to Take Advantage of the Weak

The story of Naboth in 1 Kings 21 highlights how prophets deal with injustice. Jezebel took possession of Naboth's vineyard for Ahab by setting up false witnesses and having him killed. This is an example of the powerful taking advantage of the weak. God sent a word through Elijah to Ahab that the dogs would lick his blood in the place where they licked Naboth's blood.

> And thou shalt speak unto him, saying, Thus saith the Lord, Hast thou killed, and also taken possession? And thou shalt speak unto him, saying, Thus saith the Lord, In the place where dogs licked the blood of Naboth shall dogs lick thy blood, even thine.
> —1 Kings 21:19, kjv

Another illustration of how prophets deal with injustice is found in the Bible where David took Bathsheba, Uriah's wife, and had Uriah killed. Nathan came to David and exposed this injustice. David had many flocks and herds but took from Uriah the only lamb he had. This is another example of the strong taking advantage of the weak. This was a grave injustice.

And the LORD sent Nathan unto David....And Nathan said to David, Thou art the man. Thus saith the LORD God of Israel, I anointed thee king over Israel, and I delivered thee out of the hand of Saul; and I gave thee thy master's house, and thy master's wives into thy bosom, and gave thee the house of Israel and of Judah; and if that had been too little, I would moreover have given unto thee such and such things. Wherefore hast thou despised the commandment of the LORD, to do evil in his sight? thou hast killed Uriah the Hittite with the sword, and hast taken his wife to be thy wife, and hast slain him with the sword of the children of Ammon. Now therefore the sword shall never depart from thine house; because thou hast despised me, and hast taken the wife of Uriah the Hittite to be thy wife.

—2 SAMUEL 12:1–10, KJV

A PROPHET'S VIEW OF GOD AND SOCIETY

The Sermon on the Mount found in Matthew chapter 5 serves as something like a manifesto. I call it the prophet's manifesto. A manifesto is a published verbal declaration of the intentions, motives, or views of the issuer, be it an individual, group, political party, or government. The Sermon on the Mount, delivered by Jesus thousands of years ago, provides the way in which prophets should view and deal with people. Let's take a look at this passage and break it down verse by verse.

Poor in Spirit

Prophets look for humility, the poor in spirit, those who recognize their need for God.

Blessed (happy, to be envied, and spiritually prosperous—with life-joy and satisfaction in God's favor and salvation, regardless of their outward conditions) are the poor in spirit (the humble, who rate themselves insignificant), for theirs is the kingdom of heaven!

—MATTHEW 5:3, AMPC

Mourning

Prophets grieve (mourn) over what grieves the heart of God. They also walk in the comfort of the Holy Ghost.

God blesses those people who grieve. They will find comfort!

—MATTHEW 5:4, CEV

Meekness

Meekness is important to prophets. Meekness is characterized as mild, patient, and long-suffering.

Blessed (happy, blithesome, joyous, spiritually prosperous—with life-joy and satisfaction in God's favor and salvation, regardless of their outward conditions) are the meek (the mild, patient, long-suffering), for they shall inherit the earth!

—Matthew 5:5, ampc

Righteousness

Prophets have a hunger and thirst for righteousness (justice, uprightness, right standing with God).

Blessed and fortunate and happy and spiritually prosperous (in that state in which the born-again child of God enjoys His favor and salvation) are those who hunger and thirst for righteousness (uprightness and right standing with God), for they shall be completely satisfied!

—Matthew 5:6, ampc

Mercy

Prophets will cry out against cruelty and harshness. They call for mercy and compassion for the afflicted and oppressed.

Blessed (happy, to be envied, and spiritually prosperous—with life-joy and satisfaction in God's favor and salvation, regardless of their outward conditions) are the merciful, for they shall obtain mercy!

—Matthew 5:7, ampc

Peacemaking

Prophets grieve when there is strife, hatred, fighting, contention, confusion, and division. They are lovers and promoters of peace (shalom).

Blessed (enjoying enviable happiness, spiritually prosperous—with life-joy and satisfaction in God's favor and salvation, regardless of their outward conditions) are the makers and maintainers of peace, for they shall be called the sons of God!

—Matthew 5:9, ampc

Persecution

Prophets are often persecuted for their stand for righteousness. This has always been the case. Unrighteous systems will fight against anything that threatens them.

Blessed are they which are persecuted for righteousness' sake: for theirs is the kingdom of heaven. Blessed are ye, when men shall revile you, and persecute you, and shall say all manner of evil against you falsely, for my sake. Rejoice, and be exceeding glad: for great is your reward in heaven: for so persecuted they the prophets which were before you.

—Matthew 5:10–12, kjv

Salt and light

Prophets are salt and light.

> Ye are the salt of the earth: but if the salt have lost his savour, wherewith shall it be salted? it is thenceforth good for nothing, but to be cast out, and to be trodden under foot of men. Ye are the light of the world. A city that is set on an hill cannot be hid. Neither do men light a candle, and put it under a bushel, but on a candlestick; and it giveth light unto all that are in the house. Let your light so shine before men, that they may see your good works, and glorify your Father which is in heaven.
>
> —MATTHEW 5:13–16, KJV

I know this verse is applicable to all true believers, but it is especially applicable to prophets. Prophets bring salt and light to the church and the world. Prophets cannot hide the light that God gives them. Prophets bring light to the house (the church).

Uphold justice

Prophets have a standard of righteousness. They teach and preach what is right. The greatest in the kingdom are the obedient. Read Matthew 5:17–20. Jesus upheld the law because it was righteous. He fulfilled the law and the righteousness of the law. We are now righteous through Christ.

Again, the emphasis of prophets is righteousness (justice, right standing with God).

The Pharisees were not righteous. They considered themselves the greatest, but they were the least. They were actually teaching men to break the law through their tradition. The Pharisees were hypocritical.

Motives of the heart

Prophets deal with the motives of the heart such as unjustifiable anger (murder) and calling your brother a fool, and they warn people of their consequences. The motive behind much name calling and insult is anger and hatred, which is murder. Read Matthew 5:21–26.

These verses are interesting as they show how Jesus ("a prophet like unto Moses") views unjustifiable anger. Unjustifiable anger is when you do not have a case, but you still press it. The result of anger can be court or a trial. The result is that it might backfire on you. Reconciliation is important before it goes that far. The results can be devastating (lawsuits), including judgment and prison. This is where unjustifiable anger can lead. Jesus likens it to murder.

Some people will make a case out of anything. This is an unrighteous use of the legal system. People use the legal system to destroy others (murder). Prophets try to help us keep our hearts clear of this level of anger.

Issues of the day

Prophets will deal with the issues of their day (injustice). Read Matthew 5:27–32.

Divorce was one of the issues of the day when Jesus ministered. The religious system of His day had provided a way for men to divorce their wives for almost any cause. Jesus rebuked them and exposed the real reason for these divorces—lust, adultery, and hardness of heart. The men of Christ's day were simply being cruel toward their mates in putting them away. Prophets will deal with cruelty and hardness of heart.

Malachi also dealt with this injustice and called it treachery. This was being committed by the priests in Malachi's day.

> And did not he make one? Yet had he the residue of the spirit. And wherefore one? That he might seek a godly seed. Therefore take heed to your spirit, and let none deal treacherously against the wife of his youth. For the LORD, the God of Israel, saith that he hateth putting away: for one covereth violence with his garment, saith the LORD of hosts: therefore take heed to your spirit, that ye deal not treacherously.
>
> —MALACHI 2:15–16, KJV

Again the issue was injustice. Wives were being unfairly treated by their husbands, and it was sanctioned by the religious system of the day.

> He saith unto them, Moses because of the hardness of your hearts suffered you to put away your wives: but from the beginning it was not so.
>
> —MATTHEW 19:8, KJV

They were putting away their wives for issues other than adultery, when in fact what they were doing was a form of adultery. They were trying to use Moses's words, about issuing a bill of divorcement when they divorced their wives, as a loophole to divorce without legal grounds. Moses's decree was not an endorsement of divorce, but it was a protection for the women who were being put away, that they would have something that said they were not put away because of adultery.

Divorce is also an issue today. Divorce can be unrighteous depending on the motive. Prophets hate this and all kinds of injustice and will speak against it.

Prophets are valuable members in any society. They carry solutions to complex problems, have access to divine knowledge and wisdom, and they have a love for God and for people that causes them to be filled with mercy and a passionate desire for justice.

PART III

GET ACTIVATED

CHAPTER 13

ACTIVATING PROPHETIC MINISTRY GIFTS

Let me say this to you on this wise, that you can begin now to start activating the prophetic streams from within your belly, coming out of dormancy, into the front line of what God is doing in the earth today. You can move from pathetic to prophetic and declare a new sound in this generation. But it starts within your belly and mouth.

—TIM AND THERESA EARLY[1]

To ACTIVATE SOMETHING is to start it off, trigger it, or set it in motion. Prophetic activations are spiritual exercises that use words, actions, phrases, objects, Scripture verses, worship songs and dance, prophetic prayers, and more to trigger the prophetic gifts and help believers in every area of life and ministry to flow freely as they are commissioned to release God's word in the earth. They set in motion prophetic utterances, songs, and movement that will bring great blessing to the members of local churches and ministries and the world.

Activations are designed to break down the barriers that hinder and prevent people from operating in prophecy. These barriers include fear, doubt, timidity, and ignorance. This will also provide people an opportunity to minister, some for the first time, in a safe and loving environment.

Activations rekindle and fan the flame of ministries that have become stagnant in the prophetic flow. We all need times of rekindling and reignition. Prophetic activations will ignite believers and churches to prophesy. Motionless churches need to be set in motion. Prophetic activations can get us moving again.

> That is why I would remind you to stir up (rekindle the embers of, fan the flame of, and keep burning) the [gracious] gift of God, [the inner fire] that is in you by means of the laying on of my hands [with those of the elders at your ordination].
>
> —2 TIMOTHY 1:6, AMPC

I was exposed to prophetic activations in 1989 through the ministry of Drs. Buddy and Mary Crum of Life Center Ministries. I invited them to our church.

They came and activated, trained, confirmed, and launched us in prophetic gifts and ministry. Since then I have seen the growth of our prophetic groups and teams over the years. There have been times when we became stagnant, and we had to break through to another level. But we know how to use the activations to stir up our gifts and bring revival when needed.

Now I travel all over the world—sometimes alone or with my prophetic team—activating believers in the prophetic. Some of those who are in prophetic ministry at my church have become so strong in the prophetic that they have launched their own international ministries and they too travel the world preaching and teaching, and activating and releasing prophets among the nations. God is always challenging us to come up higher and expand more.

There are many creative ways to activate believers. I have placed over one hundred of them organized in categories in the next few chapters in this book. Activations should be simple and fun. Saints should enjoy moving in the things of the Spirit. All ages can be involved. Activations will bring a new excitement to any church and also can be a catalyst for revival and glory.

The value of different activations is that they will break your limitations and give you the ability to operate in different ways. Don't be limited to your favorite way, but move in different ways and administrations. The prophetic must never become boring and routine but should always be exciting and new. God has many surprises for us, and the prophetic will always release new things.

With the diversity of gifts present in the body of Christ, activations are important because we want to see people operate correctly and accurately in their unique prophetic anointing. We don't want to release people who could potentially do damage and harm to others. We need training, and sometimes correction, in operating in prophecy. Activations provide a safe environment to help people learn how to operate in excellence in this important area. Although prophecy comes from God, it is released through human vessels, and therefore it can be tainted and sometimes delivered inaccurately. As 2 Corinthians 4:7 says, "We have this treasure in earthen vessels."

Prophetic activations are not designed to make everyone a prophet—only God can call and commission a prophet. Activations are simply designed to stir people to grow in whatever level they are called to. There may be people participating and leading activations who are prophets, some with the gift of prophecy, and some who have the spirit of prophecy as a result of being filled with the Holy Ghost, but there also may be people who are psalmists, minstrels, intercessors, counselors, preachers, teachers, and dancers in the activations. Activations will stir them and cause them all to move more in faith and inspiration.

Prophetic activations will also raise the prophetic level in a church, region, or territory. The prophetic level is measured by how many mature prophets are ministering in a region, how many believers are operating prophetically in a region, how many churches are operating in the prophetic in a region, and the level of prophetic intercession and worship in a region.

Samuel the prophet is an example of how one person can influence a region. When Samuel was born, there was no prophetic activity in the nation (1 Sam. 3:1). By the time Samuel anointed Saul, there were companies of prophets ministering (1 Sam. 10). In 1 Samuel 19 we find Samuel at Naioth in Ramah standing over the prophets. The prophetic atmosphere was so strong that everyone who came into this atmosphere began to prophesy.

Samuel was responsible for developing emerging prophets in Israel. The Bible does not give us the details of this training. There probably was musical and scriptural training involved in this training, and possibly impartation from Samuel into the lives of the prophets. Samuel brought the prophetic to a new level in Israel that outlived him and continued in generations to come. This is what I intend to do by releasing these activations to you that have been so instrumental in my personal walk with Christ as well as in the life of my church.

WHO SHOULD FACILITATE AND PARTICIPATE IN PROPHETIC ACTIVATION?

Leaders who have a desire to see the local church and the people released into a greater prophetic dimension should employ the strategy of prophetic activations. We cannot teach people how to prophesy, but we can help them to hear the voice of God and speak the words they hear with faith and confidence. Prophetic activations should be done in a loving environment where people feel comfortable. There is no better place than around loving leaders and believers who have no motive other than to bless and encourage.

If you are a leader of a ministry, small group, or church, set aside some time to do activations. If you are a member at a church that operates in the prophetic, bring this idea up to your pastor. If you attend a church that is not open to prophetic ministry, connect with a group of mature prophets and have them confirm and activate you. When you participate in prophetic activations, you will see a new momentum in your prophetic flow.

Paul admonishes the church to desire to prophesy (1 Cor. 14:1) and "covet to prophesy" (1 Cor. 14:39, KJV). Those who desire this important administration of the Holy Spirit should take the time to be a part of a prophetic activation. Activation will stir believers and help them move into a strong prophetic flow. Even those who have experience in the prophetic can benefit from activations. Sometimes people need to be restored and rekindled. We can become dormant in our gifts. We need to continually stir up these gifts.

> While every Spirit-filled believer can prophesy as a general grace God gave to the entire Church (Joel 2:28–29; Acts 2:15–18; 1 Cor. 14:31),

the measure we experience the prophetic and are able to walk in it is determined by our hunger. If we can live without it, we most likely will.

—BENJAMIN SCHAFER[2]

Those who desire to prophesy should understand the great benefits of prophecy. Prophecy can encourage, comfort, build up, confirm, strengthen, impart, release, renew, refresh, heal, deliver, illuminate, enlighten, direct, expose, warn, convict, correct, bless, quicken, and restore. These many benefits alone should cause every leader, church, and believer to desire to prophesy. I have personally seen lives transformed and changed in over eighty nations though the power of prophecy.

Prophets and prophetic people should do more than just prophesy. They should also train and teach others in this area. Every believer should be able to hear the voice of God and release a word on a consistent basis. The prophetic dimension will also affect every area of the church, including the praise and worship, prayer, preaching, teaching, counseling, evangelism, and the arts. Prophetic churches will be a blessing to their cities, nations, and communities because they release the word of the Lord and reveal the heart of God.

IN WHAT ENVIRONMENT SHOULD PROPHETIC ACTIVATIONS BE CARRIED OUT?

Prophetic activations can be done in small or large groups. Groups can consist of believers who are on different levels of the prophetic. There are people who are advanced or intermediate, and some may be beginners. It is good to have a mixture of people on different levels to sharpen and strengthen each other during the activations.

Some people will also have a stronger prophetic flow depending on their level of faith and their knowledge of the Word. Everyone can receive an impartation during a prophetic activation and become stronger in the prophetic flow.

We should follow after love and desire spiritual gifts, but we should especially desire to prophesy (1 Cor. 14:1). Not only should we desire to prophesy, but also we should desire to excel in it. First Corinthians 14:12 reads, "So, seeing that you are zealous of spiritual gifts, seek that you may *excel* to the edifying of the church" (emphasis added). Activations are designed for believers who not only have a desire to prophesy but also desire to excel in this area. *Excel* means to be exceptionally good at or proficient in an activity or subject. Prophetic people should minister in excellence. Prophetic activations are designed to help believers develop and minister with excellence and accuracy.

Prophetic activations are designed to help believers sharpen each other in the area of prophecy. Proverbs 27:17 reads, "As one piece of iron sharpens another..." (ERV). *Sharpen* means "to improve or cause to improve." There are times we need to sharpen the ax. Sometimes we can become dull in our gifting, and we need to sharpen ourselves. Ecclesiastes 10:10 reads, "If you don't sharpen your ax, it will be harder to use" (CEV).

In prophetic activations we generally place the parameters of the prophetic word to include edification, exhortation, and comfort (1 Cor. 14:3). This provides an atmosphere of safety for people who are opening themselves up to receive a word.

By doing this we are limiting the chance of error affecting a person in a negative way. We don't want people hearing words about "premature death" or "whom to marry." We don't want them to hear disturbing things such as, "I see a dark cloud following you," "Witches are after you," and so on. Although these kinds of words are possible, we leave that to more experienced prophets in a different setting.

Prophetic activations provide a safe environment for people to be stirred and activated in the area of prophecy. Prophecy does not replace prayer, preaching, teaching, praise, worship, and other areas that give a believer a balanced lifestyle. The reason why prophetic activations are necessary is because the prophetic area has often been underdeveloped, while the other aspects of the Christian life have been more developed.

During an activation it is important for the people to follow instructions. This is not the place for rebellious and spooky people to try to hijack the prophetic flow and show off their gifts. Submission to godly authority should be a core value of the prophetic ministry; rebellion is as the sin of witchcraft.

> Prophetic activation exercises are meant to equip with practical tools for hearing the voice of God. Eventually you will be able to utilize those tools in every sort of situation: during ministry time at your local church, in everyday life conversations with others, while writing emails or simply praying for others in your private time with the Lord. They will help you flow in the prophetic in your everyday life.
>
> —BENJAMIN SCHAFER[3]

When participating in the activation exercises, we should only give what we receive regardless if it makes sense or not. Don't worry if you receive something the Lord gives you that does not make sense to you. You would be surprised to learn that what does not make sense to you may be life changing to the person you are ministering to.

> When we are running a "Prophecy School" or workshop on prophecy we find that most attendees are able to operate in this gift at a basic level—the challenge then is for them to develop the gift. None of us starts off as mature in any of the gifts of the Holy Spirit and prophecy is no different. God is a loving Father and knows that we need to grow in both faith and understanding.
>
> —GEOFF AND GINA POULTER[4]

In other words, don't despise the day of small beginnings. Everyone has to start off somewhere, and usually it will be a small beginning.

Always remember that the Bible, as the perfect revelation of Jesus and the infallible Word of God, is the absolute standard for weighing and assessing all revelation (2 Tim. 3:16; Col. 2:18–19; John 1:14).

> Prophecy is not just about communicating God's mind, but also His heart.
>
> —STEVE THOMPSON[5]

CORNELIUS CONNECTIONS: WHERE TO GO AND WHAT TO DO UPON BEING ACTIVATED

> Then Peter went down to the men who were sent to him by Cornelius and said, "Here I am, the one you are seeking. Why have you come?" They said, "Cornelius, a centurion, a man who is righteous and fears God and is of good report throughout the nation of the Jews, was directed by a holy angel to summon you to his house to hear your words."
>
> —ACTS 10:21–22

God will connect you with people who need the word of the Lord that is in your mouth.

Supernaturally people have dreamed my name and heard that they needed to contact me and have me pray for them and minister to them.

As you begin to activate and stir up your gift, God will begin to supernaturally connect you with people who need your anointing, who need the word of the Lord that is in your mouth.

This is the supernatural lifestyle God gives prophets and prophetic people. This is the exciting life of a prophet. I've found myself in cities and countries I never thought I'd be, places I've never heard of... but it was a divine connection because of the word I have in my mouth and that I carry with me all the time, so when I got there I was able to release the word of the Lord.

Some people want to be sent out to all kinds of places, but what word are they carrying that will take them into the place that God has for them? Make sure you are consistently stirring up the gift that is within you so that you will be able to minister to people when they call.

There are 125 activations in this book that will get you well on your way to developing your gift to flow effectively in prophetic ministry. They can be followed in order or chosen based on the time element and what the leader desires to do. These activations will stretch you and give you the ability to operate in different dimensions of prophecy.

CHAPTER 14

BEGINNING ACTIVATIONS

We have diverse gifts according to the grace that is given to us: if prophecy, according to the proportion of faith.

—ROMANS 12:6

As IT SAYS in the verse above, there are many gifts in the body of Christ that are given through grace, but prophecy is given according to the proportion of faith. You must have a measure of faith in order to operate in the prophetic. These beginning activations help to "prime the pump." They will help to get the river to flow by increasing your measure of faith. Your faith must be accompanied by desire, as I mentioned above. You must desire to prophesy and then begin to stir up the gift of God within you, as it says in 2 Timothy 1:6. As the gift is stirred, it will begin to flow out of your belly, your spirit, like rivers of living water (John 7:37), bringing life to those who hear.

Now understand that these activations are not designed to teach you how to prophesy, per se, but how to hear from God and release what you hear. These activations are designed to encourage you to hear from God, to listen to the Spirit, and to step out in faith and get the river flowing. As you do that, you will develop your prophetic gift.

You will be challenged and stretched as you, by faith, embark on these activation exercises and dive deeper into the prophetic. As you get around others, there is a greater faith level, and it helps you launch out in the prophetic. Others can help you move in faith and by the Spirit of God.

Prophetic activation #1: read a scripture; release a prophetic word

In this activation you read or quote a verse of Scripture the Lord gives you for the person you are ministering to, and then you launch from that verse and minister prophetically to the person. This is a powerful exercise that will help your prophetic flow.

For example, 2 Timothy 1:7 says, "For God has not given us the spirit of fear..." You might hear the Lord say, "My son (or My daughter), don't be afraid; I am with You..."

Prophetic activation #2: receive one word; release a prophetic word

This activation is simple. When you stand before a person, believe God for just one word. It could be *grace, power, love,* or *mercy.* Launch from the one word God gives you into the prophetic. Sometimes God gives us one word, and as we speak prophetically, the word will expand and flow.

If the Lord gives you the word *power,* you might be led to say something like, "My son (or My daughter), My power is available to you. Don't be afraid to walk in My power. As you walk in power, you will see many miracles and breakthroughs in the days to come."

Prophetic activation #3: kick-start: pray in the Spirit; release a prophetic word

As you begin to minister, pray in the Spirit, allow the Lord to give you a word or a picture when you are praying, then launch into the prophetic. This tunes your spirit to what God wants to say to the person. Speaking in tongues is a good way to "kick-start" the prophetic flow.

Prophetic activation #4: see a picture; release a prophetic word

This exercise involves the seeing aspect of the prophetic. Some people are more visionary. Ask the Lord for a picture, and launch into the prophetic word. This exercise will sharpen the visionary aspect of the prophetic. The pictures you can receive are limitless.

Prophetic activation #5: play music; sing a prophetic word

This activation requires music and will activate the prophetic song. Follow the music and sing prophetically to the person. Anointed music is a catalyst to the prophetic flow.

Prophetic activation #6: use an object; release a prophetic word

Common objects: watch, phone, keys, Bible, and so on. With the object in hand, launch into the prophetic flow. This activation will stretch your faith to speak in different areas of a person's life and increases the visual aspect of the prophetic flow.

Here are a few examples on how this could flow: 1) With a watch you may prophesy to the person concerning God's timing. 2) With a pen you may release a word about writing. 3) With keys you may release a word about God unlocking and opening doors for them, and so on.

Prophetic activation #7: bless the person; release a prophetic word

This activation begins with blessing the person you are ministering to. For example, you may say, "I bless you with..." peace, favor, shalom, and the like. Then you would launch into a prophetic word. You should hear a word when you are blessing them. This helps you flow into the power of prophetic blessing.

Prophetic activation #8: beginning with a "don't" word

This activation begins by speaking "don't." For example, "Don't be afraid," "Don't worry," "Don't be ashamed," or "Don't look back." This activation is an exercise in what God does not want us to do. The beginning of the prophetic word is with a "don't," and you launch into the prophecy and develop the word.

Prophetic activation #9: beginning with a question

Questions such as "Am I not your God?" "Am I not with you?" "Have I been faithful to you?" "Have I not called you?" would begin an activation like this.

Sometimes the prophetic word begins with a question, and then the Lord speaks to us based on the question. In this activation you begin by allowing the Lord to give you a question for the person you are ministering to, and then you launch with a prophetic word.

> Have you not known? Have you not heard? Has it not been told to you from the beginning? Have you not understood from the foundations of the earth?
>
> —Isaiah 40:21

Prophetic activation #10: "if" prophecies

These are prophecies that are conditional—"If you seek me, then I will…," "If you continue to worship me, then I will…," "If you are faithful, then I will…," and so on.

This activation begins with an *if*. Ask the Lord to give you a word beginning with *if* for the person you are ministering to, and launch into the prophetic flow. This activation challenges the recipient to obey and be blessed.

> If you are willing and obedient, you shall eat the good of the land.
>
> —Isaiah 1:19

CHAPTER 15

CREATIVE ACTIVATIONS

God has chosen the foolish things of the world to con-
found the wise. God has chosen the weak things of the
world to confound the things which are mighty.

—1 CORINTHIANS 1:27

C REATIVE ACTIVATIONS ARE designed to stretch you beyond the normal way you would hear and release a prophetic word. These are designed to have you prophesy on things you wouldn't normally prophesy on. Most people prophesy on hope, faith, and other words, but to prophesy on things like "the ear" causes you to have to rely on the creativity and innovation of the Spirit. Prophets are, by nature, very creative and innovative. Those attributes are part of the prophet's mantle. God is the Creator, and He dwells in a place of new things and uncommon, divine creativity. He wants His prophets in that place with Him, ready to hear and act on His spontaneous word.

Prophetic activation #11: new thing prophecy

This activation begins with praying for God to do something new in the person's life you are ministering to. As you pray, believe God for a word that will release something new in the person's life, and then launch into the prophetic. You can prophesy new doors, new anointing, new relationships, new health, new revelation, and the like.

Prophecy is a powerful way to see the release of new things.

> See, the former things have come to pass, and new things I declare; before they spring forth I tell you of them.
>
> —ISAIAH 42:9

Prophetic activation #12: creation prophecies

This activation begins by asking God what He is creating for the person you are ministering to, or what they have been created for (their purpose), and then launching into the prophetic flow. God's word is creative because God is creative.

> You have heard; see all this. And will you not declare it? I have shown you new things from this time, even hidden things, and you did not

know them. They are created now and not from the beginning; even before the day when you did not hear them, lest you should say, "Yes, I knew them."

—Isaiah 48:6–7

But now, thus says the Lord who created you, O Jacob, and He who formed you, O Israel: Do not fear, for I have redeemed you; I have called you by your name; you are Mine.

—Isaiah 43:1

Prophetic activation #13: prophesying in rhyme

This activation is designed to minster to the person poetically. Prophecy can be poetic, and it is a powerful way to minster to people. Ask the Lord to give you a rhyme for the person you are ministering to, and launch into the prophetic. Take your time in this activation and let the Holy Spirit give you the words. Here's an example of what prophetic rhyme looks like:

I am with you today;
　　don't be afraid.
I will go with you;
　　your future I have made.
I speak to you today.
　　You now hear my voice.
Don't be sad.
　　It is time to rejoice.

Prophetic activation #14: the ear

This activation focuses on the ear of the person you are ministering to. God often speaks to us concerning our ear (hearing). Touch the person's ear and pray for their spiritual hearing and then launch into the prophetic word. Here are a couple examples of how you would prophesy about someone's ear: "I am opening your ear to hear My voice," or "I am closing your ear to the voice of the enemy."

Give ear, O my people, to my teaching: incline your ears to the words of my mouth.

—Psalm 78:1

Prophetic activation #15: the eye

This activation focuses on the eyes of the person you are ministering to. Pray for the person's eyes and ask the Lord to give you a word. Then launch into the prophetic. The eyes are related to vision, discernment, revelation, insight, focus, etc.

> Your eyes shall see the King in His beauty; they shall see the land that is very far away.
>
> —Isaiah 33:17

Prophetic activation #16: the mouth or tongue

This activation focuses on the mouth and tongue. Pray for the person's mouth and tongue, ask the Lord to give you a word, and then launch into the prophetic. Words for this prophetic flow can include preaching, teaching, singing, prophesying, praying, public speaking, wisdom, and the like.

> Then the lame man shall leap as a deer, and the tongue of the mute sing for joy. For in the wilderness waters shall break out and streams in the desert.
>
> —Isaiah 35:6

Prophetic activation #17: the hands

Hold the person by the hand and pray for their hands while asking the Lord to give you a word, then launch in the prophetic flow. Examples of words given during this activation can include healing hands, God holding their hands, God lifting their hands, God using their hands, and the like.

> Thus says the Lord to Cyrus, His anointed, whose right hand I have held—to subdue nations before him and to loosen the loins of kings, to open before him so that the gates will not be shut.
>
> —Isaiah 45:1

Prophetic activation #18: the heart

This activation focuses on the person's heart, their innermost being. Pray for the person's heart, and ask the Lord to show you their heart. When you receive a word, launch into the prophetic word. Words here can include a pure heart, new heart, courageous heart, healing your heart, and the like.

> Say to those who are of a fearful heart, "Be strong, fear not. Your God will come with vengeance, even God with a recompense; He will come and save you."
>
> —Isaiah 35:4

Prophetic activation #19: the mind

Lay your hand on the person's head and pray for their mind and thought life. Ask the Lord to give you a word for their mind and thoughts, and launch into the prophetic word. Words can include knowledge, intelligence, creativity, order, restoration, and the like.

> Search me, O God, and know my heart: try me, and know my thoughts.
>
> —Psalm 139:23, kjv

Prophetic activation #20: the feet

Pray for the feet of the person. The feet represent the person's walk, path, and journey. Ask the Lord to give you a word, and launch into the prophetic. Words that can be released during this kind of activation can include new feet, beautiful feet, new path, different path, travel, and so on.

> So I prophesied as He commanded me, and the breath came into them, and they lived and stood up upon their feet, an exceeding great army.
> —Ezekiel 37:10

CHAPTER 16

ACTIVATIONS PROMPTED BY THE NAMES OF GOD

Moses said to God, "... When they say to me, 'What is His name?' what shall I say to them?" And God said to Moses, "I AM WHO I AM."
—EXODUS 3:13–14

THE FOLLOWING ACTIVATIONS are released from the name of God. God drops His word when we publish the name of the Lord. In Deuteronomy 32:2–3, the Bible says, "My teaching will drop [Hebrew word *nataph*, meaning "to prophesy"] like the rain, my sayings will distill as the dew, as the droplets on the grass, and as the showers on the herb. For I will proclaim the name of the Lord: Ascribe greatness to our God!"

Prophetic activation #21: Jehovah Jireh

This activation launches on the name *Jehovah Jireh* (the Lord My Provider). God drops His word (*nataph*—to drop, prophesy) when we publish His name and ascribe greatness to Him. Ascribe greatness to the name Jehovah Jireh by verbally declaring His greatness, allow and wait for God to drop His word, then launch into the prophetic. Possible prophetic words that flow out of this activation include challenges to give, to trust, or to have faith in God's provision. Jehovah Will Provide is the name given by Abraham at the place where he had been at the point of almost slaying his son Isaac. (See Genesis 22:14.)

Prophetic activation #22: Jehovah Rapha

This activation launches on the name *Jehovah Rapha* (the Lord my Healer). This is a great way to release a healing word that can include physical or inner healing. It was God who brought Israel to Marah. It was at this place that the Lord became known as "the LORD who heals you" (Exod. 15:26). He brought them here to teach them and to make Himself known to them, and He causes us to reflect back on that place to teach us and make Himself known to us (1 Cor. 10:11) as our healer.

For example, you may hear the Lord say to you on behalf of the person, "Son/daughter, I am your healer. I am healing you now from the past, binding up your wounds, and causing new life to flow through your mind, body, and spirit. You don't have to wonder; it is My desire to bring healing to every area of your life that is hurting."

Prophetic activation #23: Jehovah Shalom

The name *Jehovah Shalom* means "the Lord My Peace." The peace of God, or shalom, includes prosperity, health, and wholeness. The words launched from this activation will bring peace and wholeness to those you minister to. Gideon named the place where God confirmed his victory over the Midianites "the Lord Is Peace," and he built an altar (Judg. 6:24).

You may be led to say something like this: "My son/My daughter, I am Your peace. Cast your cares upon Me. My peace I give to you. I don't give you peace that the world gives. You will have My peace that passes all understanding. Let not your heart be troubled."

Prophetic activation #24: Jehovah Shammah

Jehovah Shammah means "the Lord Is Present." These words confirm the presence of God with a person and the benefits of His presence. *Jehovah Shammah* is a Christian transliteration of the Hebrew, meaning "Jehovah is there," the name given to the city in Ezekiel's vision in Ezekiel 48:35.

For this activation you may hear the Lord say something like, "My son/My daughter, I am with you. I am in the midst of your troubles. I am in the midst of your storm. I am with you even until the end."

Prophetic activation #25: El Shaddai

El Shaddai means "Mighty God." These words can speak of God's power and might in a person's life and release faith to believe for God's mighty acts. In the Old Testament *El Shaddai* occurs seven times. *El Shaddai* is first used in Genesis 17:1.

An example of what this activation may release may be something like this: "My son/My daughter, get ready to see Me perform mighty acts in your life. Get ready to see a move of My power over your situation. I am Almighty God."

Prophetic activation #26: I AM

I AM THAT I AM was revealed to Moses. This name of God provides an unlimited number of words that can be released through revealing who God is to the person you are ministering to. You could begin by declaring to the person that God is their shield, deliverer, healer, provider, friend, and so on, as the Lord reveals to you His position in the person's life.

When Moses saw the burning bush in the desert, He asked God, "When they say to me, 'What is His name?' what shall I say to them?" (Exod. 3:13). God answered his question by the revelation of His name as the "I Am." "And God said to Moses, 'I AM WHO I AM,' and He said, 'You will say this to the children of Israel, "I AM has sent me to you"'" (Exod. 3:14).

Prophetic activation #27: Jehovah M'Kaddesh

This name means "the God who sanctifies." A God separate from all that is evil requires that the people who follow Him be cleansed from all evil. This activation is launched with a word of sanctification, holiness, and separation.

> Speak also to the children of Israel, saying, "You must surely keep My Sabbaths, for it is a sign between Me and you throughout your generations, that you may know that I am the LORD who sanctifies you."
> —EXODUS 31:13

An example of a word launched from this activation may be something like, "My son/My daughter, I am sanctifying you, making you holy, and setting you apart for my use. Let Me purify you that you may be holy. Let Me wash you that you may be clean."

Prophetic activation #28: Jehovah Nissi

Jehovah Nissi means "the Lord My Banner." Words of victory and triumph are released through this activation.

> Then Moses built an altar and called the name of it, The LORD Is My Banner.
> —EXODUS 17:15

An example of a word released from this activation is, "I am Your banner. Be encouraged, for today I am giving you victory over all your enemies. By the power of My name you have overcome."

Prophetic activation #29: Jehovah Roi

Jehovah Roi means "the Lord My Shepherd." In this activation you would be challenged to release words that speak of the Lord's protection, leading, feeding, and the like. The most extensive reference to "the Lord Our Shepherd" is Psalm 23.

Prophetic activation #30: Wonderful

God is a God of wonders. This activation will cause you to speak words that tell of the wonderful works of God in the life of the person you are ministering to. *Wonderful* means "inspiring delight, pleasure, or admiration; extremely good; marvelous."

NAMES OF GOD[1]

El Shaddai (Lord God Almighty)—Gen. 17:1; 28:3; 35:11; 43:14; 48:3

El Elyon (The Most High God)—Gen. 14:18–20, 22; Ps. 57:2; 78:35

Adonai (Lord, Master)—*Adonai* occurs 434 times in the Old Testament. There are many uses of *Adonai* in Isaiah as "Adonai Jehovah." *Adonai* is found two hundred times in Ezekiel and eleven times in Daniel chapter 9.

Yahweh (Lord, Jehovah)—Used more than any other name of God, Yahweh occurs in the New Testament 6,519 times. It is first used in Genesis 2:4.

Jehovah Nissi (The Lord My Banner)—Exodus 17:15

Jehovah Roi (The Lord My Shepherd)—Psalm 23, also Jehovah Rohi, Jehovah Raah, or Jehovah Ro'eh

Jehovah Rapha (The Lord That Heals)—Exodus 15:26

Jehovah Shammah (The Lord Is There)—Ezekiel 48:35

Jehovah Tsidkenu (The Lord Our Righteousness)—Jer. 23:6; 33:16

Jehovah M'Kaddesh (The Lord Who Sanctifies You)—also Jehovah Mekoddishkem; Exod. 31:13; Lev. 20:8

El Olam (The Everlasting God)—Gen. 21:33; Jer. 10:10; Isa. 26:4

Elohim (God)—*Elohim* occurs over two thousand times in the Old Testament. *Elohim* is in the very first verse of the Bible, Genesis 1:1.

Qanna (Jealous)—Exod. 20:5; 34:14; Deut. 4:24; 5:9; 6:15

Jehovah Jireh (The Lord Will Provide)—Gen. 22:14

Jehovah Shalom (The Lord Is Peace)—Judg. 6:24

Jehovah Sabaoth (The Lord of Hosts)—1 Sam. 1:11; 17:45; 2 Sam. 6:18; 7:27; 1 Kings 19:14; 2 Kings 3:14; 1 Chron. 11:9; Ps. 24:10; 48:8; 80:4, 19; 84:3; Isa. 1:24; 3:15; 5:16; 6:5; 9:19; 10:26; 14:22; Jer. 9:15; 48:1; Hosea 12:5; Amos 3:13; Micah 4:4; Nah. 3:5; Hab. 2:13; Zeph. 2:9; Hag. 2:6; Zech. 1:3; Mal. 1:6

CHAPTER 17

ACTIVATIONS PROMPTED BY SPIRITUAL VIRTUES

So now abide faith, hope, and love, these
three. But the greatest of these is love.
—1 CORINTHIANS 13:13

GOD OFTEN CHALLENGES us through the prophetic word in the areas of spiritual virtues such as love, faith, hope, or holiness. These areas are very important to a believer. The word of the Lord will often challenge, encourage, and help in these areas of our lives, causing us to be strong and fully developed. These kinds of words are very important for a believer to hear from the Lord. Some people need to be healed, to be corrected, or to refocus on these areas. The prophetic word will do that. Some people also need to be commended in these areas. The word of the Lord will come and let them know that they are doing well.

Prophetic activation #31: love

Focus on the love of God for the person you are ministering to. Speak words of love over the person and launch into the prophetic flow. These words confirm and remind people of the love of God for them and challenge them to walk in love, compassion, and forgiveness. This activation releases the prophetic minister to operate in the love of God in the prophetic flow.

Anyone who does not love does not know God, for God is love.

—1 JOHN 4:8

Prophetic activation #32: faith

Focus on the area of faith, speak words concerning faith, and then launch into the prophetic word. Faith is an important part of the believer's life, and God will often speak to us and challenge us in this area. These words challenge people in the area of faith and exhort them to remove doubt and unbelief from their lives.

And without faith it is impossible to please God, for he who comes to God must believe that He exists and that He is a rewarder of those who diligently seek Him.

—HEBREWS 11:6

Prophetic activation #33: mercy

Focus on the mercy of God. Speak the mercy of God over the person you are ministering to, then launch into the prophetic word. These words remind people of God's mercy and forgiveness, and deliver them from guilt, condemnation, and shame. This activation helps the prophetic minister to operate in the mercy and compassion of the Lord when ministering.

> Oh, give thanks unto the Lord, for He is good, for His mercy endures forever!
> —Psalm 107:1

Prophetic activation #34: hope

Focus on the subject of hope, pray over the person's hopes and dreams, and then launch into the prophetic word. Use this word to stir people to hope and dream. This activation helps the prophetic minister release hope and encouragement.

> Now may the God of hope fill you with all joy and peace in believing, so that you may abound in hope, through the power of the Holy Spirit.
> —Romans 15:13

Prophetic activation #35: holiness

Pray for the person's holiness and sanctification, and launch into the prophetic word. These words challenge people to walk in purity and to remove impurities from their lives. This activation helps the prophetic minister stand for righteousness and purity.

> Pursue peace with all men, and the holiness without which no one will see the Lord.
> —Hebrews 12:14

Prophetic activation #36: power

Pray for the person to walk in the power of God, and then launch into the prophetic word. These words challenge people to walk in power and demonstration of the Spirit. This activation reminds the prophetic minister that the prophetic ministry is not in word only but also in power. Sometimes the power of God is released during this activation to release a miracle in the life of the person ministered to.

> He gives power to the faint, and to those who have no might He increases strength.
> —Isaiah 40:29

Prophetic activation #37: authority

Focus on the authority of the believer through Christ, pray for the authority of Christ to increase, and launch into the prophetic word. These words exhort people to walk in and exercise their authority in Christ. This activation also increases the authority in which the prophetic minister prophesies.

> Then He called His twelve disciples together and gave them power and authority over all demons and to cure diseases.
>
> —LUKE 9:1

Prophetic activation #38: humility

Focus on the virtue of humility, pray for the person to walk in humility, and launch into the prophetic flow. These words exhort people to walk in humility and warn against the dangers of pride. This activation reminds the prophetic minister of the virus of pride versus the anointing that comes with humility—and the need for it, especially in prophecy.

> Likewise you younger ones, submit yourselves to the elders. Yes, all of you be submissive one to another and clothe yourselves with humility, because "God resists the proud, but gives grace to the humble."
>
> —1 PETER 5:5

Prophetic activation #39: joy

Focus on the joy of the Lord (you can even laugh during this activation), and launch into the prophetic flow. These words remind people of the importance of joy and come against situations that steal joy. This activation releases the prophetic minister to minister the prophetic word with joy.

> Then he said to them, "Go your way. Eat the fat, drink the sweet drink, and send portions to those for whom nothing is prepared; for this day is holy to our Lord. Do not be grieved, for the joy of the LORD is your strength."
>
> —NEHEMIAH 8:10

Prophetic activation #40: favor

Focus on the favor of God, speak favor over the person's life, and launch into the prophetic flow. These words release the favor of God for blessing and promotion. This impartation helps the prophetic minister release favor.

> For You, LORD, will bless the righteous; You surround him with favor like a shield.
>
> —PSALM 5:12

CHAPTER 18

TEAM MINISTRY ACTIVATIONS

He called to Him the twelve, and began to send them
out two by two, and gave them authority...
—MARK 6:7

ROPHETS CAN ALSO work together in teams. Teams help keep prophets balanced, and teamwork provides a healthy barrier against pride, isolation, and exclusiveness. We have many recognized prophets in our local assembly, and they understand that teamwork is the way to go. We need to be connected with people who flow strongly in prophetic ministry.

The following activations are for training prophets and prophetic people how to minister in groups of three or with the help of a more experienced prophetic minister.

Prophetic activation #41: follow the prophetic word of another (piggyback)

These activations will pair you with someone who is stronger and more experienced in the prophetic ministry. This will help you receive an impartation as you work with this partner. They can evaluate your prophetic flow and help you overcome any obstacles or challenges you experience as you begin to operate in the prophetic.

In this activation you will allow the more experienced person to go first in ministry, and you will follow them (piggyback) in ministering to the person. Listen carefully to them minister, allow the Holy Spirit to highlight a word or a phrase that they release, and then launch into the prophetic based on what the Holy Spirit highlights to you. You will simply move in the flow and strength of what has been released. Don't be intimidated. Simply speak what the Lord gives you after they turn it over to you.

Prophetic activation #42: initiate the prophetic word and then follow

In this activation you will go first, and the more experienced person will follow and expand on what you minister. This activation will help you see how much deeper the word that you began can go. You will then follow with a word that continues to expand what you originally began. These activations will teach you that the prophetic is like a river that continues to flow.

Prophetic activation #43: receive an impartation then prophesy

In this activation the more experienced prophetic person lays hands on you and releases an impartation by faith, then releases you to minister to the person. After receiving the impartation, launch into the prophetic flow and believe for a stronger release.

Prophetic activation #44: prophesy to the other prophetic minister, then to the third party

In this activation you will pray for the more experienced prophetic minister and encourage them with a word. After you share with them, you will turn and minister to the other person. This will stretch you to minister to more than one person.

Prophetic activation #45: receive a word and release a word

In this activation you allow the more experienced prophetic minister to minister to you, and then you will turn and minister to the other person. This activation will stir you because after you receive a word, you will be inspired to release a word.

Prophetic activation #46: insight from the more experienced minister

In this activation ask the more experienced prophetic minister for any instruction that can help you in your prophetic flow. The more experienced prophetic minister should be able to assist you in any adjustments you need to make, and then release you to minister again.

Prophetic activation #47: start, stop, start

In this activation you will start by praying and ministering to the third party, and when the more experienced minister says stop, you will stop, and then turn to the experienced minister and start to minster to them. When the minister says stop, you will then turn to the other person and resume ministering to them until you are told to stop. This activation helps us understand that the spirit of the prophet is subject to the prophet and that you can resume in the prophetic flow. (See 1 Corinthians 14:32.)

Prophetic activation #48: minister to both

In this activation have the other two hold hands, pray over them, and release a word to both at the same time. In other words, you are believing for a word that applies to both of them. This is a mini-corporate word. This helps to move you into the corporate flow. Some words are for individuals, and some are for groups.

Prophetic activation #49: release a word to the minister after they share

You will allow the more experienced minister to minister to the third party, and when they finish, you will minister again to the minister.

Your prophetic flow should be stronger by now, and the minister after receiving will minster to you. The word is usually an encouragement to you in your prophetic adventure. This also can be a time of more impartation from the more experienced minister.

Prophetic activation #50: release a word to the experienced minister and then the third party again—twice

You will begin by praying for and launching into the prophetic flow, beginning with the more experienced minister, then when the minister says, "Switch," you will turn and begin ministering to the third party. The experienced minister will say, "Switch," again, and you will return to ministering prophetically to the experienced minister. The minister will say "Switch," again and you will return to ministering to the third party. This activation will stretch you with the help of a more experienced prophetic minister.

CHAPTER 19

BIBLE-BASED ACTIVATIONS

All Scripture is inspired by God and is profitable for teaching, for reproof, for correction, and for instruction in righteousness, that the man of God may be complete, thoroughly equipped for every good work.
—2 TIMOTHY 3:16–17

I N ORDER TO take advantage of these next activations, you must have some basic knowledge about what different Bible symbols mean. These may be more for intermediate or advanced prophetic people who have had more time in the Word. It's important to understand that the Bible is a prophetic book and is full of prophetic symbols to launch from.

Prophetic activation #51: Bible names

The names of people in the Bible are very prophetic, and the Lord will often give a person a word using people in the Bible. The most common are Abraham, Joseph, Moses, Joshua, Samuel, David, Elijah, and Esther.

Begin this activation by praying for the person and asking the Lord to give you a Bible name, then launch into the prophetic. Even Jezebel can come up in referring to someone being delivered from the attacks of Jezebel. This activation will help the prophetic minister be open to God's use of names as symbols while prophesying. It is also possible to prophesy a new name over a person.

Prophetic activation #52: books of the Bible

Each book of the Bible carries a message or theme. For example:

- Genesis—the beginning
- Psalms—praise
- Proverbs—wisdom
- Galatians—liberty
- Revelation—the kingdom

Pray for the person and ask the Lord to give you a book of the Bible, then launch into the prophetic. This will require some basic knowledge of the books of the Bible. Sometimes you will call out the person's favorite Bible book, or even encourage them to study a certain book.

Prophetic activation #53: Bible minerals

God will often use minerals or elements (gold, silver, brass, diamond, ruby, emerald, wood) to give a message. Pray for the person and ask God to give you a mineral, then launch into the prophetic flow. This will require a basic knowledge of minerals, their meaning, and how they are referenced in the Bible.

Prophetic activation #54: Bible colors

Colors are also prophetic. Bible colors include:

- Purple—royalty
- White—purity
- Red—redemption
- Green—prosperity
- Black—mystery, hidden
- Blue—heavenly

Pray for the person and ask the Lord to give you a Bible color, then launch into the prophetic word. This activation will help the prophetic minister be open to God giving colors as symbols when prophesying.

Prophetic activation #55: Bible numbers

Numbers are also prophetic. Common biblical numbers include:

- One—beginning, God
- Two—double, witness, agreement
- Five—grace, goodness, favor
- Seven—completion
- Eight—new beginning
- Twelve—government, apostolic
- Thirteen—rebellion, lawlessness
- Forty—testing, trial, generation
- Fifty—jubilee, freedom, Holy Spirit, Pentecost
- One thousand—perfection

Ask the Lord to give you a Bible number and launch into the prophetic flow. This activation will help the prophetic ministry to be open to God showing numbers when ministering.

Prophetic activation #56: Bible elements

Elements are strong symbols of the prophetic. These include wind, fire, water, and earth. Pray for the person, asking the Lord to give you one of these elements, and launch into the prophetic flow. This can also include rivers, mountains, and storms.

Prophetic activation #57: Bible creatures

Eagles, lions, horses, hawks, ants, serpents, wolves, sheep, and others can all be prophetic symbols. Pray for the person, ask the Lord to give you a Bible creature, and launch into the prophetic flow. Each animal has a certain characteristic, and even a serpent can be a picture of wisdom. This activation will help the prophetic minister to be open to receive animals as symbols when ministering.

Prophetic activation #58: Bible miracles

There are many miracles in the Bible that have prophetic messages. One of my favorites is Lazarus being raised from the dead. Miracles of healing, deliverance, and provision are abundant in Scripture. Pray for the person, ask the Lord to give you a Bible miracle, and launch into the prophetic flow.

Prophetic activation #59: Bible sounds

Sounds like the sound of wind blowing, rain falling, praise, joy, war, trumpets, shouting, and clapping can also be prophetic. Pray for the person, listen as a sound is released in your ear, and launch into the prophetic flow. This activation will break the limitation of the prophetic minister from just hearing a word or seeing a picture.

BIBLE PROPHETS— NAMES AND MEANINGS

Amos—"burden bearer"

Anna—"favor" or "grace"

Asaph—"convener" or collector"

Barnabas—"son of consolation"

Daniel—"God is my Judge"

David—"beloved"

Elijah—"whose God is Jehovah"

Elisha—"God his salvation"

Ezekiel—"dedication"

Gad—"fortune"

Habakkuk—"God will strengthen"

Haggai—"embrace"

Heman—"faithful"

Hosea—"salvation"

Isaiah—"festive"

Jeduthun—"lauder" or "praising"

Jeremiah—"raised up or appointed by Jehovah"

Joel—"Jehovah is his God"

Jonah—"a dove"

Malachi—"messenger" or "angel"

Micah—"who is like Jehovah"

Micaiah—"who is like Jah"

Nahum—"consolation"

Nathan—"gift from God"

Obadiah—"servant of the Lord"

Samuel—"heard of God"

Zechariah—"Jehovah is renowned or remembered"

Zephaniah—"the Lord conceals"

Prophetic activation #60: Bible prophets

Each Bible prophet is unique and symbolizes a different aspect of the prophetic ministry. There are also lesser-known prophets such as Asaph, Heman, and Jeduthun—all musical prophets. There are also governmental prophets such as Daniel, Elijah, Isaiah, Ezekiel, Jeremiah, and John, prophets whom most believers are familiar with. Pray for the person, ask the Lord to give you a biblical prophet, and launch into the prophetic flow.

> As we eat the Lord, enjoy Him, drink Him, breathe Him in, and meet with the saints, there's something bubbling in us, some words that are coming out of us for building up! As we practice to speak in the meetings again and again, we are perfected in our prophesying for the building up of the church as the Body of Christ.
>
> —STEFAN MISARAS[1]

CHAPTER 20

PROPHETIC PRAYER ACTIVATIONS

Pray in the Spirit always with all kinds of prayer and supplication.
—EPHESIANS 6:18

THIS NEXT SET of activations are some of the easiest activations to do because everybody can pray. Prayer is like a bridge into the prophetic. These are prophetic prayer activations that serve as a foundation to launch into the prophetic flow. These activations help the minister to pray prophetically. Often when you are praying for people, God will begin to give you a word for them. Learning to pray prophetically is basically praying what God is revealing to you at the time. This is spontaneous-type prayer, or praying by inspiration, then releasing what God is saying.

Prophetic activation #61: finances

This activation includes praying prophetically for the person's finances. Allow the Holy Spirit to give you what to pray. You may be inspired to pray for increase, business, saving, adjustments, debt, investments, new job, new career, and the like. You can then launch into the prophetic word concerning their finances.

Prophetic activation #62: health

This activation includes praying for someone's health. Allow the Holy Spirit to give you what to pray. You may be inspired to pray for healing, strength, restoration, rest, stress, eating habits, tiredness, and other things that affect a person's health. You can then launch into the prophetic flow.

Prophetic activation #63: ministry

This activation includes praying for the person's place in the body of Christ. Focus on Romans 12, Ephesians 4, and 1 Corinthians 12—the chapters in the Bible that outline the gifts and ministries of the Spirit—and allow the Holy Spirit to give you what to pray. You can be inspired to pray for their ministry, calling, gifts (revelation, power, utterance), and anointing. You can then launch into the prophetic flow.

Prophetic activation #64: family

This activation includes praying for the person's family. Allow the Holy Spirit to give you what to pray. You can be inspired to pray for salvation, unity, marriages, children, men, women, and other things related to the family. You can then launch into the prophetic flow.

Prophetic activation #65: city

This activation includes praying for the city the person is from. Allow the Lord to give you what to pray. You may be inspired to pray for the economy, educational system, youth, churches, spiritual climate, and so on. You can then launch into the prophetic flow.

Prophetic activation #66: destiny

This activation includes praying for the person's destiny and future. Allow the Lord to give you what to pray. You may be inspired to pray for their purpose, path, decisions, relationships, doors, career, and so on. You can then launch into the prophetic flow.

Prophetic activation #67: relationships

This activation includes praying for the person's relations. Allow the Lord to give you what to pray. You may be inspired to pray for new relationships, old relationships, broken relationships, restored relationships, bad relationships, and the like. You can then launch into the prophetic flow.

Prophetic activation #68: marital status

This activation includes praying for the person's marital status (married, single, or divorced). Allow the Lord to give you what to pray. You may be inspired to pray for restoration, patience, healing, blessing, and the like. You can then launch into the prophetic flow.

Prophetic activation #69: career

This activation includes praying for the person's career. Allow the Lord to give you what to pray. You may be inspired to pray for promotion, a new career, employment, change in career, education, and the like. You can then launch into the prophetic flow.

Prophetic activation #70: dreams and vision

This activation includes praying for the person's dreams and vision for their life. Allow the Lord to give you what to pray. You may be inspired to pray for a wide variety of things because there are so many different dreams and hopes that people carry. You can then launch into the prophetic flow.

CHAPTER 21

Prophetic Songs and Worship Activations

Speak to one another in psalms, hymns, and spiritual songs,
singing and making melody in your heart to the Lord.
—Ephesians 5:19

THESE ACTIVATIONS REQUIRE singing. You do not have to be a great singer to participate. Prophecy can be spoken or sung. These activations will help the prophetic minister flow in the various songs of the Lord. Every praise and worship team should be activated this way. The song of the Lord is simply the Lord Jesus singing through us to the person, revealing His heart to them. Prophetic songs are powerful because they go deep into the heart of the recipient.

Prophetic activation #71: new song

This activation is simple and requires you to sing a new song. Ask the Lord for a melody or follow a minstrel, and launch into the prophetic song.

Prophetic activation #72: song of love

This is simply a love song from the Lord to the person you are ministering to. Speak the love of God over the person and launch into the prophetic flow. Allow the Lord to sing about His love for the person through your voice.

Prophetic activation #73: song of encouragement

This song is to encourage the person. Ask the Lord what area the person needs encouragement in, and launch into a prophetic song of encouragement. Allow the Lord to sing through you a song of encouragement.

Prophetic activation #74: song of healing

Ask the Lord what areas the person needs healing in—physical, emotional, the past, and the like—and launch into a prophetic song of healing. Miracles of healing can occur through this activation, and it trains the minister to be sensitive in this area of ministering to the hurts and pains of people.

Prophetic activation #75: song of deliverance

Ask the Lord what area the person may need deliverance in—hurt, fear, rejection, unforgiveness, and so on. Use wisdom in this area, for there may be things you do not have to call out by name, then launch into the prophetic song about freedom, liberation, chains being broken, feet untied, or whatever the Lord leads you to sing to bring deliverance to the person's life. God sends His word to heal and deliver (Ps. 107:20).

> Thou art my hiding place; thou shalt preserve me from trouble; thou shalt compass me about with songs of deliverance. Selah.
>
> —Psalm 32:7, kjv

Prophetic activation #76: song of commendation

This song commends what the person is doing right or good. Ask the Lord what areas He wants to commend the person, and then launch into the prophetic song. God often speaks well over us through the prophetic song.

Prophetic activation #77: song of victory

The prophet Moses sang a song of victory after coming through the Red Sea (Exod. 15:1). Ask the Lord in what area He wants to bring victory to the person's life, and launch into the prophetic song. This song will celebrate the victory of the Lord in the person's life.

Prophetic activation #78: song of ascent

Songs of Ascent (Psalms 120–134) were songs that Israel sang when they were ascending to Jerusalem to worship. This song calls the person to move up higher in different areas of their life. Ask the Lord in what areas He wants the person to come higher—faith, hope, love, worship, prayer, holiness—and launch into the prophetic song. This song will challenge the person to ascend into a new place.

Prophetic activation #79: scripture song

This is simply singing over them from the Scriptures. Select a scripture that the Lord lays on your heart and begin to sing it over the person, and then launch from there into the prophetic song. This trains the prophetic minister to be open to using Scripture in singing the song of the Lord.

> Thy statutes have been my songs in the house of my pilgrimage.
>
> —Psalm 119:54, kjv

Prophetic activation #80: song of restoration

Ask the Lord what area the person may need restoration in, and then speak restoration over them (i.e., finances, health, relationships, family, ministry) and allow the Lord to sing through you a song of restoration. Much of the prophetic ministry has to do with restoration, and this activation will train the prophetic minister to be a vessel of restoration.

CHAPTER 22

ACTIVATIONS THAT INVOLVE MOVEMENT AND DEMONSTRATION

My speech and my preaching was not with enticing words of man's wisdom, but in demonstration of the Spirit and of power.
—1 CORINTHIANS 2:4

T HESE ACTIVATIONS INVOLVE movement and demonstration. Prophetic people can use movement. An example of this is when Elisha told the king to take arrows and smite the ground before he released a prophetic word. In this prophetic demonstration the prophet Elisha used movement and action to show the king what it would take for him to see victory over his enemy:

Now Elisha had become sick with the illness of which he would die. So Joash the king of Israel went down to him and wept before him, and said, "My father, my father, the chariot of Israel and its horsemen."

Elisha said to him, "Take a bow and arrows." So he took a bow and arrows. Then he said to the king of Israel, "Draw the bow." So he drew it. Elisha put his hands on the king's hands.

Then he said, "Open the east window." So he opened it. Then Elisha said, "Shoot." So he shot. Then he said, "The arrow of the deliverance of the LORD, and the arrow of deliverance from Aram; for *you must strike Aram in Aphek until you have destroyed them.*"

Then he said, "Take the arrows." So he took them. Then he said to the king of Israel, "Strike the ground." So he struck it three times and stood there. Then the man of God was angry with him and said, "You should have struck it five or six times. Then you would have stricken Aram until you had finished them. Now you will strike Aram just three times."
—2 KINGS 13:14–19, EMPHASIS ADDED

The activations in this chapter will help the prophetic minister to be sensitive to inspired movements that God sometimes uses in demonstrating a prophetic word. We have seen prophets use all kinds of movements in delivering the word with powerful results.

Prophetic activation #81: stomp the feet

Stomping the feet can symbolize crushing the enemy, putting your foot down, and the like. Have the person you are ministering to stomp their feet, and then launch in the prophetic flow.

Prophetic activation #82: lift the hands

Lifting the hands can represent worship, surrender to God, or the Lord lifting us. Lift the person's hands, receive a word, and launch into the prophetic flow.

Prophetic activation #83: turnaround

Turn the person around, receive a word, and launch into the prophetic flow. Words of turnaround are powerful in causing a person to see divine turnaround.

Prophetic activation #84: one step forward

Have the person you are ministering to take one step forward; then receive a word and launch into the prophetic flow. This can represent stepping out of old things, moving forward, stepping into new realms, and so on.

Prophetic activation #85: open the hands

Have the person open their hands, receive a word, and launch into the prophetic flow. Open hands can symbolize receiving from God, opening up to God, releasing your gifts, and so on.

Prophetic activation #86: pouring

Put your hands above the person's head and move as if you are pouring something on their head, receive a word, and launch into the prophetic flow. This can represent outpouring, new oil and new water coming upon the person, or the Lord filling them up.

Prophetic activation #87: loosing the hands

Have the person put their hands together, then loose them quickly. Receive a word, and launch into the prophetic flow. This can symbolize God loosing their hands for ministry, for finances, for healing, and so on.

Prophetic activation #88: hands on shoulder

Place your hand on their shoulder, receive a word, and launch into the prophetic flow. The shoulders represent carrying a burden, a ministry, a responsibility, and the like.

Prophetic activation #89: crown them

Symbolically place a crown on their head, receive a word, and launch into the prophetic flow. God can crown people with glory, honor, authority, favor, and the like.

Prophetic activation #90: circle the person

Walk around the person, receive a word, and launch into the prophetic flow. Circling a person can represent protection, presence, walls coming down, and the like.

CHAPTER 23

ACTIVATIONS PROMPTED
BY COMMON OBJECTS

*So handkerchiefs or aprons he had touched were brought to the sick,
and the diseases left them, and the evil spirits went out of them.*

—ACTS 19:12

THESE ACTIVATIONS USE objects that are common in prophetic churches, such as dance teams, to help the minister with inspiration in using common objects that are prophetic. There are many objects you can use. These are generally used by prophetic churches in worship.

Prophetic activation #91: use a fan

Use a fan or a piece of paper to fan the person, receive a word, and launch into the prophetic flow. Fans produce wind and can represent stirring, kindling, refreshing, breath, or wind.

Prophetic activation #92: anoint with oil

Anoint the person with oil, receive a word, and launch into the prophetic flow. You can anoint the forehead (thinking), ears (hearing), throat (speaking, singing), hands (ministering), or feet (travel, walking). These words often release a new anointing or stir up the anointing upon the recipient.

Prophetic activation #93: use a sword

Place a sword in the person's hand, receive a word, and launch into the prophetic flow. The sword represents battle, authority, angelic intervention, or cutting.

Prophetic activation #94: use a shofar

Place a shofar in the hand of the person, receive a word, and launch into the prophetic flow. A shofar is a trumpet representing gathering, warning, calling, warfare, victory, and the like.

Prophetic activation #95: use a tambourine

Place a tambourine in the hand of the person, receive a prophetic word, and launch into the prophetic flow. The tambourine reprints praise, celebration, or victory.

Prophetic activation #96: use a banner or flag

Place a small banner or flag in the hand of the person, receive a word, and launch into the prophetic flow. Flags and banners represent armies, victory, and the Lord Our Banner (Jehovah Nissi).

Prophetic activation #97: use a mantle

A mantle is a cloak that was worn by the prophets. Use a coat or cloth and place it on the person's shoulders, receive a word, and launch into the prophetic flow. Mantles represent anointings, callings, coverings, or spiritual garments.

Prophetic activation #98: use a badge

A badge represents authority. Place the badge in the person's hand, receive a word, and launch into the prophetic flow. Badges can also represent rank, access, or power.

Prophetic activation #99: use a fruit

Fruit can represent character, sweetness, and prosperity. Put the fruit in the hand of the person, receive a word, and launch into the prophetic flow.

Prophetic activation #100: use a candle

Use a candle (don't light it!), put it in the person's hand, receive a word, and launch into the prophetic flow. Candles represent light, illumination, and the spirit of a man.

CHAPTER 24

ACTIVATIONS PROMPTED BY FOUNDATIONAL SCRIPTURE PASSAGES

For the word of God is alive, and active, and sharper than any two-edged sword, piercing even to the division of soul and spirit, of joints and marrow, and able to judge the thoughts and intents of the heart.

—HEBREWS 4:12

THESE ACTIVATIONS USE scriptures that are highly prophetic as a foundation for ministering to others. The prophetic minister will benefit from these activations by being sensitive to using Scripture as a means to launch into the prophetic flow.

Prophetic activation #101: Psalm 23

The LORD is my shepherd; I shall not want.
> He makes me lie down in green pastures;
He leads me beside still waters.
> He restores my soul;
He leads me in paths of righteousness
> for His name's sake.
Even though I walk
> through the valley of the shadow of death,
I will fear no evil;
> for You are with me;
Your rod and Your staff,
> they comfort me.
You prepare a table before me
> in the presence of my enemies;
You anoint my head with oil;
> my cup runs over.
Surely goodness and mercy shall follow me
> all the days of my life,

and I will dwell in the house of the LORD
> forever.

Allow the Holy Spirit to illuminate a portion of this psalm to speak to the person. There are fourteen points in this psalm you can launch from. They are:

1. The shepherd
2. No lack
3. Green pastures, which represent a place of feeding or prosperity
4. Lie down, rest
5. Restoration
6. Path of righteousness
7. No fear
8. Comfort
9. Overcoming your enemies
10. A fresh anointing or being anointed
11. Overflow
12. Goodness
13. Mercy
14. House of the Lord

Which of these points does the Holy Spirit highlight to you? Psalm 23 is the most recognizable psalm in Scripture, and this psalm has ministered to most people at one time or another. Read the psalm, and launch into the prophetic flow. This activation helps the prophetic minister to launch from Scripture.

Prophetic activation #102: Psalm 27
This activation is taken from Psalm 27:1–6:

> The LORD is my light and my salvation;
> > whom will I fear?
> The LORD is the strength of my life;
> > of whom will I be afraid?
> When the wicked came against me
> > to eat my flesh—
> my enemies and my foes—
> > they stumbled and fell.
> Though an army should encamp against me,
> > my heart will not fear;
> though war should rise against me,

in this will I be confident.
One thing I have asked from the LORD,
    that will I seek after—
for me to dwell in the house of the LORD
    all the days of my life,
to see the beauty of the LORD,
    and to inquire in His temple.
For in the time of trouble
    He will hide me in His pavilion;
in the shelter of His tabernacle He will hide me;
    He will set me up on a rock.
Now my head will be lifted up
    above my enemies encircling me;
therefore I will offer sacrifices of joy in His tabernacle;
    I will sing, yes, I will sing praises to the LORD.

There are at least thirteen points in this psalm you can launch from; they are:

1. No fear
2. Strength
3. Overcoming your enemies
4. Confidence
5. The beauty of the Lord
6. Being hidden by God
7. Exaltation—head lifted up above your enemies
8. Mercy
9. Seeking God
10. Help
11. Being led by God
12. Faith
13. Waiting on the Lord

Which points in the psalm does the Holy Spirit highlight to you as you read the scripture over the person you are ministering to? Launch into the prophetic flow when the Holy Spirit quickens a portion of this psalm to you.

Prophetic activation #103: Isaiah 60
This activation is taken from Isaiah 60:1–5:

Arise, shine, for your light has come,
and the glory of the LORD has risen upon you.
For the darkness shall cover the earth
and deep darkness the peoples;
but the LORD shall rise upon you,
and His glory shall be seen upon you.
The nations shall come to your light
and kings to the brightness of your rising.
Lift up your eyes all around, and see:
They all gather themselves together; they come to you;
your sons shall come from afar,
and your daughters shall be carried at your side.
Then you shall see and be radiant,
and your heart shall thrill and rejoice
because the abundance of the sea shall be converted to you,
the wealth of the nations shall come to you.

These scriptures highlight the glory. There are at least thirteen points in this portion of Scripture you can launch from. They are:

1. Arising
2. Shining
3. The glory of the Lord
4. Overcoming darkness
5. People attracted to the light in your life
6. Leaders coming
7. Sons and daughters coming, people gathering to you
8. Enlargement
9. Abundance
10. Conversion
11. Wealth
12. Nations coming
13. Joy

Which point does the Holy Spirit highlight? Read the verses over the person, and launch into the prophetic flow.

Prophetic activation #104: Psalm 29
This activation is taken from Psalm 29:3–9:

The voice of the Lord is over the waters;
>   the God of glory thunders;
>   the Lord is over many waters.
The voice of the Lord sounds with strength;
>   the voice of the Lord—with majesty.
The voice of the Lord breaks the cedars;
>   the Lord breaks the cedars of Lebanon.
He makes them skip like a calf,
>   Lebanon and Sirion like a wild ox.
The voice of the Lord flashes
>   like flames of fire.
The voice of the Lord shakes the wilderness;
>   the Lord shakes the Wilderness of Kadesh.
The voice of the Lord makes the deer to give birth,
>   and strips the forests bare;
and in His temple everyone says, "Glory!

This passage emphasizes the voice of the Lord. Read the passage over the person you are ministering to, and launch into the prophetic flow. Be sensitive to the points the Holy Spirit highlights to you.

Prophetic activation #105: Joel 3

This activation is taken from Joel 3:18:

And it will be that in that day the mountains will drip sweet
>   wine,
>   and the hills will flow with milk,
>   and all the streambeds of Judah will flow with water;
a spring will proceed from the house of the Lord
>   and will water the Valley of Shittim.

This verse is chosen because it's rich in prophetic imagery. There are at least six points you can launch from. They are:

1. New wine
2. Milk, which represents prosperity
3. Rivers of Judah, praise
4. Water or refreshing
5. Fountain, life
6. Water in dry places

Read the verse over the person you are ministering to, and launch into the prophetic flow. Be sensitive to the points the Holy Spirit highlights. This activation will help the prophetic minister use Scripture, which is rich in symbolism.

Prophetic activation #106: the river of God—Psalm 46:4–5; John 7:37–38

Using a theme that is common in the prophetic, this activation is based on the river of God. Read these verses over the person you are ministering to, allow the Holy Spirit to highlight a portion, and then launch into the prophetic flow.

> There is a river whose streams make glad the city of God, the holy dwelling place of the Most High. God is in the midst of her; she will not be moved; God will help her in the early dawn.
>
> —Psalm 46:4–5

> On the last and greatest day of the feast, Jesus stood and cried out, "If anyone is thirsty, let him come to Me and drink. He who believes in Me, as the Scripture has said, out of his heart shall flow rivers of living water."
>
> —John 7:37–38

Prophetic activation #107: dry bones—Ezekiel 37:1–10

This activation emphasizes the life-giving aspect of the prophetic and another common prophetic theme of dry bones coming to life. Read the verses over the person, allow the Lord to highlight some point, and launch into the prophetic flow.

> The hand of the Lord was upon me, and He carried me out in the Spirit of the Lord and set me down in the midst of the valley which was full of bones, and He caused me to pass among them all around. And there were very many in the open valley. And they were very dry. He said to me, "Son of man, can these bones live?"
>
> And I answered, "O Lord God, You know."
>
> Again He said to me, "Prophesy over these bones and say to them, O dry bones, hear the word of the Lord. Thus says the Lord God to these bones: I will cause breath to enter you so that you live. And I will lay sinews upon you and will grow back flesh upon you and cover you with skin and put breath in you so that you live. Then you shall know that I am the Lord."
>
> So I prophesied as I was commanded. And as I prophesied, there was a noise and a shaking. And the bones came together, bone to its bone. When I looked, the sinews and the flesh grew upon them, and the skin covered them. But there was no breath in them.

Then He said to me, "Prophesy to the wind; prophesy, son of man, and say to the wind: Thus says the Lord GOD: Come from the four winds, O breath, and breathe upon these slain so that they live." So I prophesied as He commanded me, and the breath came into them, and they lived and stood up upon their feet, an exceeding great army.

Prophetic activation #108: new thing—Isaiah 42:9; 43:19; 48:6

This activation is based on "new thing" scriptures in Isaiah. Prophecy releases new things. Read these verses over the person you are ministering to, allow the Holy Spirit to highlight one of the points, and then launch into the prophetic flow.

See, the former things have come to pass, and new things I declare; before they spring forth I tell you of them.

—ISAIAH 42:9

See, I will do a new thing, now it shall spring forth; shall you not be aware of it? I will even make a way in the wilderness, and rivers in the desert.

—ISAIAH 43:19

You have heard; see all this. And will you not declare it? I have shown you new things from this time, even hidden things, and you did not know them.

—ISAIAH 48:6

Prophetic activation #109: the eagle—Exodus 19:4; Psalm 103:5; Isaiah 40:31

This activation uses eagle scriptures to launch. The eagle is a symbol of the prophetic, and the Lord uses this creature often in prophetic utterances. Read the verses over the person you are ministering to, allow the Lord to give you a word, and launch into the prophetic flow. This activation helps the prophetic minister to be sensitive to the symbols of creatures used in the prophetic flow.

You have seen what I did to the Egyptians, and how I lifted you up on eagles' wings, and brought you to Myself.

—EXODUS 19:4

...who satisfies your mouth with good things, so that your youth is renewed like the eagle's.

—PSALM 103:5

...but those who wait upon the LORD shall renew their strength; they shall mount up with wings as eagles, they shall run and not be weary, and they shall walk and not faint.

—ISAIAH 40:31

Prophetic activation #110: the lion—Genesis 49:9; Proverbs 28:1; 30:30; Amos 3:8; Hebrews 11:33

This activation is based on scriptures with the word *lion*. The lion is another symbol that is often used in prophetic utterances. Read the scriptures over the person, allow the Holy Spirit to highlight, and then launch in the prophetic flow.

> Judah is a lion's cub; from the prey, my son, you have gone up. He crouches and lies down like a lion; and as a lion, who dares rouse him?
>
> —Genesis 49:9

> The wicked flee when no man pursues, but the righteous are bold as a lion.
>
> —Proverbs 28:1

> ...a lion which is strongest among beasts, and does not turn away for any.
>
> —Proverbs 30:30

> The lion has roared; who will not fear? The Lord God has spoken; who can but prophesy?
>
> —Amos 3:8

> ...who through faith subdued kingdoms, administered justice, obtained promises, stopped the mouths of lions.
>
> —Hebrews 11:33

Faith Activations Based on the Word

I call these faith activations because they use scriptures on faith to launch into the prophetic flow. Faith is such an important part of the believer's life that God often speaks to us in this area, and prophetic ministers often challenge people in the area of faith through the prophetic word. These activations use a portion of faith scriptures as diving boards to get into the prophetic flow.

Prophetic activation #111: Luke 1:37

> For with God nothing will be impossible.

This activation launches on Luke 1:37. Speak this word over the recipient, and launch into the prophetic flow. Many prophecies call people to believe for the impossible. This activation will sharpen the prophetic minister's sensitivity to the importance of faith when prophesying.

Prophetic activation #112: Matthew 17:20

> Faith as a grain of mustard seed...

What a powerful word from the mouth of Jesus. Speak this over the recipient, and launch into the prophetic flow. There are an infinite number of words that can be given in the context of this scripture.

Prophetic activation #113: Mark 11:22

Have faith in God.

This is another activation that challenges the recipient in the area of faith. Speak these words over the recipient, and launch into the prophetic flow. Prophecy can encourage people to believe for miracles and great breakthroughs.

Prophetic activation #114: Mark 9:23

All things are possible to him who believes.

Speak this word over the recipient, receive a word, and launch into the prophetic flow. The prophetic word can move people into the realm of possibility.

Prophetic activation #115: 2 Corinthians 5:7

For we walk by faith, not by sight.

Speak this word over the recipient, receive a word, then step into the prophetic flow. This is another activation that tunes the prophetic minister's ears to hear and release words about faith and believing.

CHAPTER 25

CORPORATE MINISTRY ACTIVATIONS

*But the manifestation of the Spirit is given
to everyone for the common good.*
—1 CORINTHIANS 12:7

THESE GROUP ACTIVATIONS will stretch you to be able to minster to more than one person. They will help increase your flow and your faith. Requiring flexibility and spontaneity, they will show you how to switch and change from ministering to one person and then moving on quickly to the next person with a fresh word specifically for them. This group of activations increases faith because the prophet will have to receive a word for more than one person. These activations won't leave you much time to think or have your mind interfere with what's happening in the spirit.

Prophetic activation #116: around the circle

Form a circle of about three to seven people. The team leader selects a person who will prophesy to the circle member directly to his/her left or right. The person who receives ministry then ministers to the person on his/her other side. This chainlike ministry continues all the way around the circle. This activation requires everyone in the circle to minister, and everyone receives a word.

Prophetic activation #117: all on one

Each person in the circle takes a turn in ministering to one circle member. The result will be an in-depth ministry to a single person. This activation demonstrates the flow of prophetic ministry, and activates the prophetic minister to operate with a team.

Prophetic activation #118: one on all

This activation is designed to "stretch" a minister past his/her usual limitations. The minister is required to prophesy to each member of the circle. This exercise will build faith and confidence in the minister.

Prophetic activation #119: one prophetic word

A minister is required to give a single prophetic word to everyone in his/her circle. Each circle member ministers in this way. Circle members are to write down only the words that were given directly to them by the others. After everyone in the circle has ministered, each circle member is to read each of the words that were spoken and determine what the Lord is saying through all the words put together.

Prophetic activation #120: switch/change

At the command of the group leader the person will switch/change between two people he/she is ministering to. Sometimes the change will be quick at the command of the leader, and sometimes slow. A quick change helps develop accuracy and quick concentration, and a slow change will force the prophetic ministry to go deeper and longer. The spontaneous switching of ministers will exercise the ministers' ability to hold a prophetic word and their ability to minister at a moment's notice. The team leader simply says, "Switch," and the minister turns and ministers to the next person, and when "Switch" is said again, the minister returns to ministering to the first person.

Prophetic activation #121: group prophecy

A minister from the circle is chosen to give a common prophecy that pertains to all the circle members. This exercise is designed to help the minister become comfortable with ministering to whole groups of people such as a congregation.

Prophetic activation #122: popcorn

The team leader will select a minister and up to five circle members. The prophetic minister is required to prophesy to all five within three minutes. The leader will stop the minister when time is up. The time limit and number of words to the five people may vary, but it must be completed in three minutes. This exercise helps overcome timidity and thought interference. This forces the minister to "dive in" and flow from their spirit when prophesying.

Prophetic activation #123: tunnel

Form two lines with circle members facing each other. Select one person to walk between the lines. As the person walks between the lines, each person will lay hands on them and prophesy. Those at the end of the line "tunnel" should listen to the words that come before their turn comes to minister and then launch into the prophetic flow when the person arrives to them.

Prophetic activation #124: one word, develop the word

In this activation the prophetic minister again gives one word to each member of the group. The members write down the word. After giving a single word to each of the members, the prophetic minister then returns to the first person and develops the word, launching into the prophetic flow from that one word. The minister continues this with each member in the group until completing the circle.

Prophetic activation #125: the blind prophet

The prophetic minister turns his/her back to the group. Each group member steps up behind the person one at a time. The prophetic minister releases a word to the person whom they are unable to see. This "stretches" the prophetic minister to prophesy by faith and not to be moved by what they see (or don't see).

PART IV

STAY IN THE FLOW

CHAPTER 26

Resist the Urge to Run

Now the word of the LORD came to Jonah son of Amittai,
saying, "Get up, go to Nineveh, the great city, and cry out against
it, because their wickedness has come up before Me." But Jonah
got up to flee to Tarshish from the presence of the LORD.

—JONAH 1:1–3

THE LORD GAVE me a word in this season for all the Jonahs: Stop running from your call and assignment; you will end up in the belly of a whale. As soon as you obey, that whale will spit you out so you can complete your assignment.

Where shall I go from Your spirit, or where shall I flee from Your presence? If I ascend to heaven, You are there; if I make my bed in Sheol, You are there. If I take the wings of the morning and dwell at the end of the sea, even there Your hand shall guide me, and Your right hand shall take hold of me.

If I say, "Surely the darkness shall cover me, and the light shall be as night about me," even the darkness is not dark to You, but the night shines as the day, for the darkness is like light to You.

—PSALM 139:7–12

ARE YOU A JONAH?

Are you a prophet on the run? Are you running away from your assignment to speak the word of the Lord? Are you running from the presence of the Lord? Are you hiding? You can run, but you cannot hide from God.

The Lord is calling the Jonahs. You will not be the first and you will not be the last. There are Jonahs in every generation. There are prophets running from God today. Don't be a prophet on the run. You have been called to bless your generation. Don't run and hide from the call. Embrace it and obey God today.

For those who don't want to speak for the Lord, I pray that His word in your heart will be like fire shut up in your bones (Jer. 20:9)!

God told Jonah to arise and go to Nineveh. Jonah instead went the other way. Jonah ran from the presence of the Lord. There are many prophets who are like Jonah. I call them prophets on the run. They sense and know the call of God to be a prophet, but they say, "I cannot handle that calling."

If you are a prophet on the run, then you know that you cannot hide from God. You cannot hide in the bottom of the ship like Jonah. You cannot hide from the presence of the Lord.

In Psalm 139:8–9, 12 David wrote, "If I ascend to heaven, You are there; if I make my bed in Sheol, You are there. If I take the wings of the morning and dwell at the end of the sea…even the darkness is not dark to You, but the night shines as the day, for the darkness is like light to You."

Even the darkness cannot hide from God. Jonah tried to hide, but God knew where he was. God knows where His Jonahs are. He knows where every prophet is.

ARISE AND GO TO NINEVEH!

Jonah did go to Nineveh. Jonah did speak the word of the Lord to that city. The results were astonishing. The whole city repented and was spared.

Jonah's assignment was to speak to a city. What is your assignment? How many lives hang in the balance as a result of your calling? How many people will be blessed when you obey God?

This is a call for the Jonahs to arise and go to Nineveh. Where is your Nineveh? Whom are you sent to? These are questions every prophet has to answer.

YOUR JONAH EXPERIENCE HAS PROPHETIC SIGNIFICANCE

Even Jonah's experience was prophetic. He was in the belly of the whale three days and three nights. This was a picture of Christ being in the heart of the earth three days and three nights.

> For as Jonah was three days and three nights in the belly of the great fish, so will the Son of Man be three days and three nights in the heart of the earth.
>
> —MATTHEW 12:40

When you are prophetic, even your experiences will be prophetic. Jonah was prophetic even when he was running away from the call. Prophet, you can't escape. You have been designed by God to be a prophet. You will see things even when you are running from the call.

> Then they said to Jonah, "What shall we do to you, so that the sea may quiet down for us?" For the sea was growing stormier. So Jonah said to them, "Pick me up and toss me into the sea. Then the sea will

quiet down for you. For I know that it is on my account this great
storm has come upon you."

—JONAH 1:11–12

Jonah knew what was going on when the storm came. The men on the ship
did not know, but Jonah knew. Prophets know when they are running. They
know the trouble of running from the call. Jonah told the men to throw him
overboard. Then he was swallowed by a big fish. Jonah cried out to God from
the belly of the big fish. He promised God he would pay his vows.

Prophets, many of you have vowed to serve and obey the Lord, but you are
running the other way. It is time to keep your vows, promises, dedications,
obligations....

But I will sacrifice to You with the voice of thanksgiving; I will pay
what I have vowed. Salvation is of the LORD!

—JONAH 2:9

Your vows are on me, O God; I will complete them with thank
offerings to You.

—PSALM 56:12

The story of Jonah shows us the importance of the call of the prophet.
Prophets are different. Prophets are unique. Prophets don't ask to be called or
chosen. Prophets are called from the womb. Prophets pay a price for running
and hiding. Jonah ended up in the belly of a great fish.

NECESSITY IS LAID UPON YOU

Though I preach the gospel, I have nothing to boast of, for the
requirement is laid upon me. Yes, woe unto me if I do not preach the
gospel!

—1 CORINTHIANS 9:16

Arise and obey, Jonah. Don't get yourself in trouble. Necessity is laid upon you.
You have to obey God. You have to arise. Jonah prayed and God brought him
out of the fish's belly. God will bring you forth when you pray.

There are many ministers who have accepted the call to preach but are
running from the prophetic calling. Maybe your group does not believe in
prophets. Maybe you have seen people call themselves prophets who did not
have good character. Maybe you have seen false prophets. These are reasons
why some run from the call.

God is calling and transitioning many of His ministers. Many have been
called to be prophets, but they are fearful. Don't be a Jonah. Don't run from
the call. Embrace it. The prophet's ministry is designed to bring deliverance and
salvation to many. Nineveh was spared and blessed because Jonah went there.

No Excuses for Prophets

The call to be a prophet can seem intimidating. The prophet's call is a great responsibility. Some prophets come up with excuses, but God does not want to hear them.

Jeremiah said, "I am too young." Moses said, "I am not eloquent." God answered them both.

> And Moses said unto the LORD, O my LORD, I am not eloquent, neither heretofore, nor since thou hast spoken unto thy servant: but I am slow of speech, and of a slow tongue. And the LORD said unto him, Who hath made man's mouth? or who maketh the dumb, or deaf, or the seeing, or the blind? have not I the LORD?
> —EXODUS 4:10–11, KJV

> But the LORD said unto me, Say not, I am a child: for thou shalt go to all that I shall send thee, and whatsoever I command thee thou shalt speak.
> —JEREMIAH 1:7, KJV

God will make a way for you too, and He will back you up when He calls you. God's grace is sufficient. Don't be afraid. You can do this.

Appeal to the Jonahs

If you have been running, then you need to repent and turn around. Don't waste another day not doing what God has called you to do. Make a decision today. Obey God. Don't obey your flesh. Don't submit to your fears. Don't be rebellious. Repent before it is too late. Repent like Jonah. Jonah cried unto the Lord, and God heard him. It is better to say no, and then turn around, than to say yes and never do it. Notice the parable of Jesus in Matthew's Gospel:

> But what think ye? A certain man had two sons; and he came to the first, and said, Son, go work to day in my vineyard. He answered and said, I will not: but afterward he repented, and went. And he came to the second, and said likewise. And he answered and said, I go, sir: and went not. Whether of them twain did the will of his father? They say unto him, The first. Jesus saith unto them, Verily I say unto you, That the publicans and the harlots go into the kingdom of God before you.
> —MATTHEW 21:28–31, KJV

The son who said, "I will not," but later repented and went into the vineyard did the will of his father. Repent and do the will of the Father. Go into the vineyard and work.

PRAYERS OF REPENTANCE FOR JONAHS

Lord, I repent for running from my calling. I will turn around and obey the call. I will not be rebellious anymore. I will not allow fear or rebellion to cause me to run from the prophet's call. I submit my life to You, Lord. I submit my tongue to speak Your word. I submit my eyes to see Your vision. I submit my life and time to being a prophetic voice. I accept my assignment and the grace I need to fulfill it. I will not be a Jonah. I will go to my Nineveh. I will speak Your word. Let any trouble I have experienced in running from the call leave my life. Let Your peace return to my life. Let Your joy return to my life. I renounce and turn away from any behavior that is contrary to the prophet's call. I turn away from any religious tradition that would keep me from obeying this call. I will not be afraid to do what I have been sent to do.

CHAPTER 27

STAND STRONG AGAINST OPPOSITION

*Therefore take up the whole armor of God that you may be able
to resist in the evil day, and having done all, to stand.*
—EPHESIANS 6:13

As a prophet you will run into opposition. The Lord will put you in situations where you must overcome things such as fear, criticism, rejection, jealous people, and the like. This is a part of the consequence of such a strong anointing. The Lord will build courage in you. You will have to make decisions that some people won't agree with. You will have to take a stand. You cannot please everyone, and you may lose some relationships.

But more than the people you see, realize that the battles you face to maintain your anointing have more to do with what you don't see. The Bible says that "our fight is not against flesh and blood, but against principalities, against powers, against the rulers of the darkness of this world, and against spiritual forces of evil in the heavenly places" (Eph. 6:12). This verse is about the devil and his demons.

Demons hate prophets. Witches and warlocks hate prophets. Jezebel hates prophets. Prophets are a threat to the works of darkness. Prophets expose the works of the enemy. Prophets are on the enemy's hit list. God protects His prophets. God sustains them. Don't be afraid of the enemy. No weapon formed against you will prosper.

> No weapon that is formed against you shall prosper, and every tongue that shall rise against you in judgment, you shall condemn. This is the heritage of the servants of the LORD, and their vindication is from Me, says the LORD.
>
> —ISAIAH 54:17

> When Jezebel killed the prophets of the LORD, Obadiah took a hundred prophets and hid them in groups of fifty in a cave and fed them with bread and water.
>
> —1 KINGS 18:4

Even in the midst of trial and hardship God sustains prophets. They don't have to depend on men and religious systems to survive. Prophets depend on God. They must be free to speak for the Lord. True prophets don't eat at Jezebel's table.

> Arise, go to Zarephath, which belongs to Sidon, and live there. I have commanded a widow there to provide for you.
>
> —1 Kings 17:9

> Now send word out and gather for me all Israel on Mount Carmel, along with the four hundred and fifty prophets of Baal and the four hundred prophets of Asherah who eat at Jezebel's table.
>
> —1 Kings 18:19

Elijah was fed by ravens. God was his source and provider. Prophets depend on God for sustenance. Prophets need God's sustenance because they are often rejected by men. Prophet, expect to receive miraculous provision from God.

> "Go from here and turn eastward and hide by the Kerith brook, which is east of the Jordan. You shall drink from the brook, and I have commanded the ravens to feed you there." So he went and did according to the word of the LORD, for he went and lived by the Kerith brook, which is east of the Jordan.
>
> —1 Kings 17:3–5

God preserves His prophets. Don't be fooled, Jezebel; you cannot kill them all.

> Was it not told my lord what I did when Jezebel slew the prophets of the LORD, how I hid an hundred men of the LORD's prophets by fifty in a cave, and fed them with bread and water?
>
> —1 Kings 18:13, KJV

God hates when His prophets are mistreated. Prophets can be mistreated, persecuted, ignored, called crazy, rejected, overlooked, isolated, muzzled, and passed over. Prophets are often persecuted by the systems they cry out against. This is nothing new. God vindicates His prophets, defends them, and deals with the systems that mistreat them.

> Saying, "Do not touch my anointed ones, and do no harm to my prophets."
>
> —Psalm 105:15

> Now Jeremiah was still coming in and going out among the people, for they had not yet put him into prison.
>
> —Jeremiah 37:4

Now that you know God's position concerning the difficult seasons in your life and ministry as a prophet, let's look at what your responsibility is when it comes to standing firm against opposition.

OVERCOME THE FEAR OF MAN

This can be a major battle for prophets. The fear of man brings a snare. You cannot fear man, the call, criticism, rejection, persecution, or intimidation and be strong in the prophetic. Fear will short-circuit your prophetic flow. Everyone has to overcome some kind of fear. You are not alone. God will deliver you from all your fears and give you the courage you need.

> "Do not be afraid of their faces. For I am with you to deliver you," says the LORD.
>
> —JEREMIAH 1:8

> Do not fear those who kill the body but are not able to kill the soul. But rather fear Him who is able to destroy both soul and body in hell.
>
> —MATTHEW 10:28

> The fear of man brings a snare, but whoever puts his trust in the LORD will be safe.
>
> —PROVERBS 29:25

You can't be a people-pleaser.

> For am I now seeking the approval of men or of God? Or am I trying to please men? For if I were still trying to please men, I would not be the servant of Christ.
>
> —GALATIANS 1:10

The prophet's desire is to please God, not men. You cannot be a servant of Christ and please men. Prophets don't seek the approval of men. The prophet's priority is to please God. Inordinate people pleasing brings you into bondage by enslaving you to everyone whom you desire to please.

You must obey God.

> Peter and the other apostles answered, "We must obey God rather than men."
>
> —ACTS 5:29

Although this is spoken by an apostle (and it applies to apostles as well), this describes a prophet perfectly. When confronted with a choice, the prophet will obey God. Man cannot be above God to the prophet. God's commands trump all.

You cannot live off people's praise and approval.

Men love the acknowledgments of men, particularly prestigious men, but we have got to be weaned away from that necessity. It is a process; it does not take place in a day. Every time that God brings us to that place of weaning, we have got to submit to it, until we come to the place where we do not need it. We need to come to the place where we are not only indifferent to the applause of men, but also to their criticisms and reproaches.

—Art Katz[1]

For they loved the praise of men more than the praise of God.

—John 12:43

But he is a Jew who is one inwardly. And circumcision is of the heart, by the Spirit, and not by the letter. His praise is not from men, but from God.

—Romans 2:29

Don't look for people to honor you.

Jesus did not look for or receive honor from men. Jesus received honor from the Father. Prophets have always had to live without honor from men. God does not want you to depend on man's honor. The Father's honor is the most important thing to prophets.

Jesus said to them, "A prophet is not without honor, except in his own country, and among his own relatives, and in his own house."

—Mark 6:4

I do not receive honor from men.

—John 5:41

Jesus answered, "If I glorify Myself, My glory is nothing. It is My Father who glorifies Me, of whom you say that He is your God."

—John 8:54

Be ready to stand alone.

Fear will cause men to run and hide. Just ask Jesus and Paul.

"But all this was done that the Scriptures of the prophets might be fulfilled." Then all the disciples forsook Him and fled.

—Matthew 26:56

At my first defense no one stood with me, but everyone forsook me. May it not be charged against them.

—2 Timothy 4:16

Be ready when some churches reject your ministry.

The fear of excommunication—of being put out of the synagogue, of being put out of the church or denomination—has always been a way that religious systems control men. The Pharisees threatened anyone who confessed Christ with excommunication. Are you willing to be excommunicated because of the truth?

The early church leaders were excommunicated. Martin Luther and John Hus were excommunicated. The reformers were excommunicated.

Excommunication is really a kind of banishment, a punishment that's handed out by a church when one of its members breaks some important church rule. The Latin root is *excommunicare*, meaning "put out of the community," which is just what happens when a person is excommunicated.

> His parents said this, because they feared the Jews. For the Jews had already agreed that if anyone confessed that He was the Christ, he would be put out of the synagogue.
>
> —JOHN 9:22

> They will put you out of the synagogues. Yes, the time is coming that whoever kills you will think that he is offering a service to God.
>
> —JOHN 16:2

Be ready to confront.

> Go to Pharaoh in the morning as he goes out to the river. Confront him on the bank of the Nile, and take in your hand the staff that was changed into a snake.
>
> —EXODUS 7:15, NIV

> Son of man, confront Jerusalem with her detestable practices.
>
> —EZEKIEL 16:2, NIV

A prophet cannot operate with integrity if his or her loyalties are placed in the wrong person. Fear of man leads to compromise, pride, rejection, and so much more.

DEMONS THAT ATTACK PROPHETS

The most well-known spirit set up to tear down prophets and prophetic ministry is the spirit of Jezebel. This spirit hates prophets and attempts to wipe them out. In the Bible, Jezebel was a witch. Her idolatry and witchcrafts were many. Other spirits that attack prophets include:

- Rejection (self-rejection, fear of rejection)
- Fear
- Intimidation
- Witchcraft
- Loneliness

- Isolation
- Discouragement
- Hurt
- Depression
- Frustration
- Weariness
- Pride
- Confusion
- Jealousy (against prophets)
- Burnout
- Tiredness
- Bitterness
- Unforgiveness

- Anger
- Insecurity
- Inferiority
- Disappointment
- Timidity
- Shyness
- Lust
- Deception (self-deception)
- Withdrawal
- Grief
- Sadness
- Infirmity

Loose yourself from these spirits. You may not be attacked by them all, but the ones that have affected you need to be dealt with.

WHEN PEOPLE TRY TO SHUT YOU DOWN

People will use all kinds of means to shut down prophets, including false accusations and even misquoting Scripture and the character of God to protect them from your seeing into their hearts.

Prophets are sometimes accused of being crazy and having a devil. Jesus was called a Samaritan and accused of having a devil. Prophets are often called "rebellious," "religious," "deep," "spooky," and "crazy," especially by religious systems that are confronted with the truth.

> The Jews there answered, "We say you are a Samaritan. We say a demon is making you crazy! Are we not right when we say this?"
> —JOHN 8:48, ERV

> Then the Jews said to Him, "Now we know that You have a demon. Abraham and the prophets died, and You say, 'If a man keeps My word, he shall never taste death.'"
> —JOHN 8:52

People will use the verse "judge not" to shut the mouths of prophets. A similar verse people use to break the flow of prophetic judgement or warning is "God is love."

Regarding "judge not," Jesus was referring to a critical, condemning, fault-finding, nitpicking, and self-righteous spirit (outer judgment). The biblical reference to "judge not" does not mean that wickedness and evil should not be exposed and rebuked. Jesus is referring to unrighteous judgment and not to righteous judgment. Jesus exposed and rebuked the Pharisees for their wickedness.

> Do not judge and criticize and condemn others, so that you may not be judged and criticized and condemned yourselves.
>
> —Matthew 7:1, ampc

> Do not judge according to appearance, but practice righteous judgment.
>
> —John 7:24

How to Stay in the Fight

Get tough.

Prophets must develop some toughness. Be prepared to put on the camel's hair and eat locusts and wild honey.

> And the same John had his raiment of camel's hair, and a leathern girdle about his loins; and his meat was locusts and wild honey.
>
> —Matthew 3:4, kjv

You must be tough, strong enough to withstand adverse conditions or rough or careless handling.

Shake off the dust.

Prophets have to learn how to "shake off the dust." Prophets want everyone to receive the truth and be blessed, but sometimes it just does not happen that way. You can't make people do what the Lord says. Sometimes you have to leave and "shake off the dust."

> And whosoever shall not receive you, nor hear your words, when ye depart out of that house or city, shake off the dust of your feet.
>
> —Matthew 10:14, kjv

Remember, it's not about you.

If you are rejected, don't pick up demons of hurt and rejection. Don't let those demons in your life. Remember the word of the Lord to Samuel:

> And the Lord said unto Samuel…for they have not rejected thee, but they have rejected me, that I should not reign over them.
>
> —1 Samuel 8:7, kjv

It's not about you; it's about the Lord. Rejoice, and be exceedingly glad.

Blessed are you when men revile you, and persecute you, and say all kinds of evil against you falsely for My sake. Rejoice and be very glad, because great is your reward in heaven, for in this manner they persecuted the prophets who were before you.

—MATTHEW 5:11–12

Rejoice!

Prophets know what it is to weep. Prophets know what it is to grieve. Prophets also need to rejoice. Prophets must learn to rejoice even when things don't look good. Learn from the prophet Habakkuk and the psalmist.

Although the fig tree shall not blossom, neither shall fruit be in the vines; the labour of the olive shall fail, and the fields shall yield no meat; the flock shall be cut off from the fold, and there shall be no herd in the stalls: Yet I will rejoice in the LORD, I will joy in the God of my salvation. The LORD God is my strength, and he will make my feet like hinds' feet, and he will make me to walk upon mine high places. To the chief singer on my stringed instruments.

—HABAKKUK 3:17–19, KJV

For his anger endureth but a moment; in his favour is life: weeping may endure for a night, but joy cometh in the morning.

—PSALM 30:5, KJV

Don't despair.

John was a prophet crying in the wilderness. He was in the desert. The desert represents isolation and separation. The people came to the wilderness to hear him. Don't despair, prophet. Those who want to hear will hear.

For this is he that was spoken of by the prophet Esaias, saying, The voice of one crying in the wilderness, Prepare ye the way of the Lord, make his paths straight.... Then went out to him Jerusalem, and all Judaea, and all the region round about Jordan.

—MATTHEW 3:3, 5, KJV

Roll your works upon the Lord.

Roll your works upon the Lord [commit and trust them wholly to Him; He will cause your thoughts to become agreeable to His will, and] so shall your plans be established and succeed.

—PROVERBS 16:3, AMPC

A man's heart devises his way, but the LORD directs his steps.

—PROVERBS 16:9

CHAPTER 28

SEEK PROPHETIC COMMUNITY

*Let us not forsake the assembling of ourselves together, as is
the manner of some, but let us exhort one another.*
—HEBREWS 10:25

I N THE NEW Testament the apostle Paul mentions the prophetic presbytery
as a function in the early church. There is great need for local churches
to have prophetic presbyteries that will strengthen, release, and help the
church move into a greater level of breakthrough and ministry. I am surprised
by the number of churches that have never had a time for prophetic presbytery,
although this was practiced in the early church and has been restored to the
modern church for over fifty years.

> Do not neglect the gift that is in you, which was given to you by
> prophecy, with the laying on of hands by the elders. Meditate on these
> things. Give yourself completely to them, that your progress may be
> known to everyone.
>
> —1 TIMOTHY 4:14–15

Churches must have a revelation of the power of prophetic presbyteries and
then set aside time for them periodically. David Blomgren's book *Prophetic
Gatherings in the Church* is a classic on the subject of prophetic presbyteries.
Unfortunately it is now out of print. I will be referring to his book in this chapter.

WHAT IS PROPHETIC PRESBYTERY?

A prophetic presbytery is composed of presbyters, or elders, of a local church
who are also apostles and prophets and who have the resident gift of prophecy.
When a prophetic presbytery is held, these presbyters (elders) lay hands on and
prophesy over selected believers to speak the will of God over them, impart gifts,
and release them into their membership ministries. The presbyters do not have to
be from the local church where the presbytery is being held. In other words, local
churches can call in presbyters from other churches to conduct the presbytery.

Bill Hamon defines *prophetic presbytery* as "a time when two or more
prophets or prophetic ministers lay hands on and prophesy over individuals at

a specified time and place."[1] Prophetic presbyteries are conducted for several reasons:

1. For revealing a saint's membership ministry in the body of Christ

2. For ministering a prophetic rhema word of God to individuals

3. For the impartation and activation of divinely ordained gifts, graces, and callings

4. For revelation, clarification, and confirmation of leadership ministry in the local church

5. For the laying on of hands and prophecy over those who have been called and properly prepared to be an ordained minister serving in one of the fivefold gifts

A prophetic presbytery is different from receiving prophetic words from a prophetic team. Prophetic presbyteries are governmental because they are conducted by the authority (elders) of the church. Presbyteries are to deliver prophetic words to the people they have gathered to pray for, but prophetic presbyteries have more of a "setting and releasing" aspect for those receiving ministry. Candidates for receiving ministry are chosen by the leadership of the church. Prophetic presbytery is not a time for anyone and everyone to receive a word.

Presbytery team

The presbytery team can consist of two or more presbyters, although it is ideal to have three or four presbyters on the team. Each presbyter takes time to prophesy over the candidates before the entire congregation. Each presbyter has a portion of the word to release; no one presbyter will have the entire word of the Lord. Presbyters must work together as a team. There is no competition between the presbyters, particularly because they should all be mature (elders).

The presbytery is led by a senior presbyter (usually an apostle with the most experience and maturity among the presbyters). Apostles will be able to prophesy with authority and revelation from their apostolic office. They also have an anointing to set. Prophets, however, are much needed in a presbytery because they bring detail and clarity by releasing the word of the Lord from the prophet's office. Apostles and prophets make a powerful team in a presbytery.

Presbyters with a resident gift of prophecy can prophesy on a regular basis to God's people. They do not have to wait for a special anointing to prophesy; they can prophesy because of the resident gift of prophecy. The simple gift of prophecy is for edification, exhortation, and comfort, but apostles and prophets can go beyond these and speak direction, correction, and revelation. They can do this because of other gifts, such as the word of wisdom, the word of knowledge, and faith, which operate through their offices. Therefore a prophetic presbytery will go beyond edification, exhortation, and comfort. It will include impartation, direction, confirmation, and revelation because of the combination of the resident gift of prophecy in the presbyters and the strength and anointing of their offices.

The strength of a particular prophetic presbytery will depend upon the presbyters and candidates. The more mature and gifted the presbyters are, and the more qualified the candidates are, the stronger the prophetic flow will be. The strength of the presbytery, in part created through prayer, fasting, and worship, will be determined by the faith of the church and the spiritual atmosphere.

Strong utterances and impartations should be expected if a presbytery is conducted properly. God desires for churches to have strong prophetic gatherings. These should be times of great refreshing and blessing for the entire church. Even those not receiving ministry can rejoice and be blessed as they watch and listen while others in the body receive so much from the Lord. It is always the case that when others in the body are strengthened and released, the entire church is blessed.

Who should attend?

The entire leadership of the church should be present during a presbytery. They need to hear the prophetic words spoken over people who are under their leadership. The leadership of a church is responsible to oversee the members and has a responsibility to help guide the candidates after they receive prophetic ministry. Members should also be encouraged to come and give their support. The corporate anointing helps to enable a strong presbytery to take place. Those who are not receiving ministry should not sit idly by as mere spectators of what is transpiring. They should help create an atmosphere through their faith and prayer that will assist the presbyters and candidates to receive the full blessing of the Lord.

It is wise to invite presbyters who are new to the church and not too familiar with the people receiving ministry. It is also good to have a presbyter return who has functioned as a presbyter before (if this is not the first presbytery). There may be leaders within the local church who can function on a presbytery, but it is recommended that the leadership bring in presbyters from outside the local church who are not familiar with the candidates.

After each presbyter has prophesied (although it is not necessary for all the presbyters to prophesy over each candidate), it is time for the presbytery to lay hands on and pray over the candidate (or candidates, if a couple). This is a time of impartation and the transfer of gifts and anointing. The candidate will be encouraged, confirmed, strengthened, and released into a greater sphere of ministry as a result of prophetic presbytery. The church will also be blessed by hearing the prophetic word that was spoken over the candidates. This will help the church and leadership to discern the gifting and calling upon the candidates. The church will be built up because key people (candidates) have received prophetic presbytery.

Candidates

Candidates should be members of the local church who have been selected by its leadership. They should be saved and Spirit filled, and they should evidence spiritual maturity. It is recommended that the candidates be members of a local church for at least a year to prevent people from joining a church just to receive this kind of ministry. Prophetic presbytery is not a time to fix problems that believers may have. It is unfair to the presbyters to select people who are not qualified to receive the specific kind of ministry that they have to offer.

While all believers can receive prophecy and churches today are raising up prophetic teams to accomplish this, prophetic presbytery is a time during which only a select few receive in-depth prophetic ministry. It is recommended that the number be limited to between three and seven. After candidates receive prophetic presbytery, time can be given to call people from the congregation and prophesy over them. This is to encourage believers, but it is not the main reason why the presbyters have come. The church can also receive corporate words during a time of prophetic presbytery.

Believers of a local church can request to be candidates for prophetic presbytery. However, the leadership bears the responsibility of selecting the candidates. Those who are chosen should be told beforehand in order to prepare spiritually for the prophetic presbytery. Fasting on the part of the candidates and the presbyters will always enhance the strength and accuracy of the prophetic word. The whole church can be encouraged to fast prior to a presbytery. This will create an atmosphere for the Holy Spirit to speak to the church.

That being said, it should also be made clear that people who do not desire prophetic presbytery should not be forced to receive it. If a husband or wife desires to become a candidate for prophetic presbytery but his or her mate does not, this does not represent a disqualification. However, if one mate is not as qualified as the other and yet both desire ministry, it is advisable for them still to receive ministry as a couple (provided that both are saved). If a mate is unsaved, the believing mate can still receive ministry from the presbytery alone.

Candidates should be people whom the leadership of the church feels are about to enter into a new level of ministry. They can be potential leaders or potential ministers of the church. Large churches will have an abundance of candidates, and they must be chosen carefully and prayerfully. There may be a tendency for some people to feel overlooked, but the time frame must be understood by all, and no one should take offense if they are not chosen.

Location and duration

The presbytery should occur in the local church setting. It should not be done in a cell group or home meeting. The entire church should understand the importance of this time and participate if possible. A short message can be given before a presbytery, and worship should be done at intervals to keep the prophetic spirit strong. All prophecies should be recorded and later reviewed by the leadership. The candidate has the responsibility to take heed to the word spoken.

The presbytery can take place over several days. It takes time to minister in prophetic presbytery. This is not a time to call in prophets to prophesy over everything moving in your church.

A church can have a presbytery yearly or biyearly depending on the need. Leaders should spend time teaching and preparing the church if they have never had a presbytery. The church needs to have revelation and understand the importance of such a time.

RESTORATION OF THE PROPHETIC PRESBYTERY

The practice of the ministry of prophetic presbyteries remained absent from the church for many generations after the early church was dispersed until the Latter Rain Movement of the 1940s in North America. Many churches began to operate in presbyteries during the Latter Rain Movement. However, after a short time, the practice again declined significantly. One of the reasons for this is that very few books were written by leaders of the Latter Rain Movement.

We are living in times of restoration. Prophetic presbytery is a part of restoration truth that churches should receive and operate in. Restoration churches are recovering truth, revelation, and ministry that have been absent or neglected in the church for generations. With restored truth comes a greater ability for breakthrough and release of ministry.

Prophetic presbytery is like a "spiritual technology" that the enemy desires to keep from the local church because it can be so effective in strengthening the church. I have a heart to see it restored fully. I have seen firsthand the benefits of prophetic presbytery in Crusaders Church, over which I am the apostolic overseer.

Benefits of prophecy in a presbytery

David Blomgren mentions nine benefits of prophecy in a presbytery as follows:

1. Edification (1 Cor. 14:3)
2. Exhortation (1 Cor. 14:3)
3. Comfort (1 Cor. 14:3)
4. Direction (Acts 13:1–2)
5. Conferral (1 Tim. 4:14)
6. Confirmation (Acts 15:32)
7. Correction (1 Cor. 14:31; *learn* means "corrective learning")

8. Judgment (Hosea 6:5)

9. Equipping of the saints (Eph. 4:11–12)[2]

Prophetic presbytery releases great grace to the hearers. The prophetic word is able to build us up and release our inheritances unto us.

> Now, brothers, I commend you to God and to the word of His grace, which is able to build you up and give you an inheritance among all who are sanctified.
>
> —Acts 20:32

Believers need grace in order to serve God. Believers need an abundance of grace so they can "reign in life" (Rom. 5:17). One sign of an abundance of grace is an abundance of gifts (1 Cor. 1:4–7), and both gifts and grace are imparted during a prophetic presbytery.

The prophetic word is more than information. The prophetic word releases life (breath). Remember the experience of the prophet Ezekiel:

> So I prophesied as he commanded me, and the breath came into them, and they lived, and stood up upon their feet, an exceeding great army.
>
> —Ezekiel 37:10

Prophetic presbytery is a time in which life is breathed into the recipient. The gifts and destiny of the candidate are revealed and activated. It causes believers to rise up and stand on their own feet. It is a key to raising up a strong army of believers.

Leaders are changed when they come into contact with the company of the prophets. Saul was released as the first king of Israel through the prophetic anointing:

> After that you will come to the hill of God, where the garrison of the Philistines is. And when you come there to the city, you will meet a group of prophets....And they will prophesy. And the Spirit of the LORD will come upon you, and you will prophesy with them. And you will be turned into another man.
>
> —1 Samuel 10:5–6

Prophetic presbytery is a time to release potential leaders into their callings and ministries. The strength of prophetic presbytery is the joining together of the anointings of the team. The team members strengthen and stir up one another as they minister together.

Prophetic presbytery is a time for learning the will of God and being comforted. It is a time to allow the prophets to speak. The presbyters minister as a team:

Let two or three prophets speak, and let the others judge. If anything is revealed to another that sits by, let the first keep silent. For you may all prophesy one by one, that all may learn and all may be encouraged.

—1 Corinthians 14:29–31

As one ministers, others can receive revelation concerning the candidates. In this way the candidates benefit from the ministry of several prophets.

As I mentioned above, I believe that prophetic presbytery is a spiritual technology from God that is designed to help leaders build strong churches. This is a day of restoration. Churches must appropriate all the benefits that God's gifts bring to the church.

I believe that as churches around the world take advantage of prophetic presbytery, they will move into apostolic strength and power.

Empowering through the laying on of hands

The Hebrew word for *lay* is *camak*,[3] and the word for *laying on of hands* for an ordination or a sacrifice is *semicha*.[4] The Greek word for *laying on of hands* is *epitithemi*. This word implies contact, which is a channel for transmission.[5] Prophecy is a channel through which grace and gifts are transferred. The person receiving has the responsibility and obligation to steward the gifts and grace received. Timothy received a gift through prophecy with the laying on of hands of the presbytery.

This command I commit to you, my son Timothy, according to the prophecies that were previously given to you, that by them you might fight a good fight.

—1 Timothy 1:18

The prophecies Timothy received helped him to war a good warfare. Paul reminded (charged) him according to these prophecies. Prophetic presbytery is not to be taken lightly by the recipient. Unto whom much is given, much is also required. The recipient has the responsibility and obligation to war with the prophetic word. Prophetic words recorded during a presbytery should be meditated upon and used by the candidate as a weapon against the enemy.

David Blomgren mentions thirteen benefits of the laying on of hands and prophecy by the presbytery:[6]

1. A greater realization of each one's responsibility to function in a ministry
2. A greater appreciation for the various ministries in the body of Christ and the need for them
3. A "setting in" of ministries in the local assembly
4. Finding one's place in the body of Christ
5. The confirmation of the will of God for the candidate

6. The further development of ministries within the local body

7. Specialized assistance through prophetic revelation and individual lives

8. The strengthening of the whole church in a better understanding of God's ways through receiving prophetic ministry

9. The raising of the spiritual level of the whole church through seeking the Lord in fasting and prayer

10. The receiving of prophetic direction for the whole church

11. The imparting of gifts and blessings to believers by the laying on of hands

12. A greater recognition of God's order in the authority of the local leadership as overseers of the lives of the people

13. A deposit of faith in the hearts of the congregation to see God's purposes fulfilled

Prophetic gatherings are times when destinies are revealed and released. Prophecy has always been a vehicle through which the Lord has given direction, blessing, activation, and impartation to His people. This can be seen when Jacob gathered his sons together. Jacob spoke prophetically to his sons and detailed their destinies and inheritance:

> Jacob called to his sons and said, "Gather yourselves together, so that I may tell you what will befall you in the last days. Gather yourselves together and hear, sons of Jacob, and listen to your father Israel."
> —GENESIS 49:1–2

It is important for churches and believers to set aside times for prophetic gatherings. These can be times of power and release when accompanied by prayer and fasting and with the laying on of hands, which is one of the principle doctrines of the church (Heb. 6:1–2).

Sometimes the prophetic word spoken during a time of presbytery will not be fully fulfilled until years later. With prophetic presbytery believers can prepare for the future by aligning themselves with the Word of the Lord. The Word of the Lord will be tested, but a believer walking in faith and fulfillment will see the desired result.

Moses prophesied over the tribes of Israel. The Word of God calls it a blessing:

> Now this is the blessing with which Moses, the man of God, blessed the children of Israel before his death.
> —DEUTERONOMY 33:1

Prophetic presbytery is a time of blessing. *Blessing* is the Hebrew word *berakah*, meaning "a benediction." Moses was a prophet. Prophets have the grace, authority, and ability to release tremendous blessings. This is why presbyteries should consist of prophets who have the office of prophet as opposed to people with the gift of prophecy. Prophets have more grace and authority to release and bless people concerning their destinies.

What If Your Church Does Not Have Prophetic Gatherings or Training

I have been asked this question many times as I have begun to facilitate prophetic roundtables around the country. Some have wondered if they should just start their own church or move to a different church because the church they attend does not operate in the prophetic. Unless you have a grace to start a church, I wouldn't recommend that you start a church. Starting churches is really an apostolic function, although prophets can start churches. I don't recommend that you become a fringe group away from the local church, where you only meet outside the church, but get a core group of people together who are also interested in the prophetic and who will pray and study together. Get some books on the subject. Start a reading club. Read the books. Come together and discuss them. Use the group to stay sharpened, connected, and inspired so that you won't dry up and die spiritually.

I also recommend that you get activated. You can attend a prophetic conference to get activated, even if you have to travel outside of your city to find one. Then get connected with a prophetic association or network so that you can consistently stay in contact with mature prophetic people, but you still need to be submitted to a local church as well just to be able to hear the Word. ElijahList.com/links has a listing of prophetic ministries that you can access. But again, you still need to be submitted to a local church as well to be able to hear the Word. Also, consider connecting with the authors of the books you are reading to receive activation and impartation.

Even if your church doesn't flow prophetically but they preach and teach the Word, have good worship, and are a fellowship filled with love, I think it is important you remain connected and accountable. You don't want to be a renegade prophet who is not connected or accountable to anybody, not submitted to any authority. Prophets who are all alone and don't listen to anyone are sometimes walking in rebellion. They are proud and independent. This is where a prophetic person can really get into trouble because if they are off on their own and are operating in error, no one can correct them.

Being a part of a prophetic team, a prophetic company, or a prophetic church will bring you into accountability with other prophets. First Corinthians 14:29 says, "Let two or three prophets speak, and let the others judge." Prophets can judge each other because prophets know prophets. They can tell when a prophet is wrong or when a prophet is bitter, rebellious, independent, getting into false doctrine, or becoming controlling.

I know prophets can be persecuted and rejected, but if someone is always saying, "Nobody loves me. I am persecuted. Nobody trusts me," it could be that they are just rebellious and won't submit to anybody. I am very wary of people who have no friends, no relationships, no accountability, and no local church and never submit. They just want to pop up and prophesy.

Remember now, prophets are *a part of the church*. "God has put these in the church...prophets..." (1 Cor. 12:28). Remember that under the old covenant prophets were primarily often isolated and alone because they were dealing with an apostate nation. Now in the new covenant the church is different. The church is a place full of people who are born again, new creatures, and who are also filled with the Spirit of God. A prophet can never say, "I'm outside the church," even though he or she can't be in certain churches because they don't accept it or they fight it. I understand that. But the prophet is supposed to be part of the church, functioning inside the church. The prophet is a part of the body. Your hand does not run off and say, "I'm not part of the body anymore."

I am a pastor. I am a shepherd. I believe in the local church. I love the local church, and even though the local church can vex me, I never separate myself from the local church. Even as an apostle, I am accountable to other leaders, and I am accountable my elders. I don't say, "I am the apostle. You don't tell me anything." No. If I get off and if my lifestyle is not right, they have a right to correct me and challenge me.

So it is very important that you remain connected to a good Bible-believing fellowship, where the Word of God is honored and taught. If there is no openness to the prophetic, get with other prophetic believers and pray and study together, as I have already stated. Join a network of prophets. Buy prophetic books. Attend prophetic conferences. Buy CDs, listen to podcasts, and follow strong prophetic leaders in social media so that you continue to stir and strengthen your gift. Then pray and believe God to raise the prophetic level in your region. Remember, even as Elijah thought he was the only one, God reminded him, "I have seven thousand in Israel." Sometimes you may think you are the only one, but there is always a remnant moving with God.

PLACES WHERE PROPHETS GROW AND FLOURISH

Prophetic activations allow you to be among those who prophesy. Being around those who prophesy can pull you into the prophetic flow. This is what happened to Saul. The prophet Samuel said to Saul: "...you will meet a group of prophets coming down from the high place with a harp, a tambourine, a flute, and a lyre before them. And they will prophesy. And the Spirit of the LORD will come upon you, and you will prophesy with them. And you will be turned into another man" (1 Sam. 10:5–6).

There are certain places and atmospheres that cause prophets to grow and flourish—places geared toward prophetic activation, training, equipping, impartation, and confirmation.

Prophetic families

God can raise up your children to be prophets. God called Jeremiah when he was a child. Prophetic children must be handled differently. They are not like every other child. They are unique and very sensitive to the Spirit of God and the spirit realm.

> I raised up some of your sons as prophets, and some of your young men as Nazirites. Is it not so, O children of Israel? says the LORD.
>
> —AMOS 2:11

> But the LORD said to me, "Do not say, 'I am a youth.' For you shall go everywhere that I send you, and whatever I command you, you shall speak."
>
> —JEREMIAH 1:7

Prophetic communities: a company of prophets

> When they came to the hill, a group of prophets met him. And the Spirit of God came upon him, and he prophesied among them.
>
> —1 SAMUEL 10:10

First Samuel 10:10 is the first mention of "a company (cord, chain, or band) of prophets" (Nabhis). There were previously individual prophets. And on one occasion the seventy elders prophesied (Numbers 11:25), and Moses said, "Would God that all the Lord's people were prophets, and that the Lord would put his Spirit upon them." But until the time of Samuel there was no association or community, college or school, of prophets. [The prophet Samuel's] language shows his intimate relation to this "company," of which he was doubtless the founder…Its formation was due to a newly awakened religious life among the people, and intended as a means of deepening and extending it.

[The company] arose about the same time as the establishment of the monarchy, and furnished a regular succession of prophets, by whom the word of the Lord was spoken for the guidance and restraint of the king. "Samuel saw the need of providing a new system of training for those who should be his successors in the prophetic office, and formed into fixed societies the sharers of the mystic gift, which was plainly capable of cultivation and enlargement."

They formed a "company," a voluntary, organised society, apparently dwelling together in the same place, and pursuing the same mode of life. The bond of their union was the common spirit they possessed; and their association contributed to their preservation and prosperity.... "They presented the unifying, associative power of the prophetic spirit over against the disruption of the theocratic life, which was a legacy of the time of the judges."[7]

This community of prophets was also active at the time of Elijah and Elisha. These companies consisted of women as well, like Huldah the prophetess in 2 Kings 22:14:

> So Hilkiah the priest, Ahikam, Akbor, Shaphan, and Asaiah went to Huldah the prophetess, wife of Shallum, son of Tikvah, son of Harhas, keeper of the wardrobe (she lived in Jerusalem in the second quarter), and they spoke with her.

These prophets came together in community to encourage each other and build up their gifts. They worshipped together, ate together, and sometimes lived together. The strength of their gifts did not develop in a vacuum. They were nurtured and confirmed by other like-minded people.

Let there be companies (groups) of prophets in every city and church. Prophet, you are not alone.

> Then Saul sent messengers to take David, but when they saw the company of the prophets prophesying and Samuel taking his stand over them, the Spirit of God came upon the messengers of Saul and they also prophesied.
>
> —1 SAMUEL 19:20

Prophetic houses

Strong prophetic churches will activate and release large numbers of prophets and prophetic people because of a strong prophetic atmosphere that is conducive to nurturing and developing prophets. Every city and region needs these kinds of churches to be established in order for the territory to receive the blessing of prophets and prophetic utterances. These churches will be strong in worship and prophecy and will have strong prophetic leaders to help mature emerging prophetic gifts. We are seeing more and more of these kinds of churches being established around the globe.

Prophets need a loving faith community where they are embraced, trained, and released. This is an atmosphere conducive to their growth and development. (See 1 Samuel 19:20.)

Prophetic hubs

Many churches will become prophetic hubs for their cities and regions. A hub is a center of activity or interest, a focal point, or a center around which other things revolve or from which they radiate. These hubs will be places of encouragement, training, activation, and impartation for prophets and prophetic people. Ramah was a prophetic hub under the leadership of Samuel (1 Sam. 19:18–20).

Pray for these hubs to be established in your region. Find a hub to be encouraged and released into the prophetic flow.

> Now David fled, and he escaped and came to Samuel at Ramah. And he reported to him all that Saul had done to him. And he and Samuel went and stayed in Naioth. It was told Saul, saying, "David is at Naioth in Ramah."
>
> —1 SAMUEL 19:18–19

Prophetic teams

> When people flow together in prophetic teams, it is easy to stir up and flow in prophecy. There is the prophetic influence that is established over the team, so that each finds it easy to release prophecy. Also, each one adds to the flow and experience of the prophetic.
>
> —ASHISH RAICHUR[8]

Prophetic teams are good in helping young prophetic ministries work with more experienced prophetic ministers. This helps younger ministers develop and become stronger by being around those who are more mature and stronger. There is also an impartation that can be received and valuable experience that helps people develop faith in ministering prophetically.

School of the prophets

> It was under the administration of the Prophet/Judge Samuel, that we find the development of the school of the prophets. In this particular time period, about 931–1050 B.C., there were many false prophets that arose with false mediums of revelation. Samuel, who was raised as a boy by a priest named Eli, established training centers where young men would be taught the Law of Moses, responding to the Spirit of God and worship.
>
> While one cannot be taught how to prophesy, the schools were geared to instruct the sons of the prophets how to flow with the Spirit when He came upon them.[9]

Prophetic caves

The church needs more Obadiah-type leaders. Obadiah protected, fed, and sheltered the prophets in caves when Jezebel was trying to destroy them. Some churches will have leaders with this Obadiah-type anointing, and they will become prophetic caves to hide, shelter, nourish, and protect prophets.

When Jezebel killed the prophets of the LORD, Obadiah took a hundred prophets and hid them in groups of fifty in a cave and fed them with bread and water.

—1 KINGS 18:4

Prophetic wildernesses

Many prophets are developed in the wilderness because there is no place for development in the church. John was developed in the wilderness. There was no place for him to be developed in the religious system of Jerusalem.

In those days John the Baptist came, preaching in the wilderness of Judea.

—MATTHEW 3:1

Prophetstown

I drove from Illinois to Iowa some time ago and passed a town by the name of Prophetstown in Illinois. I have lived in Illinois all of my life, and I have never heard of this town. I researched it, and this is what I found:

Prophetstown is named for Wabokieshiek (White Cloud) a medicine man known as "the Prophet." [He was] also friend and adviser to Chief Black Hawk. Born in 1794 he presided over the village known as "prophet's village" on the Rock River. He was half Winnebago (Ho-Chunk) and half Sauk and had great influence over both tribes.[10]

I pray that the Lord would raise up "Prophetstowns" in every region across the globe. Let true prophets arise and come forth in every town and city. Let the Cloud of Glory (White Cloud) be in these towns.

He said to him, "Look, there is in this city a man of God, and he is highly respected. All that he speaks surely comes about. Now let us go there. Perhaps he can show us the way that we should go."

—1 SAMUEL 9:6

CHAPTER 29

STIR UP YOUR GIFT THROUGH PRAYER AND DECLARATION

*Then your light shall break forth as the morning, and your
healing shall spring forth quickly, and your righteousness shall
go before you; the glory of the LORD shall be your reward.*
—ISAIAH 58:8

ONE OF THE things that can hinder a prophet from operating with power is not dealing with any kind of hurt, rejection, betrayal, and the like. Even physical illness and disease can cause a prophet to be distracted from clearly hearing from the Lord. Because prophets are subject to persecution of various kinds, many prophets are in need of healing and restoration. Prophets are very sensitive and must guard their hearts. Prophets can take rejection personally. Prophets can experience deep hurt and pain. Even Elijah, one of Israel's greatest prophets, felt alone and isolated.

> And he said, "I have been very zealous for the LORD, Lord of Hosts, for the children of Israel have forsaken Your covenant, thrown down Your altars, and killed Your prophets with the sword, and I alone am left, and they seek to take my life."
>
> —1 KINGS 19:10

Elijah was also tired after his encounter with the false prophets of Jezebel on Mount Carmel. Tired prophets need God's strength. Prophets can expend a lot of virtue in their functions. Prophets sometimes overextend themselves. Jesus said, "Come away...and rest" (Mark 6:31). There are times prophets need to be refreshed and strengthened from heaven.

Don't be discouraged, prophet. You can become tired like everyone else. God will refresh and restore you.

> The angel of the LORD came again a second time and touched him and said, "Arise and eat, because the journey is too great for you." He arose and ate and drank and went in the strength of that food forty days and forty nights to Horeb, the mountain of God.
>
> —1 KINGS 19:7–8

LOOSE THE BANDS OF YOUR NECK

Satan hates prophets and will do anything to destroy them. The prophet is a threat to the works of darkness. The prophet is a target to the powers of hell. Prophets can also slip into pride and can become too harsh and critical.

But you can arise from the dust. Shake yourself. Loose the bands of your neck. You will not be held captive by Satan or by men. You will not be held captive by religious tradition.

> Shake yourself from the dust; arise, O captive Jerusalem. Loose yourself from the bonds of your neck, O captive daughter of Zion.
> —ISAIAH 52:2

There is deliverance and restoration for prophets. There is healing from rejection and hurt. There is deliverance from fear and apprehension. There is deliverance from the assignment of the spirit of Jezebel.

MY PRAYER FOR HEALING AND DELIVERANCE TO COME TO PROPHETS

Agree with me on this prayer for you and other prophets among us. You can also rework this prayer as you are led and pray it directly over yourself to see yourself set free to accomplish the call of God on your life.

> *I pray right now, in the name of Jesus, that every curse spoken against prophets be annulled. Let every negative word spoken against you be canceled. Let every attack of witchcraft, including intimidation, be canceled.*
>
> *I command these spirits to loose the prophets and let them go. I command them to come out in the name of Jesus. I command you to be healed and restored in your emotions. I command every attack on your mind to be canceled.*
>
> *I command all spirits of fear to go. Anything that would intimidate you and make you afraid to speak the word of the Lord must go, in the name of Jesus. Fear of rejection, go. Fear of man, go. Fear of being misunderstood, go. Fear of being persecuted, go.*
>
> *All spirits attacking your mind must leave in the name of Jesus. All spirits that make you think you are crazy, go. Spirits that want to control the way you think, go.*
>
> *All spirits attacking your body, leave in the name of Jesus. All spirits of sickness and infirmity, go.*
>
> *I pray for your emotions to be healed. I command all rejection to leave in the name of Jesus. I command all hurt and deep hurt to go. I command your heart to be healed and to be made whole.*

I command your soul to be restored. Any prophet with a wounded spirit or broken heart, be healed. I pray that God would mend your heart and comfort you. I pray that all your wounds be bound up. Let the oil and wine of healing be poured into your life.

I command all spirits that make you feel inferior or unworthy to come out. All spirits of guilt, shame, and condemnation go in the name of Jesus.

I command all spirits of double-mindedness to leave in the name of Jesus. All spirits that make you waver and be inconsistent, come out in the name of Jesus.

I command all spirits of wrath and anger to go. All spirits of unforgiveness and bitterness due to hurt and rejection, go.

I command all spirits of pride to leave in the name of Jesus. All spirits of arrogance and haughtiness, go. All spirits of ego and vanity, leave.

I command all spirits of isolation and loneliness to come out in the name of Jesus. All spirits of depression and discouragement, go. Any spirit that makes you want to give up and quit, leave now.

I command any spirit that would attack you at night to leave. All spirits of insomnia and restlessness, go.

I pray that you would be healed from hurt from pastors, churches, networks, family, and friends. I pray that you would be healed from any betrayal and treachery. I pray that you would be delivered from false friends and false brethren.

I command all spirits of disappointment to leave in the name of Jesus.

Disappointment with pastors, churches, and the saints, go in the name of Jesus.

I pray that your joy would be restored and be full. I pray for the zeal of God to be restored to you. I pray that a fresh anointing to prophesy will fall upon you. I pray that you will have a fresh anointing to dream and have visions.

I pray that anything blocking or hindering your prophetic flow be removed in the name of Jesus. Let any dam that is blocking the flow of the Holy Spirit be removed.

I pray for your ears to be opened. I pray for anything stopping or blocking you from hearing the voice of God to be removed. Let your ears be unplugged. Let your ear and mind be unstopped.

Let the rivers of living water flow out of your belly. Let the prophetic bubble up and gush from you. Let the word of the Lord drop from heaven on you. Let the word fall like rain upon your life.

I pray that you would be filled with the Holy Ghost. I pray that your cup will overflow. I pray that you would be filled with Holy Ghost boldness.

I pray that you would be filled with the wisdom of God. You will have the wisdom of God to fulfill your assignment.

DECLARATIONS THAT STIR THE PROPHETIC ANOINTING

The word of the Lord gives me life and breath.

The word of the Lord gives me light and direction.

The word of the Lord gives me hope.

I will write the vision and make it plain.

Let the spirit of prophecy be strong in my life.

Let me speak the word of the Lord accurately.

The word of the Lord releases wisdom for my life.

The word of the Lord reveals the secret things to me.

The word of the Lord gives me boldness.

The word of the Lord increases my faith.

The word of the Lord challenges me to do greater things.

The word of the Lord activates and stirs up my gifts.

The word of the Lord exposes the hidden works of darkness.

Demons flee and are cast out by the word of the Lord.

The word of the Lord gives me understanding.

The word of the Lord flows like a river in and through my life.

I will speak the word of the Lord and be refreshed.

The Lord will light my candle.

Let wickedness be driven out by the word of the Lord.

Let diviners and witches be confounded by the word of the Lord.

Let conviction be released through the word of the Lord.

Let repentance come through the word of the Lord.

I bind all spirits of greed and covetousness that would operate through false prophets.

I bind and rebuke all spirits of deception that would operate through false prophets.

I bind and rebuke all spirits of manipulation and control that would operate through false prophets.

Let the prophets minister to the people with love and compassion.

Let the prophets operate in excellence.

Let the prophets operate in wisdom and knowledge.

Give the prophets strong discernment.

PRAYERS THAT RELEASE PROPHETIC REVELATION

You are a God that reveals secrets. Lord, reveal Your secrets unto me (Dan. 2:28).

Reveal to me the secret and deep things (Dan. 2:22).

Let me understand things kept secret from the foundation of the world (Matt. 13:35).

Let the seals be broken from Your Word (Dan. 12:9).

Let me understand and have revelation of Your will and purpose (Ps. 119:130).

Give me the spirit of wisdom and revelation, and let the eyes of my understanding be enlightened (Eph. 1:17).

Let me understand heavenly things (John 3:12).

Open my eyes to behold wondrous things out of Your Word (Ps. 119:18).

Let me know and understand the mysteries of the kingdom (Mark 4:11).

Let me speak to others by revelation (1 Cor. 14:6).

Reveal Your secrets to Your servants the prophets (Amos 3:7).

Let the hidden things be made manifest (Mark 4:22).

Hide Your truths from the wise and prudent, and reveal them to babes (Matt. 11:25).

Let Your arm be revealed in my life (John 12:38).

Reveal the things that belong to me (Deut. 29:29).

Let Your Word be revealed unto me (1 Sam. 3:7).

Let Your glory be revealed in my life (Isa. 40:5).

Let Your righteousness be revealed in my life (Isa. 56:1).

Let me receive visions and revelations of the Lord (2 Cor. 12:1).

Let me receive an abundance of revelations (2 Cor. 12:7).

Let me be a good steward of Your revelations (1 Cor. 4:1).

Let me speak the mystery of Christ (Col. 4:3).

Let me receive and understand Your hidden wisdom (1 Cor. 2:7).

Hide not Your commandments from me (Ps. 119:19).

Let me speak the wisdom of God in a mystery (1 Cor. 2:7).

Let me make known the mystery of the gospel (Eph. 6:19).

Make known unto me the mystery of Your will (Eph. 1:9).

Open Your dark sayings upon the harp (Ps. 49:4).

Let me understand Your parables and the words of the wise and their dark sayings (Prov. 1:6).

Lord, light my candle and enlighten my darkness (Ps. 18:28).

Make darkness light before me (Isa. 42:16).

Give me the treasures of darkness and hidden riches in secret places (Isa. 45:3).

Let Your candle shine upon my head (Job 29:3).

My spirit is the candle of the Lord, searching all the inward parts of the belly (Prov. 20:27).

Let me understand the deep things of God (1 Cor. 2:10).

Let me understand Your deep thoughts (Ps. 92:5).

Let my eyes be enlightened with Your Word (Ps. 19:8).

My eyes are blessed to see (Luke 10:23).

Let all spiritual cataracts and scales be removed from my eyes (Acts 9:18).

Let me comprehend with all saints what is the breadth and length and depth and height of Your love (Eph. 3:18).

Let my reins instruct me in the night season, and let me awaken with revelation (Ps. 16:7).

Prayers That Break the Power of Jezebel

I loose the hounds of heaven against Jezebel (1 Kings 21:23).

I rebuke and bind the spirits of witchcraft, lust, seduction, intimidation, idolatry, and whoredom connected to Jezebel.

I release the spirit of Jehu against Jezebel and her cohorts (2 Kings 9:30–33).

I command Jezebel to be thrown down and eaten by the hounds of heaven.

I rebuke all spirits of false teaching, false prophecy, idolatry, and perversion connected with Jezebel (Rev. 2:20).

I loose tribulation against the kingdom of Jezebel (Rev. 2:22).

I cut off the assignment of Jezebel against the ministers of God (1 Kings 19:2).

I cut off and break the powers of every word released by Jezebel against my life.

I cut off Jezebel's table and reject all food from it (1 Kings 18:19).

I cut off and loose myself from all curses of Jezebel and spirits of Jezebel operating in my bloodline.

I cut off the assignment of Jezebel and her daughters to corrupt the church.

I rebuke and cut off the spirit of Athaliah that attempts to destroy the royal seed (2 Kings 11:1).

I come against the spirit of Herodias and cut off the assignment to kill the prophets (Mark 6:22–24).

I rebuke and cut off the spirit of whoredoms (Hosea 4:12).

I rebuke and cut off Jezebel and her witchcrafts in the name of Jesus (2 Kings 9:22).

I rebuke and cut off the harlot and mistress of witchcrafts and break her power over my life and family (Nah. 3:4).

I cut off witchcrafts out of the hands (Mic. 5:12).

I overcome Jezebel and receive power over the nations (Rev. 2:26).

CHAPTER 30

Draw From the Anointing

And Jesus said, Somebody hath touched me: for I perceive that virtue is gone out of me.

—Luke 8:46, kjv

I am finding out that God is always ready. I know there are seasons and times and different moves of God, but I also know there are many people who have always spoken before their time. An example of this would be Bishop Charles Mason, founder of the Church of God in Christ.

Bishop Mason flowed in some heavy things. He was so many years ahead of the Church of God in Christ. He was singing in tongues and singing in the Spirit before miracles occurred, while most people had not gone beyond clapping and dancing. Smith Wigglesworth raised people from the dead. These men always seemed out of place. They would always get into the flow of something before others did.

It is good to have the move of God come into a city. It is good to have the timing of God when the Spirit of God says it is time to move and it suits the whole body of Christ.

However, when you press into the prophetic move of God, when you stir that up, when you flow, God is not going to withhold something from you just because others are not ready to accept it.

The Bible says if you ask, it shall be given unto you. If you seek, you shall find. If you knock, the doors are going to open. God is not going to have you asking, seeking, and knocking and then say, "Well, I'm sorry. I can't open the door right now because it's just not time for that."

God will say, "Fine, you want it; I will give it to you even though I am not going to release this thing upon the whole body of Christ until maybe twenty years from now." God will drop that anointing on you, and you will be a church or a people ahead of your time. Then, years down the road, the whole body of Christ will come into it; they will all get the revelation. They can wait for that time if they want to, but I am not going to wait for it because I am convinced that before Jesus Christ comes back, we are going to be flowing in the prophetic. The whole body of Christ will be flowing in miracles and deliverance because He is coming back for a glorious church. It is going to take a move of God, but He is able!

If there is a demand for the prophetic, if there is a hunger for miracles, I am going to tap into that anointing and flow in it now, even though it may not seem like the proper season for it.

The Spirit of God has given me the revelation that you can flow in things ahead of your time. When Jesus's mother told Him there was no more wine at the wedding, He prophetically told her that His hour had not yet come (John 2:4). In other words, "It's not the time for this." Yet He still performed the miracle.

There is always a group of people ahead of their time. Take, for instance, the Wright brothers. They were flying airplanes ahead of their time. Everyone thought they were crazy. Now we are flying all over the world. People probably said, "They are crazy. Look at poor Wilbur and Orville." That is what people will say when you get ahead of your time in the Spirit.

The rest of the people always catch up with the move of God after about ten years have passed. For example, in the church God already moved people to get into the Word. We got into teaching. We were "Word churches." But there are still some churches that are not in the Word. That wave has passed them. They are still on the beach with their surfboards, looking for the wave.

What I am saying is that when the wave comes, you better jump and ride it! Do it then—or do it early. Where prophetic culture is concerned, stir it up, even if nobody else wants to. Maybe you can break it open for the rest of your local body of Christ.

Get Where the Anointing Is

One very important way to make sure you are part of God's flow and not an idle bystander is to get to where the anointing is. Like the woman with the issue of blood, touch the mantle of one who carries the anointing you need.

> For she said within herself, "If I may just touch His garment, I shall be healed."
>
> —Matthew 9:21

The Rotherham translation says, "If only I touch his mantle."[1] The mantle represents the *anointing*. As we have noted earlier, Elisha received the anointing of Elijah both when Elijah called him by casting his mantle on him (1 Kings 19:19) and when Elijah was taken up by the heavenly chariot, dropping his mantle for Elisha to pick up (2 Kings 2:13). This represented the anointing coming upon him to stand in the office of a prophet. We call this the *prophetic mantle*.

Jesus walked and ministered as a prophet of God. He ministered under a prophetic mantle. This mantle also included healing and miracles. The woman with the issue of blood pressed through the crowd to touch His mantle. She was putting a demand upon His prophetic mantle. As a result, she received a miracle.

Different spiritual mantles have been given to different people. As you touch the mantle of a particular office, you will draw virtue and power from that anointing. You don't always have to touch a person physically; you can draw from them *spiritually* whether or not physical touch is involved.

Faith is the channel through which you draw the anointing. It is the pipeline.

Keep begging

> And when the men of that place had knowledge of him, they sent out into all that country round about, and brought unto him all that were diseased; and *besought* him that they might only touch the hem of his garment: and as many as touched were made perfectly whole.
>
> —MATTHEW 14:35–36, KJV, EMPHASIS ADDED

One translation says they "kept begging him" (ISV). Have you ever had someone continue to beg you? They are demanding something of you. This is how you put a demand on the anointing.

According to *Webster's*, to *beseech* means "to beg for urgently or anxiously, to request earnestly, to implore, to make supplication."[2] It means "to seek." It is the laying aside of pride. You admit you have a need and beseech someone who has the ability to help you. Unless you recognize your need for and utter dependence upon the anointing, you will never put a demand on it.

> And whithersoever he entered, into villages, or cities, or country, they laid the sick in the streets, and *besought* him that they might touch if it were but the border of his garment: and as many as touched him were made whole.
>
> —MARK 6:56, KJV, EMPHASIS ADDED

Everywhere Jesus went, people were putting a demand on the anointing. They besought Him to touch His garment. They drew the healing and miracles out of Him. You may say, "This happened in every city because it was a sovereign move of God." You may think the people had nothing to do with it. But remember, it didn't happen in His hometown of Nazareth. They did not beseech to touch Him in Nazareth. These miracles didn't occur in Nazareth because the people didn't put a demand on the anointing. In other villages and cities they did, and they were made whole.

Jesus always responded to people who put a demand on Him through their hunger for the things of God. He never turned them away empty. The spiritual principle here is what I call the law of supply and demand. Where there is no demand, there is no supply. Apathetic, passive Christians don't receive much from the gifts of God.

Creating a demand

People came to hear Jesus because He created a demand by setting people free. (See for example Mark 1:26–34.) When people hear of miracles, they will gather to hear the word of God. They will come with expectancy and faith and draw from the anointing of the servant of God.

There is no substitute for miracles. They will cause a hunger to come into the hearts of people. Hungry hearts will always gather and put a demand on the anointing. Unbelievers will not put a demand on the anointing, but believers will.

If we want hungry people, we must have miracles. Some churches wonder why their people are so unconcerned and apathetic about serving God. People drag themselves to services. Some pastors will try all kinds of programs to raise the excitement of the people, but there is no substitute for doing it God's way. Where there are miracles, the people will gather willingly. Their faith level will rise, and they will put a demand on the anointing for more.

> Immediately many were gathered together, so that there was no room to receive them, not even at the door. And He preached the word to them.
>
> —MARK 2:2

Some only show up because the pastor tells them to or because they are just in the habit of going to church. Then miracles, prophecies, and healing will not flow out of the servant of God to the extent that they will where there is a demand. Of course a minister can stir up the gifts of God and minister by faith. However, when the faith of the *people* is high, it is much easier to minister. Jesus could in His own hometown do no mighty work because of their unbelief. Unbelief always hinders the flow of the anointing. Faith releases the flow.

FAITH PUTS A DEMAND ON THE ANOINTING

Faith releases the anointing. Unbelief blocks the anointing. The woman with the issue of blood put a demand on the anointing with her faith:

> At once, Jesus knew within Himself that power had gone out of Him. He turned around in the crowd and said, "Who touched My garments?"
>
> —MARK 5:30

> He said to her, "Daughter, your faith has made you well. Go in peace, and be healed of your affliction."
>
> —MARK 5:34

Faith is like a vacuum that draws the anointing. Jesus not only ministered with the anointing, but He also let the people know He was anointed (Luke 4:18). When they heard He was anointed, it was their responsibility to believe and receive from His anointing. The people of Nazareth did not believe and could not draw from His anointing. He could do no mighty work in Nazareth because of their unbelief. If they would have believed, they could have drawn from His anointing.

Faith comes by hearing (Rom. 10:17). That is why we need to *hear* about the anointing. We need teaching concerning the anointing.

What is the anointing?

The words *unction* and *anointing* here are taken from the same Greek word *charisma*.[3] *Charisma* means "an unguent or smearing (represented by smearing with oil)." It also means "an endowment of the Holy Spirit." An endowment is a gift of the Holy Spirit. It is the power or ability of God. There are diversities of gifts (endowments or miraculous faculties).

> But you have an anointing from the Holy One, and you know all things.
>
> —1 John 2:20

> But the anointing which you have received from Him remains in you.
>
> —1 John 2:27

To draw from the anointing is to receive from the gift or ability of God. You can receive healing, deliverance, and miracles in this way. Apostles, prophets, evangelists, pastors, and teachers have an anointing given to them from God. They have endowments or miraculous faculties given to them by grace. These endowments are given for the benefit of the saints. We must put a demand on these gifts and endowments.

> And Jesus said, "Somebody hath touched me: for I perceive that virtue is gone out of me."
>
> —Luke 8:46, kjv

Jesus perceived that "virtue" had left Him. The woman with the issue of blood drew virtue out of Him with her faith. As I mentioned previously in this book, the word *virtue* is the Greek word *dunamis*, which means "power, ability, strength, or might." When you put a demand on the anointing, you draw out the power of God. Power is released on your behalf. Thus, the anointing is the virtue or power of God.

> When she had heard of Jesus, she came in the crowd behind Him and touched His garment.
>
> —Mark 5:27

This woman had heard of Jesus. She had heard about the healing anointing that was upon Him. She had heard that a prophet of God was ministering in Israel.

When people hear about the anointing, their faith will increase in this area, and they will then have the knowledge and faith to put a demand on the anointing. We need to know about the apostle's anointing, the prophet's anointing, and the teacher's anointing. We need to know about the healing anointing and the miracle anointing. We need to know about special anointings given by the Holy Spirit.

The more people hear and are taught about the anointing, the greater will be their capacity to put a demand on it. As a pastor of a local church, I teach the members about different gifts and anointings. This builds their faith in that area. When ministers come to minister at our church, I tell the members about the anointing on the person's life. They then have the responsibility to draw from and put a demand on that anointing by their faith.

We cannot be passive and expect to receive from these gifts. We must be active with our faith. Passive, apathetic saints do not receive from the anointing. I have ministered in places where I had to spend the first several nights getting the people to *activate* their faith. Then they could put a demand on the anointing in my life. People have to have a hunger and thirst for the things of the Spirit. Hungry souls will always draw from the anointing.

> It happened that the father of Publius lay sick with a fever and dysentery. Paul visited him and, placing his hands on him, prayed and healed him. When this happened, the rest on the island who had diseases also came and were healed. They honored us in many ways. And when we sailed, they provided us with necessary supplies.
>
> —Acts 28:8–10

After the father of Publius was healed, the whole island of Melita came to be healed. They put a demand on the anointing in Paul's life. Notice that they honored Paul with many honors. Honoring the servant of God is a key to receiving from the anointing in his or her life. Scripture states that the people came. They came with the sick, expecting to be healed. They put action to their faith, and they came. You will find that most of the people who received miracles from Jesus either came or were brought to Him. Many besought Him.

Many in this country wonder why miracles occur so much in foreign countries. Many of the ones who attend crusades walk for miles to come to a meeting. Some travel for days. That is putting a demand on the anointing. Healing and miracles happen as a result. In America many believers will not travel two blocks—and then they wonder why they don't receive miracles.

> Believers were increasingly added to the Lord, crowds of both men and women, so that they even brought the sick out into the streets

and placed them on beds and mats, that at least the shadow of Peter passing by might touch some of them. Crowds also came out of the cities surrounding Jerusalem, bringing the sick and those who were afflicted by evil spirits, and they were all healed.

—ACTS 5:14–16

Here we see people coming "out of the cities surrounding Jerusalem." Where there is a demand, there is a supply. There was enough anointing available to heal *everyone*. These people put a demand on the anointing that flowed from the apostles. When people come to meetings, sometimes from long distances, and put a demand on the gift, they will receive miracles.

On a certain day, as He was teaching, Pharisees and teachers of the law were sitting nearby, who had come from every town of Galilee and Judea and from Jerusalem. And the *power* of the Lord was present to heal the sick.

—LUKE 5:17, EMPHASIS ADDED

The word *power* here is also *dunamis* (again, the same word translated as "virtue" in Luke 8:46). The woman with the issue of blood drew virtue from the body of Jesus with her faith. So we can say that healing virtue was in the house as Jesus taught. When healing virtue (anointing) is present, we can use our faith to put a demand on that anointing. It will then be released for healing.

Now some men brought in a bed a man who was paralyzed. They searched for ways to bring him in and lay him before Him. When they could not find a way to bring him in, because of the crowd, they went up on the roof and let him down through the tiles with his bed into their midst before Jesus. When He saw their faith, He said to him, "Man, your sins are forgiven you."

—LUKE 5:18–20

They put a demand on the anointing present in that room through their faith. As a result, healing virtue was released, and the man was healed of palsy. There are times when the presence of the Lord is thick like a cloud in a service. When the anointing is present to this degree, all we need to do is use our faith to put a demand upon it. Healing and miracles come as a result of putting a demand on the anointing.

We put a demand on the anointing with our *faith*. The Lord has given us the gift of faith for this purpose. The Lord desires that we use our faith to put a demand (withdrawal) on the gifts of God. Many never use their faith for this purpose.

Congregations that are built up in faith will have a tool they can use to receive from the gifts of God. Faith is a channel through which the anointing flows. Faith is like a light switch that starts the electricity flow. It is like the starter on a car, which ignites the power that turns the engine. Faith is the spark that ignites the explosive power of God. It ignites the power gifts of faith, healing, and miracles.

Faith ignites the revelation gifts of word of wisdom, word of knowledge, and discerning of spirits. It ignites the utterance gifts of tongues, interpretation, and prophecy. Faith releases the ministry gifts of apostles, prophets, evangelists, pastors, and teachers.

Faith comes by hearing. The more people hear about the gifts of God, the more faith they will receive to draw from them. As a pastor, I teach on different operations and administrations of the Spirit. I release people with different anointings and administrations to minister to the people. I teach people concerning these gifts and release them to use their faith to put a demand on these gifts.

It is amazing how profoundly ministers are able to minister in the atmosphere that is created through teaching and releasing. The people use their faith to pull the anointing right out of them, and the flow becomes so great, we have to purposely shut it off until the next service.

How to Put a Demand on the Anointing

The woman with the issue of blood put a demand on the healing anointing and received her miracle. Too often God's people do not receive miracles and healing because they do not place a demand on the anointing. The anointing upon and within ministry gifts is a supply. We must learn how to put a demand upon that supply and draw from it.

There is available to every believer a supply of the Spirit. A supply is a storehouse or a reservoir. When I look at ministry gifts, I see a person who is a living reservoir. In that reservoir is a supply of the anointing. It is my responsibility to draw from that supply. Men and women of God have miracles, revelation, and deliverance for you in that reservoir. If you put a demand on the anointing in that reservoir, miracles will flow out of them to you. Utterances will flow out of them into you.

Virtue came out of Jesus because the people drew from His anointing:

> The whole crowd tried to touch Him, for power went out from Him and healed them all.
>
> —Luke 6:19

Spiritual Economics: Supply and Demand

The Lord spoke to my heart the fact that there is always a supply when there is a demand. The drug problems in our cities would not exist if there was no demand for drugs. Because there is a demand for drugs, there is a supply. It is the same with the anointing. If there is no demand, there will be no supply. Hungry saints who put a demand on ministry gifts will always have a supply of the anointing. I have ministered in churches where there was such a hunger and thirst for the anointing that they literally pulled the power right out of me. I have ministered in other places where there was no demand, and as a result nothing happened. The people just sat back and waited for something to happen, and nothing did. There was no hunger or expectancy for revelation, utterances, or miracles.

These people were putting a demand on the anointing. They drew it out by seeking to touch Him. You can literally pull the anointing out of ministry gifts by your faith. If these people had just sat back and waited for Jesus to put it on them, they probably would not have received anything. Many times believers just sit back and wait for the man or woman of God to do something. All the while God is waiting for us to do something. He has placed the supply in our midst, and it is up to *us* to draw from it.

Because I teach the members of our local assembly to draw from the ministry gifts that minister in our services, telling them to put a demand on the anointing of the apostles, prophets, evangelists, pastors, and teachers, they receive the anointing. I teach them that these gifts from God have a supply in them, and it is their responsibility to draw from that supply.

Many ministers who have ministered at our local church are shocked by the high level of anointing they have been able to flow in. This has happened because I have taught the people to pull it out of them. Ministers love to minister in that type of atmosphere. The flow is much easier because the people are pulling *from* you instead of blocking you.

When Jesus was passing by the two blind men, they had to make some noise and draw Jesus's attention. They also drew the disapproving attention of the crowd. But who got the miracle? It was not the ones who tried to stop the men from crying out:

> There, two blind men sitting by the road, when they heard that Jesus was passing by, cried out, "Have mercy on us, O Lord, Son of David!" The crowd rebuked them, that they should be silent. But they cried out even more, "Have mercy on us, O Lord, Son of David!"
> —MATTHEW 20:30–31

These men put a *demand* on Jesus. They cried out even when the multitude was rebuking them, telling them to be silent. They had to press past the opposition of the crowd to receive their miracle. If they had remained silent, they would not have received a miracle. They had to put a demand on the anointing. Jesus was passing by. If they did not put a demand on His anointing, He would have passed *them* by.

It is like drawing money from a bank. You must go to the teller with a withdrawal slip and make a demand on the account. If you never make a demand on the account, you will never withdraw anything from the account.

Jesus was telling the people in His hometown of Nazareth that He was anointed:

> The Spirit of the Lord is upon Me, because He has anointed Me to preach the gospel to the poor; He has sent Me to heal the brokenhearted, to preach deliverance to the captives and recovery of sight to the blind, to set at liberty those who are oppressed; to preach the acceptable year of the Lord.
>
> —Luke 4:18–19

It was up to them to put a demand on His anointing. They could have drawn the gospel, the healing, and the deliverance right out of Him. They could have pulled the virtue and power out of Him. But they didn't. Their unbelief blocked the flow of the anointing. Instead of receiving miracles, they received nothing. Then Jesus said:

> Jesus said to them, "A prophet is not without honor, except in his own country, and among his own relatives, and in his own house." He could not do any miracles there, except that He laid His hands on a few sick people and healed them.
>
> —Mark 6:4–5

There, right in their midst, was supply—a reservoir of the anointing. In that reservoir was salvation, healing, deliverance, and miracles. Jesus was a walking reservoir of the anointing. They had the chance to put a demand on it and draw from it, but they did not because of unbelief. They did not see Him as a reservoir of the anointing but rather as a carpenter: "Is this not the carpenter, the Son of Mary and the brother of James and Joseph and Judas and Simon?" (Mark 6:3). They looked at Him and judged Him in the natural. However, if they had looked at Him in the spirit, they would have seen Him as a reservoir or a pool of the anointing. They would have drawn out of Him miracles and healing by faith.

We need to learn from this. We must put a demand upon the anointing and draw the miracles out of Him. There is nothing wrong with ministers telling people what they are anointed for. If you have a healing anointing, tell the people. Give them a chance to draw from that anointing. If you have a prophetic anointing, tell the people. Let them draw the prophetic words out of you. If you have a teaching anointing, tell the people. Let them draw the knowledge, understanding, and revelation out of you.

Elisha had enough anointing *in his bones* to raise a man from the dead. Imagine the anointing that was available to Israel while he was alive! But because they did not put a demand on the anointing in his life, they did not receive the miracles they needed. Every leper in Israel needed a miracle. The Lord in His mercy saw the need and provided the man of God with His anointing. It was up to Israel to put a demand upon it. Their needs were not met because there was no demand. There was no faith. There was no honor. If they would have honored the prophet of God, they would have been healed. The anointing was available. It was strong enough. But there was no demand. Since there was no demand, there was no supply.

GET YOUR BUCKET READY!

There are other examples in Scripture of people putting a demand on the anointing:

> He came to Bethsaida. And they brought a blind man to Him and *entreated Him* to touch him.
>
> —MARK 8:22, EMPHASIS ADDED

> He went out of the synagogue and entered Simon's house. Now Simon's mother-in-law was taken ill with a high fever, and they *asked Him* about her.
>
> —LUKE 4:38, EMPHASIS ADDED

> They brought to Him one who was deaf and had difficulty speaking. And they *pleaded with Him* to put His hand on him.
>
> —MARK 7:32, EMPHASIS ADDED

> When the wine ran out, the mother of Jesus said to Him, "They have no wine." Jesus said to her, "Woman, what does this have to do with Me? My hour has not yet come." His mother said to the servants, "Whatever He says to you, do it."
>
> —JOHN 2:3–5

In the last scripture Mary drew the miracle out of Jesus by putting a demand on Him. She presented to Him a need and He responded, even though it was not His time to act.

This was the beginning of His miracle ministry. "This, the first of His signs [miracles], Jesus did in Cana of Galilee..." (John 2:11). It all began because His mother presented to Him a need for wine. Often in ministry I will begin to flow in prophecy, miracles, or healing because I sense a demand. People can present these needs to you in such a way that it will begin to cause a miracle flow to come out of you. It is like priming the pump. Once the water begins to flow, it comes gushing out.

Jesus said that out of our bellies would flow rivers of living water. All we need to do is get the flow started. It will begin when there is a demand. Once it begins, it will continue to flow until every need is met.

Draw from the well

The story of the first miracle of Jesus at Cana of Galilee is prophetic. (See John 2:6–10.) The six water pots of stone represent the earthen vessels that the Lord uses. (See 2 Corinthians 4:7.) Six is the number of man. Man was created on the sixth day. Jesus commanded that the vessels be filled with water. Water represents the Word (Eph. 5:26). Servants of God need to be filled with the Word of God. Apostles, prophets, evangelists, pastors, and teachers are to be filled with the Word. The Lord will fill you with the Word so that others can draw from you.

Jesus then told them to draw out of the vessels. As they drew out, the water was turned into wine. Wine represents the Holy Spirit. It represents the anointing of God. We are to draw out of the ministry gifts. *Draw* is the Greek word *antleo*, meaning "to dip water with a bucket or pitcher."[4]

We are to use our buckets and draw out of the earthen vessels that God has filled with His Word. When I get around anointed ministry gifts, my bucket is out and I am ready to draw. When the Lord's vessels come into the local church, we are to draw from them. We draw because we have needs. The mother of Jesus said to Him, "They have no wine" (John 2:3). There was a need at the marriage feast for wine. When there is a need for the anointing and flow of the Spirit, we must draw out of the earthen vessels the Lord has given us. We must use our faith to draw out the wine when there is a need.

Prophets must spend time filling up on the Word. Allow the Lord to fill your vessel up with the water of the Word. As you minister, allow the saints of God to draw from you. There are so many with needs. People need the wine of the Holy Ghost that will flow from us.

Truly, whether filling up or drawing from the Holy Ghost, we need the power of God flowing in our lives. It is my sincere hope and prayer that the revelation shared in this book will tremendously bless God's people to begin to receive in abundance the fullness of all the gifts of God in the body of Christ, especially the all-important prophetic gift.

Select Principles of Prophetic Ministry

Prophecy and the Word of Knowledge

The gift of the word of knowledge may be activated and begin to manifest during prophetic activations. The word of knowledge is a fact given about the person that only God can reveal. It can be a name, an event, a year, a situation, something from their past, something in their present, and so on. The word of knowledge has been described as a "spiritual pry bar" that can open up a person to the fact that what you are saying is from God. The word of knowledge is a "breaker" gift because it can break open people and situations that have been closed.

When the word of knowledge operates in the context of prophecy, it brings the prophetic word to another level. The word of knowledge is like a "twin" gift to the gift of prophecy. These two gifts operating together produce powerful breakthroughs on the behalf of the recipient and confirm that God knows the details of their life and situation. These gifts speak comfort and direction to them in their time of need.

Tongues and Prophecy

Speaking in tongues is one of the ways we edify (build up) ourselves. Prophecy builds up others. The more built up you are, the more you will be able to build up others. We can also pray in tongues to kick start a prophetic word. Paul wrote: "I desire that you all speak in tongues, but even more that you prophesy" (1 Cor. 14:5). The Greek word translated "that" is *hina. Hina* can also be translated "in order that."[1] This means that an alternative translation for the Paul's message is: "I wish that you all spoke with tongues, but rather in order that you prophesied."

> In other words, Paul is saying that he wished they all spoke with tongues so that their tongues would lead into prophecy. This indicates that tongues can be used as an effective tool to "kick-start" a prophetic word. As you pray in tongues for someone or something, God may drop something in your spirit, a vision may come to you, a certain phrase, message or word may bubble up within you etc.

which you can speak forth to bring edification, exhortation and comfort.

—Dr. Stuart Pattico[2]

Enriched in Utterance

We can be enriched by God in power of speech and depth of knowledge. This is a manifestation of the grace of God.

> By Him you are enriched in everything, in all speech and in all knowledge.
>
> —1 Corinthians 1:5

> …in that you have been enriched by him in so many ways, particularly in power of speech and depth of knowledge.
>
> —1 Corinthians 1:5, cjb

This includes being rich in the prophetic realm and in spiritual gifts of utterance.

> I thank God because in Christ you have been ·made rich [enriched] in every way, in all your ·speaking [or spiritual gifts of speaking] and in all your ·knowledge [or gifts of spiritual knowledge].
>
> —1 Corinthians 1:5, exb

The Holy Spirit will enrich each one of us in all utterance. When somebody or something has been "enriched," it has had something extra added to it. The word carries the idea of wealth or abundance. Because we have been filled with the Holy Spirit, we should abound in utterance. The Holy Spirit is a free Spirit (Ps. 51:12), which means He is liberal, generous, and magnanimous (willing to share Himself with us). He pours Himself out upon us, and His life flows out from within us. Most often the outpouring of the Holy Spirit is released in an outpouring of prophecy. That is why we are urged not to quench or limit the Holy Spirit by quenching His inspiration.

Inspired utterances are anointed by the Holy Spirit. These words carry tremendous power and authority. Anointed words can bring deliverance, healing, strength, comfort, refreshing, wisdom, and direction.

Inspired utterances have a dramatic effect upon men and women. Their lives are enriched through the prophetic words that are spoken. Mere human words could not achieve such results. Inspired utterances are not the work of a man but the work of the Holy Spirit.

The Holy Spirit speaks through us, and He puts His word in our mouths.

> The Spirit of the Lord spoke by me, and His word was on my tongue.
>
> —2 Samuel 23:2

David understood that his utterances were divinely inspired. David would even sing under inspiration while he played on his harp. With His word on your tongue, your tongue can become an instrument of the divine. God desires to release His word by means of your tongue and mine. He has given every believer the gift of the Holy Spirit to accomplish His will.

Prophecy is the result of being filled with the Holy Ghost. Zacharias was dumb and unable to speak until his tongue was loosed through the infilling of the Holy Spirit. Then he not only spoke some words for the first time in months, but he also prophesied:

> And his father Zechariah was filled with the Holy Spirit and prophesied, saying…
>
> —Luke 1:67

Spirit-filled believers and churches should prophesy. By virtue of being filled up with the Holy Spirit, we should overflow. *Filled* is the Greek word *pietho*, meaning "to imbue, influence, or supply."

Spirit-filled believers should speak by the influence of the Holy Spirit because they have been imbued, influenced, and supplied with an abundance of the life of the Spirit of God.

Under the influence of the Holy Spirit we utter words that bring edification, exhortation, and comfort, and there is always an abundant supply of such utterance given to us by the Holy Spirit.

DIFFERENT KINDS OF PROPHETIC UTTERANCE

There are different kinds of prophetic words for different situations. The prophetic word can deal with the past, present, and future. The prophetic word is able to deal with all the issues that we face in life. God has many thoughts toward us, and if we were to speak them, they cannot be numbered (Ps. 40:5). God's Word is a lamp to our feet and a light to our path (Ps. 119:105).

1. Now—addresses issues that are currently happening in a person's life. This gives understanding on what a person is dealing with and helps eliminate confusion. I also call this a word in season (Isa. 50:4).

2. Confirmation—establishes and strengthens, builds faith and removes doubt; an example is "you are on the right track."

3. Future—speaks to the next phase or stage in your life. It may map out directions or areas of preparation needed for future tasks. This can include instruction on what to do. God's words light our paths so we know where to go.

4. Past—these are words that deal with past issues, often bringing understanding and resolving things from the past. These words help launch us into our future. There are many people chained to the past, and they need to be released. Joseph understood his past was necessary for his purpose to his people.

5. New—a new word is something completely new. It may often surprise the recipient. It is usually something they were not thinking or planning (1 Cor. 2:9–10).

6. Warning—these words warn of dangers that may be ahead and what to avoid.

7. Deliverance—these words deliver people from things such as hurt, rejection, fear, and sickness and release healing and restoration to the recipient (Ps. 107:20).

8. Revelation—these words give us insight and revelation into the plans and purpose of God for our lives (Deut. 29:29).

9. Identification—these words identify and help people understand and know who they are and what God created them to be (Judg. 6:12).

10. Correction—these words correct us and cause us to make the necessary adjustments in our lives (Prov. 3:11).

11. Commendation—God commends us when we are doing what is right. Each church in Revelation was commended and then corrected.

12. Exposure—these words expose and identify the works of sin and darkness (Heb. 4:13).

13. Conditional—these words are conditional on your obedience; an example is, "If you will pray and seek My face, then I will move you into a new level of breakthrough and blessing."

14. Impartation—God uses these words, often accompanied with the laying on of hands, to impart gifts into our lives (1 Tim. 4:14).

These words can be spoken over individuals and congregations. We must be open and allow God to speak to us in these different ways. Each way will bring great blessing to the church.

Other kinds of words that bring great benefits to those who receive it include:

- Words that heal
- Words that deliver

- Words that comfort
- Words that edify
- Words that exhort
- Words that release courage
- Words that release life
- Words that refresh
- Words that open new doors
- Words that bring change
- Words that release angels
- Words that release glory
- Words that release ministries
- Words that expose the enemy
- Words that release finances
- Words that break drought
- Words that cause breakthrough
- Words that confirm
- Words that release new things
- Words that convict
- Words that bring repentance
- Words for the brokenhearted
- Words for the bruised
- Words for the poor

Utterance in prophecy has a real lifting power and gives real light on the truth to those who hear. Prophecy is never a mind reflection, it is something far deeper than this. By means of prophecy we receive that which is the mind of the Lord; and as we receive these blessed, fresh utterances through the Spirit of the Lord the whole assembly is lifted into the realm of the spiritual. Our hearts and minds and whole bodies receive a quickening through the Spirit given word. As the Spirit brings forth prophecy we find there is healing and salvation and power in every line. For this reason it is one of the gifts that we ought to covet.

—SMITH WIGGLESWORTH[3]

AUTHOR'S NOTE

Extra content is available for free for all who want to go deeper.
Go to www.prophetsmanual.com to download it today.

NOTES

CHAPTER 1
ARE YOU A PROPHET?

1. *American Heritage Dictionary of the English Language*, 5th ed. (New York: Houghton Mifflin Harcourt Publishing Company, 2016), s.v. "fervent."

2. Ibid., s.v. "radical."

3. *English Oxford Living Dictionaries*, s.v. "intense," accessed February 15, 2017, https://en.oxforddictionaries.com/definition/intense.

4. Ibid., s.v. "spontaneous," accessed March 3, 2017, https://en.oxforddictionaries.com/definition/spontaneous.

5. *Merriam-Webster's Collegiate Dictionary*, 11th ed. (Springfield, MA: Merriam-Webster Inc., 2003), s.v. "severe."

6. Sandy Warner, *Discernment: Separating the Holy From the Profane* (N.p.: SOS Publications, 2014).

7. TheFreeDictionary.com, s.v. "measure," accessed February 1, 2017, http://www.thefreedictionary.com/measure.

8. *American Heritage Dictionary of the English Language*, 5th ed., s.v. "seduce."

9. *Oxford Dictionaries,* s.v. "hypocrisy," accessed February 15, 2017, https://en.oxforddictionaries.com/definition/us/hypocrisy.

10. *American Heritage Dictionary of the English Language*, 5th ed., s.v. "deed."

11. TheFreeDictionary.com, s.v. "sincere," accessed March 4, 2017, http://www.thefreedictionary.com/sincere.

12. Dictionary.com, s.v. "tolerate," accessed February 1, 2017, http://www.dictionary.com/browse/tolerate.

13. *American Heritage Dictionary of the English Language,* 5th ed., s.v. "agree."

14. *English Oxford Living Dictionaries*, s.v. "contend," accessed February 15, 2017, https://en.oxforddictionaries.com/definition/us/contend.

CHAPTER 2
WHAT MOVES YOUR HEART?

1. David K. Blomgren, *The Song of the Lord* (Portland, OR: Bible Press, 1978), as quoted on David K. Blomgren, "The Power of Anointed Worship Music," Secret Place Ministries, accessed April 28, 2015, http://www.secretplace ministries.org/pages/journey/soaking/anointed-worship-music.html.

2. *American Heritage Dictionary of the English Language*, 5th ed., s.v. "lip service."

CHAPTER 3
WE NEED YOU

1.   Eric Rafferty, "Five-Fold Partnership: What Prophets Need," Release the Ape, August 3, 2014, accessed February 6, 2017, http://www.releasetheape.com /five-fold-partnership-what-prophets-need/#.WJkzlLYrK34.

2.   *Merriam-Webster*, s.v. "confirm," accessed April 20, 2017, https://www .merriam-webster.com/dictionary/confirm.

CHAPTER 4
MADE BY GOD

1.   Blue Letter Bible, Strong's H5197, s.v. "*nataph*," accessed February 13, 2017, https://www.blueletterbible.org/lang/lexicon/lexicon .cfm?Strongs=H5197&t=KJV.

2.   Blue Letter Bible, Strong's H5012, s.v. "*naba'*," accessed February 13, 2017, https://www.blueletterbible.org/lang/lexicon/lexicon .cfm?strongs=H5012&t=KJV.

3.   Blue Letter Bible, Strong's H5030, s.v. "*nabiy'*," accessed February 13, 2017https://www.blueletterbible.org/lang/lexicon/lexicon .cfm?Strongs=H5030&t=KJV.

4.   Blue Letter Bible, Strong's H5031, s.v. "*nebiy'ah*," accessed February 13, 2017https://www.blueletterbible.org/lang/lexicon/lexicon .cfm?Strongs=H5031&t=KJV.

5.   Blue Letter Bible, Strong's H5414, s.v. "*nathan*," accessed February 13, 2017https://www.blueletterbible.org/lang/lexicon/lexicon .cfm?Strongs=H5414&t=KJV.

6.   Blue Letter Bible, Strong's G4130, s.v. "*pimplēmi*," accessed February 13, 2017https://www.blueletterbible.org/lang/lexicon/lexicon .cfm?Strongs=G4130&t=KJV.

7.   Patricia Bootsma, "The Hidden Life of the Prophetic Voice," Catch the Fire, May 7, 2013, accessed April 28, 2015, http://revivalmag.com/article/hidden -life-prophetic-voice.

8.   "John Emerich Edward Dalberg Acton, 1st Baron Acton Quotes," Britannica.com, accessed April 28, 2015, http://www.britannica.com/Ebchecked /topic/4647/John-Emerich-Edward-Dalberg-Acton-1st-Baron-Acton.

9.   R. C. Sproul Jr., "Ask RC: Why Did the Pharisees Hate Jesus So Much?" RCSproulJr.com, accessed April 28, 2015, http://rcsprouljr.com/blog/ask-rc/rc -pharisees-hate-jesus-much/.

10.   Art Katz, "The Prophetic Function," AuthenticTheology.com, accessed April 28, 2015, http://www.authentictheology.com/blog/terms-concepts/the -prophetic-function-by-art-katz/.

11.   Ron McKenzie, "Role of the Prophet," KingWatch.co.nz, accessed April 28, 2015, http://kingwatch.co.nz/Prophetic_Ministry/role.htm.

12.   Helen Calder, "Prophetic Intercession, Its Power and Pitfalls," *Enliven* (blog), accessed March 10, 2017, http://www.enlivenpublishing.com /blog/2012/08/06/prophetic-intercession-its-power-and-pitfalls/.

13.   Michael Sullivant, "How to Stay Humble in Prophetic Ministry," Charisma Media, accessed April 10, 2015, http://www.charismamag.com/life/1370 -j15/slw-spiritual-growth-/prophecy/9594-humility-in-the-prophetic-ministry.

CHAPTER 5
HOW THE PROPHETS OPERATE TODAY

1.   Blue Letter Bible, Strong's G3874, s.v. *"paraklēsis,"* accessed February 13, 2017, https://www.blueletterbible.org/lang/lexicon/lexicon .cfm?strongs=G3874&t=KJV.

2.   Blue Letter Bible, Strong's G3875, s.v. *"paraklētos,"* accessed February 13, 2017, https://www.blueletterbible.org/lang/lexicon/lexicon .cfm?Strongs=G3875&t=KJV.

3.   Blue Letter Bible, Strong's G3889, s.v. *"paramythia,"* accessed February 13, 2017, https://www.blueletterbible.org/lang/lexicon/lexicon .cfm?strongs=G3889&t=KJV.

4.   *Merriam-Webster*, s.v. "administer," accessed February 1, 2017, https:// www.merriam-webster.com/dictionary/administer.

5.   Blue Letter Bible, Strong's H5273, s.v. *"na`iym,"* accessed February 14, 2017, https://www.blueletterbible.org/lang/lexicon/lexicon .cfm?Strongs=H5273&t=KJV.

6.   Blue Letter Bible, Strong's H7692, s.v. *"shiggayown,"* accessed March 16, 2017, https://www.blueletterbible.org/lang/lexicon/lexicon .cfm?Strongs=H7692&t=KJV.

7.   Theresa Harvard Johnson, "The Ministry of the Scribal Prophet," accessed March 10, 2017, http://chamberofthescribe.com/91-general -information/191-emotionalism-kills-godly-relationships.

8.   Joseph Mattera, "The Difference Between Apostolic and Prophetic Roles," Charisma Media, January 23, 2013, accessed April 28, 2015, http://www .charismamag.com/spirit/prophecy/16593-how-do-you-know-the-difference -between-apostolic-and-prophetic-functions.

9.   William O. Odom and Christopher D. Hayes, "Cross-Domain Synergy: Advancing Jointness," National Defense University Press, April 1, 2014, accessed February 15, 2017, http://ndupress.ndu.edu/Media/News/News-Article-View /Article/577517/jfq-73-cross-domain-synergy-advancing-jointness/.

CHAPTER 7
DECENTLY AND IN ORDER—PROPHETIC PROTOCOL

1.   Stanley M. Horton, "Rediscovering the Prophetic Role of Women," EnrichmentJournal.ag.org, accessed December 19, 2015, http://enrichmentjournal .ag.org/200102/080_prophetic_role.cfm.

CHAPTER 8
PROPHETS PROTECT

1.   Blue Letter Bible, Strong's H8104, s.v. *"shamar,"* accessed February 14, 2017, https://www.blueletterbible.org/lang/lexicon/lexicon .cfm?strongs=H8104&t=KJV.

2.   Jim Goll and Lou Engle, *Elijah's Revolution* (Shippensburg, PA: Destiny Image, 2002), 99.

3.   John Paul Jackson, *Unmasking the Jezebel Spirit* (North Sutton, NH: Streams Publications, 2002), 33.

CHAPTER 9
PROPHETS WATCH

1.   Blue Letter Bible, Strong's H1696, s.v. *"dabar,"* accessed February 14, 2917, https://www.blueletterbible.org/lang/lexicon/lexicon .cfm?Strongs=H1696&t=KJV.

2.   Blue Letter Bible, Strong's H2803, s.v. *"chashab,"* accessed February 14, 2017, https://www.blueletterbible.org/lang/lexicon/lexicon .cfm?Strongs=H2803&t=KJV.

3.   Blue Letter Bible, Strong's H4931, s.v. *"mishmereth,"* accessed February 14, 2017, https://www.blueletterbible.org/lang/lexicon/lexicon .cfm?strongs=H4931&t=KJV.

4.   Blue Letter Bible, Strong's H4929, s.v. *"mishmar,"* accessed February 14, 2017, https://www.blueletterbible.org/lang/lexicon/lexicon .cfm?Strongs=H4929&t=KJV.

5.   Blue Letter Bible, Strong's H5324, s.v. *"natsab,"* accessed February 14, 2017, https://www.blueletterbible.org/lang/lexicon/lexicon .cfm?Strongs=H5324&t=KJV.

6.   Blue Letter Bible, Strong's H6822, s.v. *"tsaphah,"* accessed February 14, 2017, https://www.blueletterbible.org/lang/lexicon/lexicon .cfm?t=kjv&strongs=h6822.

7.   Blue Letter Bible, Strong's H5341, s.v. *"natsar,"* accessed February 14, 2017, https://www.blueletterbible.org/lang/lexicon/lexicon .cfm?t=kjv&strongs=h5341.

CHAPTER 11
PROPHETS CONFIRM AND IMPART SPIRITUAL GIFTS

1.   Blue Letter Bible, Strong's G3330, s.v. *"metadidōmi,"* accessed February 14, 2017, https://www.blueletterbible.org/lang/lexicon/lexicon .cfm?t=kjv&strongs=g3330.

2.   Richard Weymouth, *The Modern Speech New Testament* (New York: The Baker and Taylor Co., 1905), 352.

3.   Ronald Knox, *Knox Bible* (N.p.: Baronius Press, 2012).

CHAPTER 12
PROPHETS ENGAGE CULTURE

1. Dennis Bratcher, "Prophets Today?" Christian Resource Institute, accessed March 30, 2015, http://www.crivoice.org/prophetstoday.html.

CHAPTER 13
ACTIVATING PROPHETIC MINISTRY GIFTS

1. Tim and Theresa Early, "Apostolic Impartation and Prophetic Activation for Destiny," ReadBag.com, accessed January 6, 2016, http://www.readbag.com /apostlesandprophets-teaching-documents-pdfs-apostolic-impartation-and -prophetic-activation-for-destiny.
2. Benjamin Schafer, "Prophetic Activation Exercises," *A Yearning Hearts Journey* (blog), accessed December 19, 2015, http://yearningheartsjourney .blogspot.com/2012/02/prophetic-activation-exercises.html.
3. Ibid.
4. Geoff and Gina Poulter, *The Gift of Prophecy for Today* (N.p.: Morning-Star Publications, 2007).
5. Steve Thompson, *You May All Prophesy* (N.p.: MorningStar Publications, 2007).

CHAPTER 16
ACTIVATIONS PROMPTED BY THE NAMES OF GOD

1. Blue Letter Bible, "The Names of God in the Old Testament," accessed December 19, 2015, https://www.blueletterbible.org/study/misc/name_god.cfm.

CHAPTER 19
BIBLE ACTIVATIONS

1. Stefan Misaras, "We All Have the Capacity to Prophesy as We Eat, Drink, and Enjoy the Lord," *A God-Man in Christ* (blog), June 7, 2012, accessed December 19, 2015, http://www.agodman.com/blog/we-all-have-the-capacity-to -prophesy-as-we-eat-drink-and-enjoy-the-lord/.

CHAPTER 27
STAND STRONG AGAINST OPPOSITION

1. Art Katz, "The Prophetic Function," AuthenticTheology.com, accessed March 25, 2015, http://www.authentictheology.com/blog/terms-concepts/the -prophetic-function-by-art-katz/.

CHAPTER 28
SEEK PROPHETIC COMMUNITY

1. Bill Hamon, *Prophets and Personal Prophecy* (Shippensburg, PA: Destiny Image, 1987).
2. David Blomgren, *Prophetic Gatherings in the Church* (Saugus, CA: Temple Publishing, 1979).

3.   Blue Letter Bible, Strong's H5564, s.v. *"camak,"* accessed March 14, 2017, https://www.blueletterbible.org/lang/lexicon/lexicon.cfm?strongs=H5564&t=KJV.

4.   Yehuda Shurpin, "What Is a Rabbi? A Brief History of Rabbinic Ordination (Semicha)," Chabad.org, accessed February 14, 2017, http://www.chabad.org/library/article_cdo/aid/1933944/jewish/What-Is-a-Rabbi.htm.

5.   Blue Letter Bible, Strong's G2007, s.v. *"epitithēmi,"* accessed February 14, 2017, https://www.blueletterbible.org/lang/lexicon/lexicon.cfm?Strongs=G2007&t=KJV.

6.   Blomgren, *Prophetic Gatherings in the Church.*

7.   B. Dale, "A Company of Prophets," Biblehub.com, accessed December 11, 2014, http://biblehub.com/sermons/auth/dale/a_company_of_prophets.htm.

8.   Ashish Raichur, *Understanding the Prophetic* (N.p.: All Peoples Church, 2010), 202.

9.   Napolean Kaufman, "School of the Prophets in the Bible," The Well Prophetic Institute, accessed March 30, 2015, http://www.thewellchurch.net/ministries/training-and-equipping/prophetic-institute/. Used by permission.

10.   Don A. Hoglund, "History of American Towns—Prophetstown, Illinois," Hubpages.com, accessed March 14, 2017, https://hubpages.com/travel/History-of-American-Towns-Part-IX-Prophetstown-Illinois.

CHAPTER 30

DRAW FROM THE ANOINTING

1.   Joseph Rotherham, *Rotherham's Emphasized Bible* (Grand Rapids, MI: Kregel Classics, 1959).

2.   Merriam-Webster, s.v. "beseech," accessed April 21, 2017, https://merriam-webster.com/dictionary/beseech.

3.   Blue Letter Bible, Strong's G5545, s.v. *"chrisma,"* accessed February 14, 2017, https://www.blueletterbible.org/lang/lexicon/lexicon.cfm?Strongs=G5545&t=KJV.

4.   Blue Letter Bible, Strong's G501, s.v. *"antleō,"* February 14, 2017, https://www.blueletterbible.org/lang/lexicon/lexicon.cfm?Strongs=G501&t=KJV.

APPENDIX

SELECT PRINCIPLES OF PROPHETIC MINISTRY

1.   Joseph H. Thayer, *Thayer's Greek-Hebrew Lexicon of the New Testament* (N.p.: Hendrickson Publishers, 1995).

2.   Stuart Pattico, "How to Prophesy and Move in the Prophetic," StuartPattico.com, accessed December 19, 2015, http://www.stuartpattico.com/how-to-prophesy-and-move-in-the-prophetic.html.

3.   Smith Wigglesworth, *Ever-Increasing Faith* (N.p.: Wigglesworth Books, 2013).